Ewha's Korean Studies Series for Globalization 4
Korean Cultural Research Institute

UNDERSTANDING KOREAN ART

From the Prehistoric through the Modern Day

Hong Sun-pyo, **Jang** Nam-won, **Oh** Jin-kyeong, **Kim** Myung-sook, **Moon** Suk-hie

Jimoondang
Seoul

Jimoondang
514-7 Munbal-ri, Gyoha-eup, Paju-si, Gyeonggi-do, 413-756, Korea
95 Waryong-dong, Jongno-gu, Seoul, 110-360, Korea
227 Suttons Lane, Edison, NJ 08817, USA
Phone: 82-2-743-0227 E-mail: edit@jimoon.co.kr
82-2-743-3192~3 E-mail: sale@jimoon.co.kr
Fax: 82-2-743-3097, 82-2-742-4657
Homepage: www.jimoon.co.kr

The National Library of Korea Cataloging-in-Publication (CIP)
Understanding Korean Art
Edited by Hong Sun-pyo, Jang Nam-won, Oh Jin-kyeong, Kim Myung-sook, Moon Suk-hie
Paju: Jimoondang, 2011
ISBN 978-89-6297-023-4 94600
978-89-6297-020-3 (set) 600.911-KDC5 700.9519-DDC21 CIP2011002261

Printed in Korea

This textbook is published with the support of the Second-Phase Specialized Programs for Korean Studies at Ewha Womans University.

On Publishing

The Korean Cultural Research Institute (KCRI) was established in 1958 for the purpose of unearthing and researching Korean culture and actively promoting the result overseas. This was the outcome of an attempt to overcome negativity towards Korean tradition, particularly in the bleak situation of the post-war era. It is also intended to renew respect for Korean culture in the midst of an inundation of foreign culture and goods. KCRI is the first research institute founded by Ewha Womans University. Since its creation, KCRI has always held in high esteem research in the fields of Korean culture and Korea studies, as well as globalization and promotion of Korean culture based on the research. More recently, one of the top priority missions for KCRI has been promoting globalization based on Korean culture.

The 21st Century is moving toward an era of globalization through academic and cultural exchange. To preserve generalities of human societies as well as the uniqueness of and diversity within each nation, we must proactively invest our effort into them. The vision of "Korea In The World" is buttressed by ceaseless studies on the core values of Korean culture. To respond to thc call of the present era, Ewha Womans University has selected and invested in specialized programs on Korea studies. Such programs are embodiments of the University's undying passion for Korea's tradition as well as its effort to employ the essence of that tradition in international communications.

Having conducted comprehensive research in various sectors of Korean studies for over 50 years, the KCRI was selected as part of the second phase of the Korea Studies Specialized Program. The 'Specialized Program for Korea Studies and Korean Culture Education' of our research institute chose as its goal the development of a comprehensive set of textbooks on Korean language, history, arts and culture that can deliver academic, yet realistic information to domestic and foreign college level students in and out of Korea, as well as Koreans living abroad. To achieve this goal, the program selected a number of Ewha faculty members who have conducted professional and in-depth research in the proposed fields. After long and arduous research, development and authoring, the program is proud to announce the publication of *Ewha's Korean Studies Series for Globalization*.

Ewha's Korean Studies Series for Globalization is composed of textbooks covering 4 areas: *Korean Language, History, Arts and Modern Culture*. The *Korean Language* textbook is extremely practical and contains pedagogical elements designed to further enhance the understanding of, and the ability of expression in, the Korean language, and is an effective means to study Korean language and culture in an integrated manner. In the development of *Understanding Korean History* textbook, the authors conducted extensive surveys of major universities around the world and analyzed the subjects' needs and the current level of their understandings of Korean history. The authors promptly reflected the data obtained in their work. *Understanding Korean History* textbook is a great tool in rectifying any incorrect portrayal of Korean history and in conveying information in a most systematic and sensible manner. *Understanding Korean Art* is an integrated introduction to Korean arts. The textbook contains a plethora of visual and audio materials on fine arts, music and dance. Moreover the Korean Arts textbook, packed with links to Korean cultural centers and museums featuring Korean arts and artifacts, is an excellent source in which to encounter and delve into Korean arts on a higher level. *Understanding Contemporary Korean Culture* textbook focuses on the contemporary culture of Korea and related phenomena in an event-oriented manner. The textbook introduces modern Korean culture as seen through popular culture media, including literature, films, newspaper, TV and the internet.

Ewha's Korean Studies Series for Globalization will no doubt contribute immensely in promoting and in proliferating Korean culture and studies around the globe. I would like to extend my heart-felt appreciation to the faculty members and researchers who authored the texts although in less than optimal conditions. I hope their hard work will shine a light and create a better understanding of Korea in the modern world.

May, 2011
Choi Joon Sik
Director of Specialized Program for Korea Studies and Korean Culture Education &
Korean Cultural Research Institute

Introduction

Since prehistoric times and all throughout the long, ongoing history of Korea, painting, sculpture, dance, music and other forms of art developed a unique national style influenced by the kinship-based societies and climatic factors of the peninsula. Each historical period witnessed Korean art shape its own characteristics by increasing its universal appeal as well as unifying the indigenous styles through interactions with other cultures in Eurasia. Much has been said about these characteristics, but the general view is that they indicate less of a desire for ostentatious expression but rather a pursuit of inner elegance and spirituality. What runs through all Korean art is not a sense of artificial creation but an attempt to capture the vitality and sentiment that is intrinsic to nature. This common quality can be seen manifested in the trends and styles that differ depending on the tastes of the artists or patrons of art or the lifestyles of the time.

Visual arts began in prehistoric Korea with sculpture, mostly earthenware and drawings carved in rock, that served practical as well as religious purposes related to the mediumism and endemism of primitive northeast Asian art. When ancient states were founded during the Three Kingdoms and Unified Silla periods, tomb art and Buddhist art reflecting aristocratic tastes of the time were prevalent. Then in the following Goryeo and Joseon dynasties, art strongly characteristic of Confucianism and Taoism gained prominence. Since the beginning of the modern era and to this day, Korean visual art has been striving to achieve global universality through interactions with a wide range of Western art, while simultaneously trying to create a new notion of Korean beauty by unifying the nation's autonomic qualities that stem from nationalistic sentiment and its sociopolitical background.

Dance in Korea began with the act of singing and dancing performed during prehistoric farming and harvest rituals. Later, the Three Kingdoms and Unified Silla witnessed the development of the "Kiakmu" (伎樂舞), a Buddhist mask dance, and the "Cheoyongmu" (處容舞), another mask dance performed during ceremonial prayers to a guardian god of the state. In Goryeo, dance developed alongside music, largely in relation to national ceremonies, and later in Joseon, court dances and religious dances went their separate ways, which led to the emergence, in the late Joseon, of folk dances, especially those with masks, and professional dances that were performed for large audiences. By the modern era, new dances introduced from the West existed together with traditional dances inherited from the Joseon dynasty, and while this coexistence has continued on into the contemporary era, there have also been various attempts at creating new modern forms of Korean dance.

Korean music, like dance, originated from prehistoric harvest rituals, but developed as two separate types that were played in the royal courts of the Three Kingdoms and Unified Silla: *dangak* (唐樂), 'Tang music' that came from the Chinese Tang dynasty, and *hyangak* (鄕樂), the indigenous music. Then in Goryeo, *aak* (雅樂), the Confucian ritual music from the next Chinese dynasty of Song, was newly introduced into Korea, and performances combining instrumental music, singing, dancing and tricks gained popularity during national ceremonies. Early Joseon witnessed traditional music undergo a reform of incorporating *Ye* (moral order) and *ak* (music), a Confucian ideology on the correlation between civility and music, and the creation of new musical instruments. Then in late Joseon, a new traditional music was formed through the reduction of court music, as well as the proliferation of *pungnyuak* (風流樂), or 'tasteful music', by the *jungin*, a privileged middle class of professionals, and *minsokak* (民俗樂), or 'folk music', by the lower classes. In modern and contemporary times, however, traditional Korean music, now categorized as *gugak* (國樂) or 'national music', has been struggling to stay alive after Western music flowed into Korea and became the mainstream.

In this new global era, foreign interest in Korean culture, especially in Korean art, has increased. But there are still only a small number of foreign scholars who conduct academic research on Korean art, and of these few, only a small portion specializes exclusively in Korean art. Most of the researches are part of more general studies on Eastern art. Because it is difficult to find texts on Korean art in English, not to mention other foreign languages, we wanted to publish a textbook on Korean art that can provide foreign researchers and students with a comprehensive understanding of the characteristics of Korean art by looking at three of its forms: visual arts, dance, and music. This textbook is divided into seven chapters that chronologically follow the development of Korean art from prehistoric Korea, the Three Kingdoms and Unified Silla periods, the Goryeo dynasty, the early Joseon period, the late Joseon period, the modern era, to contemporary times, each chapter introducing the visual arts, dance, and music of the period in that order. In addition to the main text, this textbook comes with a glossary for each art form and a separate DVD that contains images, music and video clips, practical and specific data needed in the education of Korean art and culture.

I would like to express my sincere gratitude to those at the Korea Culture Research

Institute for their support, which made the publication of this textbook possible. Also, my deepest thanks go to all the institutions and individuals for the permission to use the valuable images, music, videos and other forms of data from their collections. Finally, I am grateful to the coauthors who have strived to bring together the different art forms of visual arts, dance, and music into one textbook, and hope to share the joy of its publication with the translators who have helped in creating the English version.

On behalf of the authors,
Oh Jin-kyeong

Contents

Ⅲ. Goryeo Period

Ⅳ. Early Joseon Period (14th–16th Century)

Ⅴ. Late Joseon Period (17th–19th Century)

Ⅵ. Modern Era (Late 19th–Early 20th Century)

Ⅶ. Contemporary Age (Late 20th Century–Present)

Prehistoric Era

I. Prehistoric Era

The prehistoric age in Korea progressed from the Paleolithic Period to the Neolithic Period to the Bronze Age and the Iron Age. The Korean peninsula and surrounding areas were first inhabited by human beings around 700,000 years ago. At this time, which corresponds to the Ice Age and the Interglacial Period, the people were nomadic hunters and gatherers who lived in caves.

Around 8,000 years ago at the end of the Ice Age, the topography on and around the Korean peninsula developed its present form and the climate were similar to what it is today. From this time, human beings made tools out of sharpened and polished stone, shaped and fired dishes out of clay, and began to cook and store food. In the Neolithic Age, they began agricultural cultivation to supplement their hunting and gathering, and in this transition from hunting to growing food for subsistence, people began to exchange their nomadic ways for a settled life.

The development of agriculture resulted in the production of surplus crops, while the dissemination of bronze tools gave rise to the concept of private property and a social rank system. Clan chiefs with wealth and power emerged as a consequence and as these chiefs developed their forces they ruled over the surrounding area, and later established states. Gojoseon, the first Korean state to grow out of a clan society, is recorded in history books such as "Samguk Yusa" (Memorabilia of the Three Kingdoms) as being founded in 2333 BCE by Dangun Wanggeom.

As indicated by the distribution of lute-shaped daggers and megaliths on the Korea peninsula, the Gojoseon Kingdom flourished around present day Liaoning, China, and gradually integrated other clan societies in the surrounding area. Around 200 BCE Gojoseon was followed by Wiman Joseon, which embraced the iron culture and consequently saw great progress in agriculture, handicraft, particularly the manufacture of weapons, and trade and commerce. Developing superior military strength, Wiman Joseon aggressively conquered other states and grew into a force strong enough to stand against the Han Dynasty, which had unified China.

Ironware was first introduced to Korea around 500 BCE, and in the following period a number of small states were established in Manchuria and all over the Korean peninsula including Buyeo, Goguryeo, Okjeo, Dongye, and the Three Han States (Mahan, Jinhan, and Byeonhan). Using iron tools, these states developed agriculture and unique social customs. Some of these states were integrated into others while others joined together to form federated states, laying the foundations for nations with centralized rule and the development of a uniquely Korean culture.

1. Art

When the formation of Korean culture is examined through extant dwelling sites, the act of painting, if defined as the visualization of objects on a two-dimensional plane, began on the Korean Peninsula in the prehistoric period, between the Neolithic Age and the Bronze Age. Before the Common Era, paintings were mainly engraved on the surfaces of rocks and metals including bronze vessels. Although works from this period include the images of a wild boar carved on pottery, which was recently excavated from the Neolithic Age remains at Bibong-ri, Bugok-myeon in Changnyeong, South Gyeongsang Province, and a deer on the pottery retrieved from shell mounds in Dongsam-dong, Busan in 1999, the most representative are petroglyphs, or rock carvings.

1) Petroglyphs, the Origin of Painting

Petroglyphs refer to pictures engraved on rock surfaces with hard stone or metal tools, compared to pictographs, which are painted onto surfaces by applying red or other pigments. Created with the techniques of pecking or grinding, petroglyphs found on the Korean Peninsula are largely distributed in the southeast region around the Yeongnam area and 15 such remains are known to exist today.

Prehistoric people on the peninsula began painting activities by carving images into the surfaces of rocks, which were held sacred at the time, to convey their wishes for survival. The images were produced by etching only the contours ("line carving" technique) or carving out the interior to create certain patterns ("surface carving" technique). Formatively, the prehistoric images are mostly two-dimensional iconographic characters that condense the overall appearance of the subject matter as much as possible. Hunting or ritual art associ-

| Fig. 1.1 Bangudae Petroglyphs (rubbing, detail), late Neolithic-early Bronze Age, 3×7～20m, Unyang-myeon, Ulju-gun, South Gyeongsang Province

ated with primitive fine arts prevail; these images can be interpreted from the perspective of mythology or folklore. As semantic paintings before characters came into use, they are assumed to have developed in connection with the belief that they are effective incantations or mediums to communicate with divine spirits or souls with transcendental power.

Major rock engravings from early times include the Bangudae Cliff petroglyphs in Ulju-gun, Ulsan, estimated to date to the late Neolithic to early Bronze Age, which comprise carvings of land or marine animals including whales, tigers, deer and wild boars <Fig. 1.1> Mixed use of the line and surface carving techniques implies that the images were created at different times. Stylistically, the Bangudae petroglyphs are related to those in such North Asia regions as northern China, Mongolia and Altai, Russia. Some of the traits of the Bangudae petroglyphs were handed down to create the petroglyphs in Cheonjeon-ri, Ulju-gun and craft paintings, which are pictorial images on bronze ritual implements. They also are regarded to have influenced the bronze horse bell pattern in Japan's Yayoi period.

Of the animal images, some are rendered in the Roentgen style from Scandinavia or Siberia, with their internal organs seen through transparent skin, but most statically depict only the basic features of the subject by summarizing their morphological characteristics. The depiction of hunting and fishing scenes, pregnant beings, and the capture of land or

| Fig. 1.2 Cheonjeon-ri Petroglyphs, early Bronze-late Bronze Age, 2.7×9.5m, Dudong-myeon, Ulju-gun, South Gyeongsang Province

| Fig. 1.3 Chilpo-ri Petroglyphs (A side), late Bronze Age, 2×3m, Mt. Gonryunsan, Heunghae-eup, Pohang-si, North Gyeongsang Province

| Fig. 1.4 Bronze Implement with Farming Scenes (back side), late Bronze Age, 7.3×12.3cm, National Museum of Korea

sea animals is interpreted as wishes for the success of the hunt, fecundity, and reproduction. Land animals are mostly carved on the right side of the rock surfaces. Whaling scenes, featuring various kinds of whales, are focused on the left side and are particularly valuable as the only petroglyphs in East Asia depicting a marine scene. The sea near the Ulju area is a famous whale habitat and whale remains have been found in the Neolithic shell mounds at the southeastern seashore. Below the school of whales is a human figure, rendered with the surface carving technique, whose limbs stretch out straight to the sides with exaggerated fingers and toes. This image is interpreted to be a frog-shaped shaman praying for a successful catch of fish. The shaman was made in the image of the amphibian frog to emphasize his/her characteristics as an intermediary connecting the human and spiritual realms. The style used for representing the shaman shares similarities with the international style found in China, Eurasia, Mongolia, North America and Siberia.

In the petroglyphs of Cheonjeon-ri, Ulju-gun, thought to be from the middle period, the whale has disappeared and instead land animals are carved along with symbolic patterns including concentric circles, intended to represent water <Fig. 1.2>. From the repeated layers and carving techniques used, the land animals are thought to date to the early Bronze Age, and the symbolic patterns to the later half to the late Bronze Age. Linked with motifs in

Scythian art, a brace of deer facing each other can be interpreted as a pictorial sign for abundant reproduction. Depiction of only characteristic parts of the subject or in semi-abstract style may well be the collective representation of a concept, a preceding phase of symbolism. Formed with curves and straight lines, the abstract images are carved in concentric circles, double zigzags, swirls or lozenge patterns. Although opinions differ on the meaning of these symbolic patterns, the prevailing view is that they represent ripples of water, the source of life, the wind, and meaningful symbols warding off evil spirits, respectively.

The later-period petroglyphs are estimated to date to the end of the Bronze Age, or beginning of the Iron Age. They generally depict shield or knife handle patterns. Opinions vary on the meaning of the trapezoid symbol decorated with short lines or dots inside. Some argue that it represents the face or body of the Sun God, while others believe it is a ceremonial decorative axe, symbolic of the power of the ruling class under the emergence of early states. This symbol, first appearing with concentric circles in the petroglyphs in Yangjeon-dong, Goryeong, was standardized in the Chilpo-ri rock-carving <Fig. 1.3> in Pohang. A more simplified form of the symbol is found in later remains in Seokjang-dong, Gyeongju, and Boseong-ri, Yeongcheon. The later-period petroglyphs are also called "Korean-style" rock carvings since they emerged and developed independently.

The painting trend toward the end of the Bronze Age can be glimpsed through the patterns incised on the surfaces of bronze ritual implements. *Danyu semungyeong*, or bronze mirrors with a fine linear design and a pair of knobs, show abstract symbolic patterns such as concentric circles and triangles, which are also found in later-period petroglyphs. They are executed elaborately with surprisingly fine workmanship and precise drafting skills. In contrast, a bronze implement with farming scenes, excavated from Daejeon, portray concrete images. At the front are birds sitting on branches in the same composition as later paintings of flowers and birds on branches (*jeolji hwajodo*), suggestive of bird worship. The back side is divided into two sections to depict a story in sequence: the right section features a plowing scene and the left the storing of crops in a container <Fig. 1.4>. Unlike rock carvings, this man-made implement is divided into framed sections, introducing the concept of a canvas and implying that the ancient people had become conscious of composition and sequence. The depiction of human figures, narrating the lifestyle of the time, signals the transition to ancient paintings.

2) Clay Figures and Earthenware: Neolithic Period, Bronze Age, Iron Age

Given the remains that show prehistoric art, prehistoric people had prominent technology in making earthenware pots and jars. The history of earthenware in the Korean

| Fig. 1.5 Pottery with Raised Design, Excavated from Amsa-dong, Neolithic Period, h. 40.5cm, The Central Museum of Kyunghee University

| Fig. 1.6 Black Burnished Earthenware (h. 22.5cm), and Red Burnished Earthenware (h. 13.2cm), Bronze Age, National Museum of Korea

peninsula began around 8,000 BCE, from the Neolithic Age, and it had been developed through the Bronze Age (BCE 1,000–BCE 300) and the Iron Age (BCE 300–) undergoing various changes in form and technique.

The most representational earthenware remains of the Neolithic Age are the raised design (隆起文) bowls and the comb-pattern (櫛文) bowls. The surface of a raised design bowl was decorated with thin mud bands, and these have been found in various places starting from the East Searegion, in Yang-yang Osan area to Busan, and also around the West Sea region around Heuksando Island.

The bottom of comb-pattern earthenware bowls was usually made in the shape of a 'U' (rounded bottom) or in the shape of a 'V' (pointed bottom), so Neolithic people could use them on a beach or a riverside setting them up after digging a shovel of soft sand, respectively. The surface of the bowls was engraved with geometric designs, being carved with thin and sharp tools such as branches or seashells.

In the Bronze Age, a much higher temperature was used to fire the earthenware, thus making it hard, and the bottoms of earthenware became flat when people moved their residential areas into inland. <Fig. 1.5>

Unlike the Neolithic period, the majority of earthenware made during the Bronze Age did not have surface patterns. During this period, there was an increase in pots made with flat bottoms, differing to those made in the Neolithic period, and the clay color was either brown or reddish-brown. Red burnished pottery (*Hong-do*, 紅陶) and black burnished pottery (*Heuk-do*, 黑陶), which were popular in China during the Neolithic period, were also being made in Korea. <Fig. 1.6>

The cultural development of the Iron Age was based on the techniques related to working with iron. Along with such developments, earthenware also advanced in technique. People began to fire earthenware with higher temperature, and the ingredients of the clay, which was used for earthenware, could be melted and combined more and more. At last, such earthenware could be solid increasingly. Furthermore, people had to develop their techniques for building kilns in order to keep higher temperature. Thanks to such techniques, the firing environment of almost 1,000℃ was created in a reduction atmosphere, and it brought the production of pottery type using ash-glaze.

On the other hand, in sites of ancient houses, small clay figures such as human and animal clay models were found. Also, shell pieces, pressed into the clay to create different surface effects known as shells (貝殼類), have been found. The shards of these particular potteries were found in excavation sites of Cheongjin Nongpo-dong and in Woonggi, Gulpo-ri. The human figurines of this age have distinct facial features and exaggerated body parts. Characteristically, these were made with succinct features, and they were used for folk beliefs acting as amulets while having the significance of a deity.

3) The Bronze Age Ritual vessels and Weapons

The inflow of bronze culture began in around 1,000 BCE in the Korean peninsula. It gradually established itself by the influence from the Liaoning (遼寧) region, a north-western

| Fig. 1.7 Liaoning Type Bronze Dagger and Korean Type Bronze Dagger, Bronze Age, h. 45.8cm, National Museum of Korea

| Fig. 1.8 Bronze Mirror with Fine Linear Design, Bronze Age, d. 21.2cm, The Korean Christian Museum at Soongsil University

| Fig. 1.9 Bronze Instrument with End Bells, Bronze Age, d. 14.4cm, National Museum of Korea

part of China. At first, the objects made from bronze were used by the ruling class or shamans to represent their status and their rituals. In their real life, they used earthenware and stoneware together.

The Bronze Age saw rapid developments in technical skills with metal which enabled the production of bronze by compounding copper and tin. Accessories and ritualistic ornaments were made from this alloy - bronze. In particular, the shape and method which were adopted for making swords show the features of their age and location.

At the start of this period, swords took after the form of the Liaoning region in China. At first, Liaoning bronze swords, which had bulging bottom had been passed, but they were localized for the Korean environment, so later the Korean swords became slim and linear unlike with the Liaoning ones. They show traditional Korean features.<Fig. 1.7>

The most representational bronze objects include the bronze mirror with geometric designs (多紐細文鏡), bronze mirror with coarse lines (多紐粗文鏡), bronze horse bell (銅鐸) and many more. The methods for making goods with metal needed molds and surface decorations with either incised or raised designs. <Fig. 1.8> In part, engraving or pecking methods were used.

Geometrical patterns were applied with close lines, concentric circle and triangles. In addition to these, there were also bronze axes, spears, shields, sword handles, weapons and buttons, bells and so on. <Fig. 1.9> On the shields, images of deer, human face, hands and farming scenes were drawn to symbolize the class distinction of the owner as well as stating the function of bronze during this period.

4) Habitation and Home

According to archaeological research, it is believed that people existed in the Korean peninsula from the prehistoric period. People had to move their residence areas continuously, so the places where they had lived were usually caves or the places shaded by rocks. When farming became developed in the Neolithic times, people began to settle down. They built homes on small hills near rivers or seas, digging the ground. The floors of such homes were flattened with mud, and the roof was covered with lots of straw after preparing rafters using pieces of wood. And they made braziers and food storage facilities in the houses. The Amsa-dong (岩寺洞) is the most well known historic site that shows Neolithic life. This is a very valuable historic site where we could found shell mounds, carbonized crops, and the implements used for picking fruits and fishing. Other tools for hunting such as arrow-shaped chiseled stones and the bones for making various implements were found. Such relics prove that they kept agriculture and fishery at one time. In the Iron Age, large communal settlements began to be established. Like the Neolithic houses, fire was located in the middle of their houses.

2. Dance

1) The Beginning of Korean Dance

Dance has its origins in the natural instinct of humans to seek out amusement, which, perhaps, is a common tendency shared by the multitudes of the world. Dance began in Korea as a part of a ritual called *jecheon*, which was conducted to worship heaven as a means of overcoming fears aroused by changes in the natural environment. In the rituals, people sing and dance while drinking. The heavenly ritual of the Korean people was an important current in the waters of the Korean spirit from the Gojoseon (ancient Joseon, 2333 BCE–108 BCE) period through to the end of the Joseon and served as a cornerstone on which Korean culture was established.

Before elucidating Korean dance, fundamental concepts such as *mu* (巫) (shaman), *mu* (舞) (dance) and *ak* (樂) (music) must be explained both in terms of etymology and fundamental notions, to facilitate an understanding of the history of Korean dance.

In particular, it may be important to clarify the conception of *mu* (巫) (shaman) that signifies the start of Korean dance. In the Chinese character *mu* "巫," the character *in* "人" is written on either side of the character *gong* "工." Pictorially the character *in* "人" looks like a dancer, and all this signifies the shaman to commit the self to god through dance. Therefore *mu* (巫) means "a person who worships god through dance." *Ak* (樂), depicts the shape of having two hands high up in the air, shaking bells while dancing. Thus, it is possible to surmise that the Chinese characters, *mu* (巫), *mu* (舞) and *ak* (樂) derive from the same origin.

2) The Course of Dance in the Prehistoric Era

In the prehistoric era when language had not been created, dance began as a way of communicating primarily for survival. Its genesis was as a means to express changes in emotion such as happiness, love, fear, and anger, and the inherent compulsions of the body.

According to the *Samguk yusa*, a collection of legends, folktales, and historical accounts related to three kingdoms of Korea, the first kingdom to be formed in Korea was founded by Dangun in 2333 BCE. Dangun was a leader who unified religion and state and took the highest status religiously and politically. Written records on Gojoseon dance are found in *Samgukyusa* and *Zhourae*, one of Confucius scriptures in the Zhou Dynasty of China, *Dongyijeon* of *Huhanseo*, history of later Han (Han Dynasty of China) and *Sagi*, historical texts of China.

Samgukyusa records Dangun as a ruler with divine power, who presided over ceremonies for the heaven and left behind the customs of dancing, singing and drinking.

Zhourae compiled by *Zhougong* of western Zhou of China, states, "Music was administered and taught in Gojoseon and that Korean dances were performed for sacrificial rites," along with the clear records of the rank and number of dancers.

Dongyijeon of *Huhanseo* reads, "*Taegang Hawusi* (the king of Wu Dynasty) lost faith and the Han people began to be on alert. However, as Emperor *Sogang* ruled, *Dongyiin* (the Korean people) started to recover their admiration, and they were invited to the royal court as guest-performers to exhibit their dance and music." These records suggest that court banquet dances for the ruling class commenced by Gojoseon people at this time.

We can find records concerning Gija-Joseon (−194 BCE), which indicates a period included in Gojoseon period in the Korean history, in *Sagi*: "King Cheonro went to the River Biryu for amusement, and instructed his court musicians to perform *youngseonak*, while having the court ladies dance the *youngseonmu*." These records suggest that during the Gojoseon period court musicians and dancers were divided and that the *youngseonmu* was in existence. *Youngseonmu* is a type of dance and the name has meaning of welcoming divine beings with supernatural power, this dance originated from the country's ancient beliefs or primitive religion.

The types of dance in the Gojoseon period include the following: first, a group dance held for heavenly sacrificial rites; second, a war dance for battle and defense; third, *jimomu*, which might have been performed with a wish for military prosperity and a rite for farming; fourth, *jurimu*, a dance for good farming; and fifth, *youngseonmu*, a banquet dance for the royal court. In the dances of the Gojoseon period, king performs a sacrificial rite for heaven through music and dance. In odder words, a king played the same role as shaman and performed dance. After the collapse of Gojoseon, kingdoms such as Buyeo, Dongae, Samhan, and others emerged. The religion of these states focused on the worship of ancestral gods, the heavenly gods and the gods of nature, and each state performed ritual ceremonies regularly.

According to the *Whijidongyijeon*, which is China's historical records included in the *Samgukji* (Romance of the Three Kingdoms) about many antient tribes and states of East, Buyeo held heavenly rituals called *Younggo* in the 12th month. In Goguryeo the heavenly ritual referred to as *Dongmaeng* was held in the 10th month and in Dongye, *Mucheon* took place. In Samhan, priests called Cheongun, were put in charge of religious rites. Ancient documents show that such heavenly rites were large festive events for the entire state, usually consisting of dance, song and drinking. The banquets were similar in character to a Thanksgiving Day gathering. Such festive events, with drink and merriment, continued in a large extent through the present day in the everyday lives of the Korean people. Of the many different records on dance types of Samhan, there is one particular dance known as *takmu*. The dance was performed by stomping on the ground in a highly disciplined manner. The dance is thought to be a form of *yunmu* (輪舞, circle dance) in which performers led by one person repeatedly sit and stand up vigorously with their hands and feet responding to each movement with bending and straightening.

Dance in the prehistoric era was closely related to the pleasures of the movement of the human body and the act of worship, later developing into a communal art form with song and dance.

3. Music

During the prehistoric era in Korea, music was performed at festivities associated with heavenly rituals. Since the age of the tribal states, Koreans have offered songs and dances to heaven and the spirits in communal ceremonies connected to agriculture. These rituals were normally held at specific times of the year. Several rituals were held according to the agricultural calendar including the first, fifth, and tenth months, which included music and dance.

1) Music of the Prehistoric Era

Because of the lack of the historic records, specific facts on musical instruments, melody, rhythm of music of this period are not known. Only a few historic records state that people gathered to sing and dance with clapping. Consequently, we can conjecture that this is related to some genres of folk entertainments such as farmers' band music *nongak* and a female circle dance of Jeolla province, *ganggangsullae*. *Nongak*, practiced mostly by farmers, was an integrated form of art centered around percussion instruments, with music, dance and play. <Fig. 1.10> *Ganggangsullae* is a folk play and involves a large number of village people participating together in song and dance. *Ganggangsullae* is a simple song with several refrains and main melody that is repeated over and over again making it easy for anyone to take part. *Ganggangsullae* begins in a slow tempo and speeds up and this help the participants to enjoy it for a long time.

Heavenly ceremonies of prehistoric era have continued until today, including *nongak* and *gut* shaman rituals. Many farming villages still hold festivals on the first and eighth full moon, fifth day of the fifth month of a year, and these are all related to ceremonies of prehistoric times.

2) String Instruments of the Prehistoric Era

String instruments existed in the southern and northern parts of the Korean peninsula in the prehistoric era. In the tombs of the northern regions, several mural wall-paintings have been found. One particular painting, which dates back to the 3rd century BCE, includes a man playing an ancient form of the *geomun-go* (six-string zither). Even though some detailed construction of the instruments are different, the drawing of the instrument is similar to

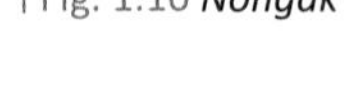

| Fig. 1.10 *Nongak*

those of today's *geomun-go*, especially in shape and playing techniques. The ancient instrument has four strings with 14 frets while today's *geomun-go* has six strings with 16 frets. The *geomun-go* is played with a small bamboo stick called *suldae*. <Fig. 1.11>

A string instrument also existed in the southern part of the peninsula. This particular instrument became the *gayageum* of Gaya state and Silla kingdom. Among the archaeological relics excavated from this region, several drawings, clay figurines, and ancient forms of the *gayageum* have been found. The *gayageum* is played by plucking or flicking with fingers. <Fig. 1.12>

| Fig. 1.11 Ancient form of *Geomun-go* from Goguryeo *Muyongchong* Tomb Mural Painting

| Fig. 1.12 The Ancient form of *Gayageum* from Silla clay pot

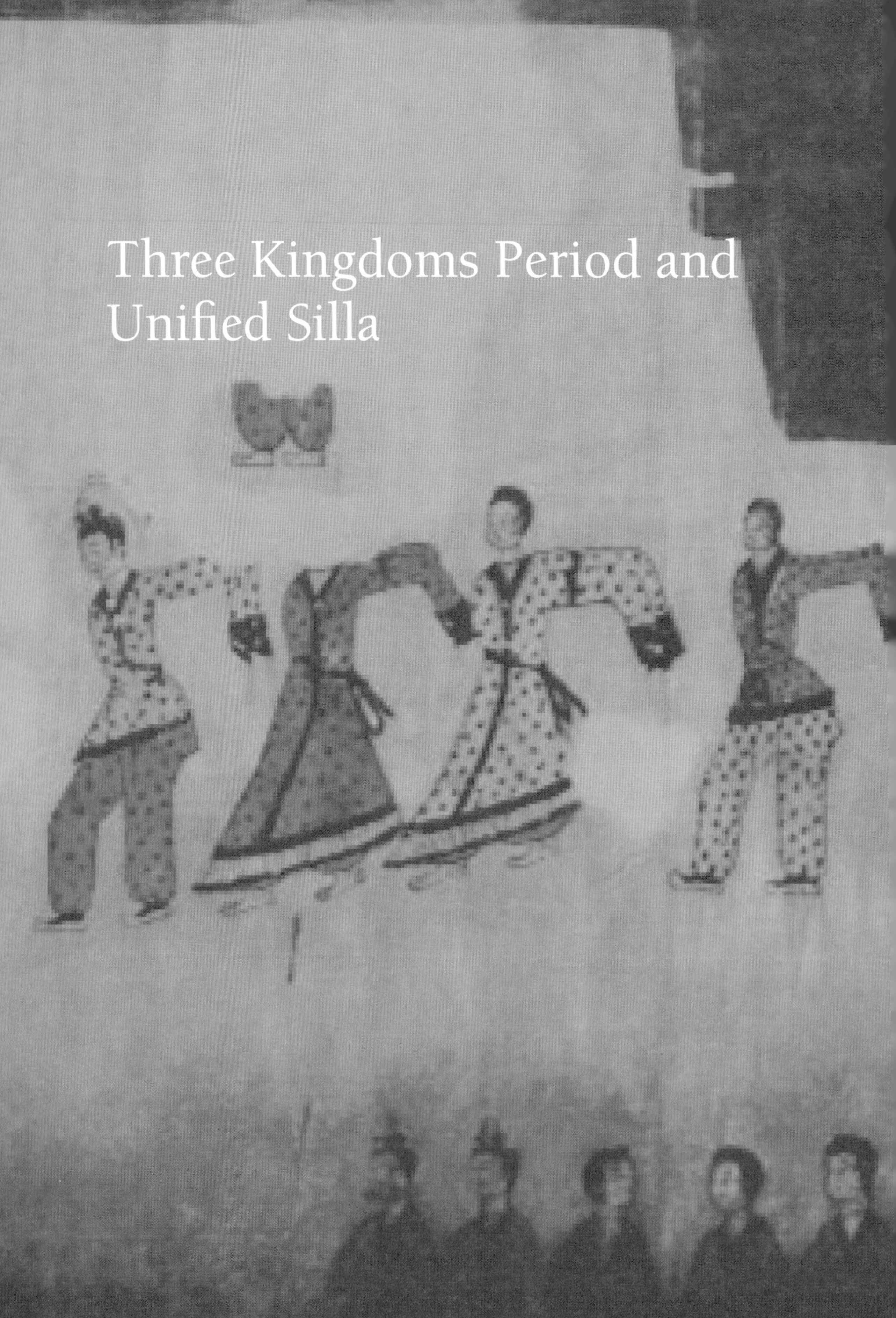

Three Kingdoms Period and Unified Silla

Ⅱ. Three Kingdoms Period and Unified Silla

Although *Samguk sagi* (History of the Three Kingdoms) states that the Three Kingdoms were founded in the order of Silla, Goguryeo, and Baekje, it was Goguryeo that first established centralized government. Founded in the Yalu River basin in 37 BCE, Goguryeo actively expanded its territory through the latter half of the 1th century during the reign of King Taejo (r. 47–165), and further strengthened the authority of the throne and central government through the latter half of the 2th century.

Baekje was founded in 18 BCE in the Han River basin by immigrants from Goguryeo who integrated with the local population. By the time of King Go-i (r. 234–286), Baekje had completely taken over the river basin area, and the foundations were laid for centralized government with the formation of a system of rule, including revision of the official rank system and introduction of official uniforms.

Silla began in 57 BCE as Saro, chiefdom within the Jinhan confederacy, based on an immigrant and local population in the Gyeongju area. In Goguryeo, the authority of the throne was very strong from the beginning, but in Silla leadership rotated among the Kim, Park and Seok clans. In the time of King Naemul (r. 356–402) in the 4th century, Silla aggressively expanded its territory, coming to occupy most of Jinhan, east of the Nakdonggang River, and then began to develop into a full-fledged kingdom.

In the Byeonhan region, downstream of the Nakdonggang River, which flows through the southeastern part of the Korean peninsula, various political groups began to appear as a result of social integration based on the iron culture. Around the 3th century, the early Gaya Confederacy grew out of the state of Geumgwan Gaya. Iron was manufactured in large quantities in this region from early times and iron trade was active, with the Gaya Confederacy also serving as a medium in iron trade between Nangnang (Lelang commandery) and Kyushu in Japan.

Having strengthened their systems of centralized government, the three kingdoms of Goguryeo, Baekje and Silla greatly expanded their territories in the 5th century. Based on plans laid during the time of King Sosurim (r. 371–384), Gwanggaeto the Great of *Goguryeo* (r. 391–413) set out to conquer Manchuria, and after driving out the Japanese, who had invaded Silla, Goguryeo's influence spread to the southern part of the country as well. Gwanggaeto was followed by King Jangsu (r. 413–491), who moved the capital to Pyeongyang, thus strengthening Goguryeo's policy of southward expansion. One consequence of this policy was the southward retreat of Baekje, which ended up moving its capital to Ungjin (Gongju, South Chungcheong Province) and then to Sabi (Buyeo, South Chungcheong Province) but continued to reform its national systems in plan for a revival. In the 6th century under the reign of King Jinheung (r. 534–576), Silla strengthened internal solidarity and expanded its territory, taking the lead in administrative matters between the Three Kingdoms. Jinheung turned Silla's elite young warriors, called *Hwarang*, into an official state organization and attempted to achieve ideological integration through reorganization of the Buddhist orders. In 676 Silla succeeded in unifying the three kingdoms.

With its increased economic and military power, Unified Silla strengthened the authority of the throne. In its centralized government the function of the ministers grew and provincial administrations were organized into nine provinces (*ju*) and five local capitals (*ogyeong*). As national affairs were stabilized and agricultural production capacity increased, the rural population began to lead better lives and handicraft, commerce and trade flourished. Unified Silla achieved a high level of culture, building on the combined culture of the Three Kingdoms and assimilating the cultures of Tang and the regions west of China. Thanks to the development of Buddhism, it also achieved a brilliant Buddhist culture. Later, Confucianism was adopted as a new ruling ideology, leading to the establishment of Confucian politics and a state school for Confucian education named *gukhak*.

1. Art

1) Painting

With the development of three ancient states, namely Goguryeo (37 BCE–668), Baekje (18 BCE–660), and Silla (57 BCE–992) in the Three Kingdoms period, importance was attached to the large-scale construction and splendid decoration of palaces and residential building. The fashionable clothing of aristocratic people, represented in tomb murals, displays the authority and power of the ruling class. The emergence of professional artists (*hwagong*) and the active use of a realistic painting style draw our attention. Realistic painting skills further improved with the introduction of Buddhist art from the second half of the fourth century and the import of the *aotufa* (concavity and convexity) technique popular during the Liang Dynasty of China around the early half of the 6th century, a method of portraying an object in a way to create a three-dimensional effect. The rapid advancement in realistic portrayal can be found in an episode in the History of the Three Kingdoms: Around 645, upon completion of the reconstruction of Hwangnyongsa Temple in Gyeongju where Solgeo had painted an old pine tree on the wall, some birds took the painting for a real tree and flew into the mural.

The professional artists were trained as government artisans (*gwanjang*) or state craftsmen (*gukgong*) belonging to a certain government institution. In Baekje, the title "baksa," meaning specialist, was awarded to professional painters and others with excellent skills to integrate them into the state organization, whereas Silla set up and operated Chaejeon (Bureau of Painting), a government institution in charge of painting. Like the ancient Todaiji Temple in Japan, it is assumed that largetemples in Korea also had professional painters as well as monk painters. Some Korean artists went to Japan and distinguished themselves there. Insaraa of Baekje, who crossed the sea to Japan around 463, is known to be Japan's first painter. Baekga and Yanggo, two professional painters from Baekje, are known to have traveled to Japan in around 588 to produce a painting on the ceiling of the Asukadera Temple. From Goguryeo, the Buddhist monk Damjing is said to have painted the mural of the main hall at the Horyuji Temple in 610. These episodes show the Three Kingdoms' contribution to the advancement of ancient painting and Buddhist painting in Japan.

(1) Development of Goguryeo Tomb Murals

Goguryeo tomb murals are very rare extant works of art that give a glimpse of painting trends at the time. The murals in 118 ancient tombs that are currently known to exist were created over some 300 years, from the 4th century when Goguryeo advanced into Liaoyang in present-day Liaoning Province, and began to emerge as a regional power in Northeast Asia. Goguryeo murals are the largest group of ancient murals in East Asia. An early Goguryeo mural depicts a massive procession of over 250 people, comprising a heavily armed cavalry, a mounted party and a musical band. They are more diverse and larger in number than similar paintings in Chinese tomb murals from the Later Han (25–220) and the Southern and Northern (221–589) Dynasties.

Reflecting the ruling class ideology of seeking immortality in life after death through the ascension of spirits and the custom of lavish burial, the Goguryeo murals share affinities with the funeral arts of East Asia in representing the after-life home of the deceased. While the Goguryeo murals are similar in style and theme to those in China and Japan, they show a distinctly indigenous tradition in pictorial expression. Depicted on the murals are portraits

| Fig. 2.1 A Figure of the Tomb Occupant's, Goguryeo, 357, Anak Tomb No. 3, Hwanghae Province, North Korea

of the tomb occupant and his wife, and the Four Guardian Deities, the four sacred animals guarding the four cardinal directions. Diverse human and animal figures and symbolic patterns related to myths, tales, customs, and events also constitute the main themes of the mural paintings. Rendered with brushes made from animal hair, bamboo or leather on the lime-plastered or stone walls of the chambers, the murals exemplify the Goguryeo painting style that reflects the enterprising spirit and international outlook of the time.

Goguryeo tomb murals developed from the first half of the fourth century through the next three centuries with significant changes occurring at intervals of about 100 years. Early murals, including those found in the Anak Tomb No. 3, dated 357, in Hwanghae Province and in the Deokheung-ri Tomb built in 408 in South Pyeongan Province, show the walls and ceilings of the multi- or double-chamber tombs, which consist of an antechamber, main chamber, and rear chamber. Depending on the existence of wings to the main chamber, a tomb is called either multi-chambered or double-chambered. Paintings on the walls depict commemorative occasions in the tomb occupant's lifetime activities or scenes from daily life or customs related to attending to the deceased, while those found on the conic ceilings with a corbelled dome or vault, representing the bowl-shaped sky, feature the heavenly world. The scenes of daily life primarily portray a large procession made up of rows of human figures including the master of the tomb and people on horseback.

From the Later Han period, the tomb occupant became the main subject of ancient tomb murals. Primarily portrayed sitting alone on a wooden bed in a curtained room, staring straight ahead, the figures are grave or solemn like the images of deities, as seen in the Anak Tomb No. 3 <Fig. 2.1>. They have similar faces but differ in size. The tomb occupant and people of high social standing were painted larger than the attendants, indicative of the use of the hierarchical portrayal technique, one of the characteristics of ancient figure painting. As seen in this example, ancient figure paintings had not yet reached the level of portraits which depict the subject as close to life as possible. The schematized front-view may be intended to embody the image of eternal life whose symbolic meaning is emphasized under the belief that life continues after death.

The murals of the Anak Tomb No. 3 exhibit the influence of the painting traditions of the Liaoyang area, presently Liaoning Province, China. In contrast, the Deokheung-ri Tomb, built 50 years later than the Anak Tomb, incorporates more diverse elements from such various areas as even the northwestern Gansu Province of China. The style of the Deokheung-ri Tomb murals shows the continuity of the Goguryeo pictorial tradition and at the same time displays new trends. Distinctive in the Deokheung-ri Tomb are landscape motifs such as mountainous terrains and trees and hunting scenes, which notably developed during the Goguryeo period. A heavenly world is unfolded on the ceiling of the antechamber, fully embellished with the sun and moon and stars, as well as the ox-herder Gyeonu and the weaving lady Jingnyeo, rarely found in tombs in other areas. Heavenly fairies, fanciful flying images of the immortals, and figures from "different worlds" such as strange but auspicious monsters and birds are of great interest. In contrast to the solemn, stiff human images on the walls, the geometric patterns on the ceiling of the antechamber are dynamically executed with accentuated strokes of varied thickness and tone.

The middle-period murals, which reflect the changes and development of Goguryeo after the kingdom moved its capital from Ji'an (presently in China) to Pyongyang in 427, include those in the Gakjeochong (Tomb of the Wrestlers), the Muyongchong (Tomb of the Dancers), the Jangcheon Tomb No. 1, the Ssangyeongchong (Tomb of the Twin Pillars), and the Susan-ri Tombs. Hence murals in these double-chambered tombs feature the regional characteristics of the two capitals. Murals in the Ji'an area notably exhibit the distinctive Goguryeo characteristics that developed through the integration of Central Asian elements. Sometimes portrayed sitting with their wives, the tomb occupants are depicted from the frontal view like the images of deities, or appear in a scene of daily life. The magnificent, official cavalry procession is replaced by a leisurely outing of a small group of people, depicted standing in a line. Such genre scenes became richer and more diverse in content with the depiction of various themes such as dancing and wrestling. The ceiling paintings feature more Buddhist themes and motifs than earlier examples, such as the twins born from a lotus flower, flying maidens in celestial robes, and scenes of Buddha worship.

The human figures in middle-period ancient murals display uniquely Goguryeo characteristics, such as a comparatively long or round face with thick chin, a conical hat with feather, dot-patterned clothing, and a rainbow-colored pleated skirt. The iconography of the "Parthian shot" tactic can also be seen, where the horseman turns his upper body round to shoot backwards, with a Goguryeo-style modification to make the horse look backwards as well. Along with these features, the painting "Warriors on Horseback" <Fig. 2.2> in the Ssangyeongchong Tomb is executed in a more concrete, natural way. The strong and confident brush strokes exhibit more advanced expressions.

In the late period tombs were reduced to the single-chamber type, as shown in the Gangseodaemyo, the Jinpa-ri Tomb No. 1, the Tonggou Sasinchong, and the Five Tombs (*Ohoebun*) No. 4 and No. 5. The murals from this period no longer include a portrait of the tomb occupant or scenes from his daily life. The four guardian deities—the Blue Dragon of the East, the White Tiger of the West, the Red Phoenix of the South, and the Black Snake-Turtle of the North—have come down from their earlier location on the ceiling to occupy the walls. The ceilings feature an array of immortals and mythological Daoist figures, implying a profound shift in motifs from Buddhist to Daoist ones and following the changes

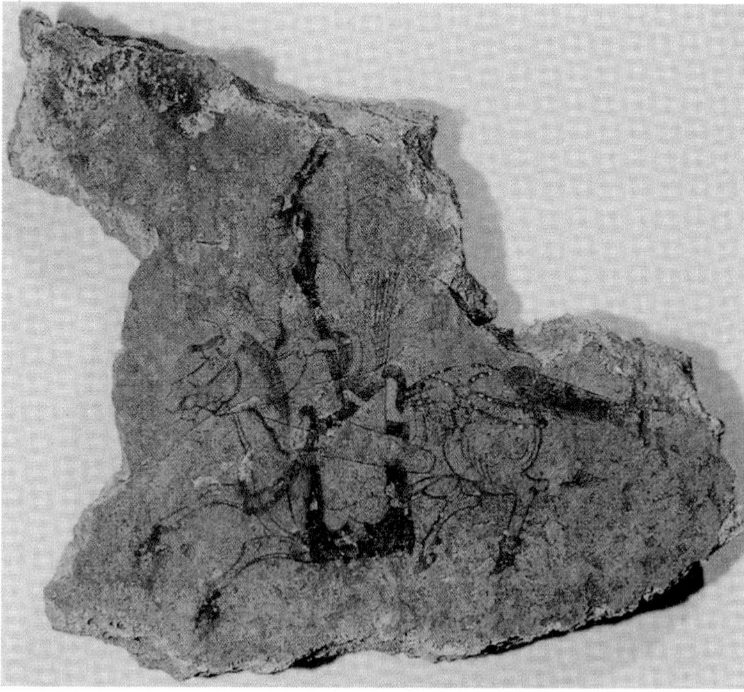

| Fig. 2.2 Mural Fragment of an Equestrian Figure from Ssangyeong-chong Tomb (Nampo-si, South Pyeongan Province, North Korea), Goguryeo, late 5th century, 44cm, National Museum of Korea

| Fig. 2.3 Black Tortoise and Serpent (black snake-turtle), Goguryeo, early 7th century, Sasin-chong Tomb, Tonggou, Ji'an, China

in the religion of the ruling class. The animal and human images are depicted in a far more realistic way under the influence of Chinese art which advanced dramatically during the Southern and Northern Dynasties. The trees and mountain peaks are rendered to give a sense of thickness, heaviness, and space. More vivid colors came into use. The decorative patterns and images covering the walls are elegant and dynamic. In particular, the painting of a black snake-turtle <Fig. 2.3> in the Sasinchong Tomb in Tonggou, China, is dramatic in that it exudes intense vitality through the energetic movements of a snake entangled with a turtle in harmony with the wave-like floating cloud patterns surrounding the mysterious figure.

| Fig. 2.4 Tile with Landscape Design, Baekje, early 7th century, 29.6×28.8cm, National Museum of Korea, Treasure No. 343

Although few examples remain extant today, Goguryeo tomb murals partially influenced the themes and execution of tomb murals and the craftwork decoration of its neighboring kingdoms, Baekje, Silla and Gaya. The tomb murals of Balhae (698–926), the kingdom founded near the Songhua River in eastern Manchuria with displaced Goguryeo people at the top of society, assimilated the Tang style to the extent that it is difficult to detect the Goguryeo tradition in them. They appear, however, to have influenced the tomb murals and decorative designs of Japan's Kofun (ca. 250–538), Asuka (538–710) and Hakuhou (645–710) periods. Although a clay tile with relief showing a landscape, dated to 7th century Baekje <Fig. 2.4>, features symmetrical, craft-like landscape design representing the ancient-style three-peaked mountains and rocks, it presages the full-fledged emergence of landscape painting as the landscape in this case is not treated as a background for human figures but as an independent motif.

(2) Development of Buddhist Painting in the Unified Silla Period

Fig. 2.5 Ui Bon collaborated with other painters, The Buddhist Illustrations in the Avatamsaka Sutra (detail), Unified Silla, 755, Gold and silver pigment on red mulberry paper, 29.2cm, Leeum, Samsung Museum of Art, National Treasure No. 196

In Unified Silla Period, painting developed in line with religious art due to the flourishing of Buddhism. As inferred from an episode regarding "Old Pine Tree" (*Nosong-do*) painted by Solgeo at the Hwangnyongsa Temple, paintings also developed to focus on "likeness of form," that is making the painting look exactly like the object, with a view to enhancing their miraculous and enlightening power. Paintings of this period are considered to have improved vastly through cultural exchange with Tang, during which time Chinese fine arts reached its first high point. The Tang court sent a folding screen as a wedding present to the royal court of its ally Silla in 596. The fact that Kim Chung-ui of Silla origin is mentioned in a Chinese textual record is of great interest in that he employed the painting style of the School of Wu Daozi, the painting sage of the Tang Dynasty. This implies that Wu's Daoist and Buddhist figure painting styles, which played a central role in the development of Tang Buddhist and Daoist figure paintings, was introduced to Silla and began to gain popularity. Silla also imported a group of paintings by Zhou Fang (c. 730–800) who was famous for his sophisticated paintings of Tang court ladies (K. *sanyeo*, Ch. shinü). The paintings of Unified Silla were introduced on the international scene around the 8th century in the form of gifts to Tang and through exports of folding screens to Japan. The Dazaifu, the administrative center of Kyushu, played an important role in importing the folding screens from Silla.

The Buddhist illustrations in the *Avatamsaka Sutra* (Flower Garland Sutra), created by various artists, including Uibon in 755, are the only extant Unified Silla paintings. The sutra frontispiece illustrations (*sagyeonghwa*), from Volumes 43–50 among the hand-copied scrolls of the 80-volume *Flower Garland Sutra*, are rendered with gold and silver powder mixed with glue on reddish-yellow mulberry paper using the *baengmyo* (Ch. baimiao, "white drawing" or "plain drawing") technique in which only the object is delicately delineated in clear, fine lines of ink. The painting of a Bodhisattva on the inside cover is based on the court painting style of Wu Daozi (680–740). It is similar in style to Japanese paintings from the Nara period and exhibits the maturity of East Asian style in the 8th century. The Buddhist-guardian spirit painting on the front cover depicts the slightly fluttering band ends and fluid folds of the garment through the skillful use of Wu's style <Fig. 2.5>. The bulging muscles of the bent legs and the tension in the knees are realistically depicted.

2) Sculpture

(1) Buddhist Sculpture

The introduction of Buddhism first began in the Three Kingdoms period (4th century), which resulted in a quickly spread to encourage the steady production of Buddhist sculptures. These developed with influences from the North and South Dynasties of China. The gilt bronze statue of Buddha is the oldest existing example <Fig. 2.6> and here the influence from the North Dynasties of China is evident; Buddha's face is long, and is wearing clothes that appear to be flattened stiffly. Such types were

| Fig. 2.6 Buddha with Inscription of "Seventh Year of *Yeonga* (延嘉)," Gilt Bronze, Goguryeo, 6th century, h. 16.2cm, National Museum of Korea, National Treasure No. 119

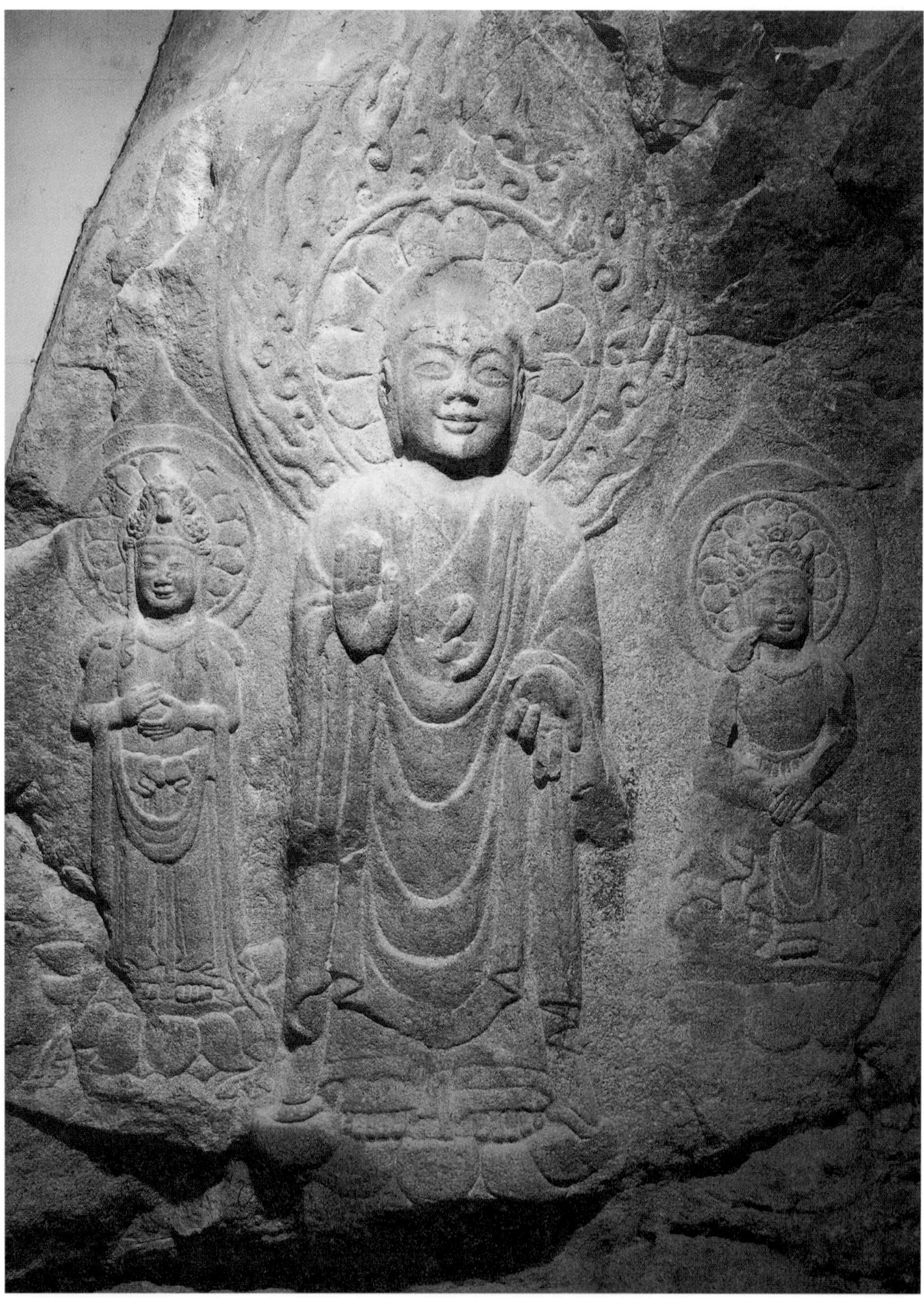

| Fig. 2.7 Buddhist Triad Carved on Rock Surface, Baekje, 7th century, h. 280cm, Unsan-myeon, Seosan, National Treasure No. 84

| Fig. 2.8 Seated Bodhisattva in Pensive Pose, Gilt Bronze, 6-7th century, h. 80cm, National Museum of Korea, National Treasure No. 78

| Fig. 2.9 Seated Bodhisattva in Pensive Pose, Gilt Bronze, 7th century, h. 93.5cm, National Museum of Korea, National Treasure No. 83

made centrally in the Goguryeo region.

Baekje (BCE 18–A.D 660) was influenced by the South Dynasties of China, as depicted in the Seosan Triad <Fig. 2.7> and the Tae-ahn Triad. Compared with the example above the folds on clothes and facial expressions are softer and smoother. The method used to carve the Goguryeo and Baekje statues of Buddha influenced those that were made in Silla. After the 7th century, influences came from the Northern Qi (北齊), Northern Zhou (北周) and Sui Dynasty (隋). Buddha statues became more three-dimensional with accentuated volume on the body. Additionally, this period saw the development of the Maitreya faith which included the image of seated Bodhisattva. Later on, this particular type became popular among all three kingdoms, resulting in the creation of master pieces such as National Treasure No. 78 <Fig. 2.8> and National Treasure No. 83 <Fig. 2.9> of gilt bronze seated Bodhisattva.

| Fig. 2.10 Buddha, Seokguram Grotto, Unified Silla, mid-8th century, h. 350cm, Mt. Tohamsan, Gyeongju, National Treasure No. 24, World Heritage

In the Unified Silla period, Buddhist related statues tended to take on a more international form with influences from the Tang (唐) Dynasty of China and also from India and other countries bordering on Western China. Balance and proportion, actual volume and detailed expressions were outstanding. Those made in the Gyeongju region around the 8th century were superior, and representational examples for this can be seen from carvings in the Seokguram (石窟庵) grotto. Religious sublimity was exressed with excellent sculpting techniques, and ideal Buddhist domain was materialized. The Seokguram grotto is a manmade space constructed using several flat and polished stones for the groined (穹窿) vault ceiling, while maintaining a balance and proportion in the stone chamber, embraces a science of divination. The structure of the Seokguram grotto is a rectangular chamber (前室) at the front connected to the main circular chamber. The two are linked by a corridor path (扉道). In the middle of the main circular chamber, there is a high-raised lotus flower pedestal with the halo of the Sakyamuni Buddha carved into the shape of a lotus flower. The structure has been made in such a way that the proportion of the entire statue appears most effective when standing in the middle of the corridor path. From

| Fig. 2.11 Indra Sakra (left) and Manjusri (right), Seokguram Grotto, Unified Silla, mid-8th century, Mt. Tohamsan, Gyeongju, National Treasure No. 24, World Heritage

this position one is able to see Buddha's halo and head. <Fig. 2.10>

The carving within the Seokguram grotto consists of all the elements related to Buddhism centered around the Sakyamuni Buddha; carvings of Bodhisattvas, deities, disciples, etc. <Fig. 2.11> Towards the latter part of the Unified Silla period, statues of Buddha were created mostly in iron rather than gilt bronze. And many seats of Buddhist idols imitated the Seokguram Sakyamuni Buddha and also the Vairocanna style statues, which continued to be popular until the beginning of the Goryeo period.

(2) Tombs Sculpture

Beginning in the Three Kingdoms period large tombs were built for kings and the nobility. Areas surrounding the tombs were constructed in uniformed styles. Most of the Goguryeo tombs are found in areas such as *Hwanin* (桓因), Tonggu (通構), Pyeongyang (平壤) and Hwanghaedo Province. In the early stages, the tombs were built with stacked stones (石塚) but after the 5th century, earth mound tombs (封土墳) became common. The early Kings' tombs were made into pyramid shapes by stacking stones into a square shape with steps (積石塚), and the most representational of this type are *Janggunchong* (將軍塚), *Taewangroong* (太王陵). In the case of *Taewangroong*, the length of one side is approximately 63m, proving that this was a large tomb with evidences of a earth wall that once surrounded the tomb. In addition to this, it seems that there was even a shrine built within the tomb location. In some cases there are traces of servants or government officials buried on the same land as the deceased lord, with two small tombs (陪塚) accompanying the main one.

During the Unified Silla period, the 12 zodiac signs replaced the four deities as tomb decorations. In order to protect the tomb, the exterior was decorated with stone statues of the 12 zodiac signs. Along with these, there were also stone guardians (儀衛) of figurines (石人) and animals (石獸). The Unified Silla (7–9th century) imitated the methods of Tang Dynasty China in constructing the stone sculptures of tombs, including the protective guardians and government officials placed outside tombs. The personified statues of the 12 zodiac signs that surround the tombs have animal features. Such structures can been seen today at Queen Seondeok's (–647) tomb, King Wonseong's (–798) tomb, King Heungdeok's (777–836) tomb and the tomb of Kim Yu-sin (595–673), who unified the Three Kingdoms.

3) Metal Work, Ceramics and Lacquer Ware

Metal and clay craft have been discovered as well as a small quantity of lacquer objects, which were excavated in the Goguryeo and Silla regions.

(1) Metal work

In terms metal works, gold works made for burial purposes are the most remarkable. From the Goguryeo period (BCE 1–A.D 7th century), metal objects decorated with plating and carving technique such as carved accessories, rice-cake steamers, pots, containers, copper vessels remain extant.

| Fig. 2.12 Incense Burner, Gilt Bronze, Baekje, mid-6th century, Excavated from Temple Site at Neungsan-ri, Buyeo, h. 62cm, Buyeo National Museum, National Treasure No. 287

| Fig. 2.13 Gold Crown, Silla, Excavated from Cheonma-chong, h. 32.5cm, Gyeongju National Museum, National Treasure No. 188

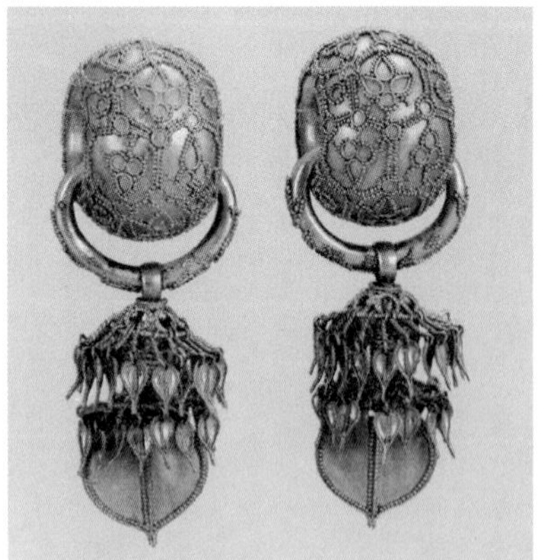

| Fig. 2.14 Gold Earrings, Silla, Excavated from Bubu-chong, Bomun-dong, Gyeongju, h. 8.7cm, National Museum of Korea, National Treasure No. 90

Gold and silver objects of Baekje were found in the Tomb of King Muryeong. The people of Baekje were famous for making precious crowns with jewels (寶冠), crown ornament (冠飾), pendants (垂下飾), earrings, bracelets, gold hair-pins, bronze burial shoes, as well as horse equipment and weapons. Baekje was also renowned for a sword with seven blades (七支刀), which is now in a collection at the Japanese Isonokami Shrine. From the excavation site of Neungsan-ri (陵山里) metal-smith workshop, metal mirrors, which a gilt bronze incense burner with a dragon, and a phoenix (龍鳳金銅大香爐) <Fig. 2.12> depicting the Baekje belief of the universe were found, each of which are examples of excellent skills in handling metal.

The locations of Byeonhan and Jinhan mark the Gaya Kingdom, and it had a strong iron based culture that is famous for producing implements related to horse-riding along with other metal accessories. In Silla, there was a hierarchical order related to the use of gold, silver, gem stones and jade (金銀珠玉). Records show evidence of gold being used for trade exchanges with other countries and also for making Buddha statues, sutras and other objects. From the crowns <Fig. 2.13>, crown decorations, gold belt (銙帶), waist pendant (腰佩), earrings <Fig. 2.14>, necklaces, bracelets and so on which were excavated from great tombs of Gyeongju showed that these were highly developed Silla's metal work technique and reflect the power and the state of the royal family. Buddhist accessories and everyday objects were made using techniques such as filigree (鏤金), inlay (象嵌), inlaying threads of metal (入絲), openwork (透彫), battery (打出) and so on.

Bell (梵鐘) were incorporated in temples for assembling people, or for notifying the time of the day, and also for ceremonies. It is said that they were first made in India and China. On the Korean peninsula, the bells made during the Silla period are the most well known. Although the size and shape vary, all of them were hung on belfries, and were struck with a wooden stick, *dangmok* (撞木). The top part of the bell was made into the shape of a dragon's head, *yongnyu* (龍紐) for hanging, the sounding device was referred to as *yongtong* (甬筒), and finally the main body was decorated in three parts. Often there would be an image of Bodhisattvas or flying apsaras[angels] engraved on the main body. In Buddhism, it was believed that listening to the sound of the bell enabled one's worries to disappear and one's wisdom to grow. Thus the variety of Buddhist iconography interpreted the deep impressive resonance of the bell. <Fig. 2.15>

| Fig. 2.15 Sacred Bell of The Great King Seongdeok, Unified Silla, 771, h. 375cm, d. 227cm, Gyeongju National Museum, National Treasure No. 29

(2) Ceramics and Lacquerware

From the Three Kingdoms to the Unified Silla period, ceramics developed rapidly. With the introduction of Chinese ceramics there was acceleration in the development of Korea wares. This was followed by advancements in kiln building techniques, increase in firing temperatures, diverse changes in material quality associated with the demands of different social classes, and the introduction of artificial glazes. Goguryeo was the first kingdom to have accepted the ceramic techniques of China, and was a forerunner with advanced techniques in making clay, using a potter's wheel, and introducing methods of carbonizing fired surfaces. <Fig. 2.16>

In Baekje, techniques in producing a grayish hard pottery developed. A custom of burying large quantities of earthenware for funerals became popular, which precipitated the production of large amounts of ceramic objects. Such objects came in a variety of forms, including jars with a long neck (長頸壺), bottles with an opening (有孔壺), mounted cups (高杯), flat cups with a cover (蓋杯), pottery with three legs (三足器), pottery ink-stones (陶硯), burial urns (骨壺) among others.

The development of earthenware in the Kingdom of Gaya was centered around the east

| Fig. 2.16 Earthenware, Goguryeo, 5-6th century, h. 53.5, Seoul National University Museum (upper) / h. 22.4cm, National Museum of Korea (under)

side of the Nakdong River. The ceramics of Gaya are characterized by a pedestal foot, supports for plates, shoes, go-carts, horses, ducks, wild geese, houses and horse-riders. They were famous for producing various forms in earthenware <Fig. 2.17>, with depictions of peoples, and animals, and also for the openwork decorations.

The Silla kingdom developed firing techniques where clay was fired to a higher temperature using natural glaze and for this the hill climbing kilns were established. Among the diverse methods applied in making earthenware of this period, many vessels were made with decorations of clay figurines and animals-these were attached onto the vessels as a form of decoration. <Fig. 2.18> And the pottery was a part of burial wares, and thus retained a high foot. These forms are understood as reflections of life itself as well as symbolizing aspirations in the after-life.

In the Unified Silla period, the burial tradition altered, and burying vast quantities of ceramic objects disappeared. In comparison to the Three Kingdoms period, large amounts of ceramics were found in habitations sites. Furthermore, influences continued to inflow from China.

| Fig. 2.17 Vessel in the Shape of Warrior on Horseback, Silla, 5-6th century, h. 23.5, 21.3cm, National Museum of Korea

| Fig. 2.18 Earthenware with Clay Figurines, Silla, Excavated from Nodong-dong Tomb, Gyeongju, h. 34cm, Gyeongju National Museum

The technique of three colors *sancai* (三彩) derived from the Tang Dynasty was introduced along with the custom of keeping ceramic urns. As a result, glazed wares began to produce for funerary urns.

The other side, Lacquerware developed in the early part of the Three Kingdoms period. According to excavation conducted in 1988 in South Gyeongsang Province, the Changwon (昌原) Daho-ri (茶戸里) tomb site revealed burial objects in lacquer, including musical instruments, swords, and for sacrificial rite *Tou* (豆). These show that lacquerware developed independently in Korea. Lacquerware has also been found in the Goguryeo the Five Tombs (*Ohhoebun*) and the Baekje Tomb of King Muryeong. From the Tomb of King Muryeong, lacquer decorations have been found on a pillow and a foot-rest. From the Silla kingdom, excavated materials show that lacquer was used for painting images and gold was applied top of lacquerware. It appears that lacquer was experimented in a number of different methods as found in the tombs of Geumgwanchong (金冠塚), Cheonmachong (天馬塚), Hwangnamdaechong (皇南大塚).

4) Architecture in Wood, Pagodas and Habitation

Ancient architecture of Korea consisted mainly of wood. This material was used together with stone and earth to form the foundation of wood architecture. The structure of roofs centered around brackets (栱包) and columns (柱) were the basic formation for royal palaces and temples, in addition to other important architectural constructions. Although they relied on function and symbol, the architectural composition was the outcome of people's conceptions that the interior space was made to appreciate an integrated view from the inside looking outward.

(1) The Capital City and the Royal Palace

It is said that during the Goguryeo period, royal chambers were embellished, fortress walls built high, and every household had small storage chambers. Furthermore, the roofs of temples, ancestral shrines (神廟), royal palaces, government offices were covered with tiles, and the custom of ordinary people was to construct the *ondol* (溫突) system which entails heating the floors in order to withstand the cold of winter. In Baekje, houses were built as residences both inside and outside the palace fortress wall, and there were a large number of priests and priestesses within the fortress grounds along with temple pagodas. In Silla, braziers were kept in rooms during winter, and in the summer food was served placed on top of ice.

With the establishment of the Three Kingdoms, cities were fortified and the royal palaces built; Goguryeo, in particular, introduced the Chinese style in city-planning, with the main north-south axis in the middle, and the placement of the royal palaces and the market in the east-west axis. The most renowned fortress palace of Goguryeo was the Ahnhak Palace (安鶴宮), located in the Daesung mountain, region of Pyeongyang. The structure of this fortress palace was laid out in a manner where the northern and southern sections were divided in relation to a central pivotal point.

Baekje also moved the capital three times, from Wirae (慰禮) to Woongjin (熊津), and then finally to Sabi (泗沘). According to the *Samguk sagi* History of the Three Kingdoms 《三國史記》, the architecture of Baekje was modest but tasteful, magnificent but in extravagant. Baekje was modest but not distasteful; it was magnificent but was not extravagant. However, records show that the Yimryugak (臨流閣) pavilion and the pond of the Woongjinseong palace (雄津城) were exquisitely dazzling. Later, when the capital city moved to Sabi, the Korean method of building fortresses was combined with those of Chinese structures, which encircle the city. An example for this is the Buso Mountain fortress (扶蘇山城), which was built in the method mentioned previously with a special format of fortifying the capital city. The Baekje skills of building palaces and gardens were transmitted to Japan.

For Silla, Gyeongju was the main city, and at first the royal palace was established within capital city Geumseong (金城) but later and the royal palace moved to Woulseong palace (月城). For 1,000 years the city of Gyeongju continued to expand gradually. With the excavation of the Silla royal palace rear garden Anapji Pond (雁鴨池). In 1975, five different lands were discovered including the Yimhaejeon (臨海殿) of Anapji site. Furthermore, there were evidences showing that the lake shores had stone masonry.

(2) Temples

The transmission of Buddhism encouraged Buddhist architecture to flourish. The layout of temples and the composition of space differed in style according to period, regional characteristics and Buddhist doctrines. In A.D. 375 Goguryeo, two temples Chomunsa Temple (肖門寺) and Yibulransa Temple (伊弗蘭寺) were first established within the fortress.

With these, Buddhist temples began to develop. At first the construction was centered around a single pagoda and building, known as Buddhist temple layout, <Fig. 2.19> but later changed to a single pagoda with two buildings in the Buddhist temple format.

Although the evidence is not entirely clear, it is believed that Buddhism influenced Baekje a year after it was transmitted to Korea, in the year A.D. 385 (the second year of King Chimryu). Baekje further developed the layout of the temple sites based on placing the middle gate, pagoda, the main building (金堂) and assembly hall in relation to a central point based on north and south directions. The site of Jeongrimsa Temple (定林寺) in Buyeo is the most representational of this layout, and Gunsuri Temple, which also has been constructed in this form, remain today. Such styles later influenced the construction

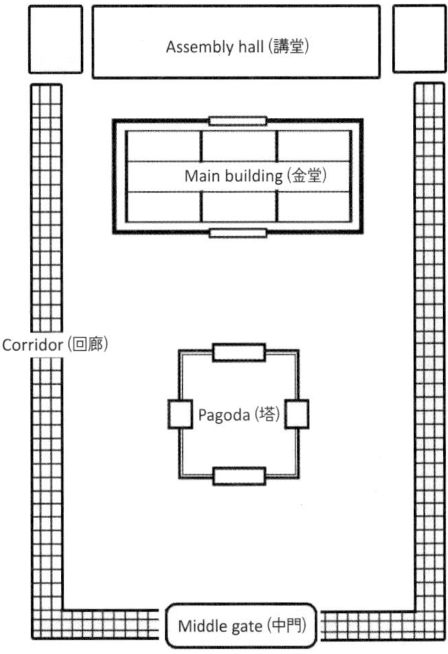

| Fig. 2.19 A Single Pagoda and Main Building *Garam* Layout, Baekje, 6th century, Mireuksa Temple Site

| Fig. 2.20 Dabotap Pagoda (left) and Seokgatap Pagoda (right), Unified Silla, Bulguksa Temple, Gyeongju, National Treasure No. 20, 21

methods of Silla and Japan.

In Silla, around the 6th century, Heungryunsa Temple (興輪寺) and Youngheungsa Temple (靈興寺) were the first temples constructed. In Hwangryongsa Temple (黃龍寺), the layout is depicted with three main buildings (三金堂式) centered around one wooden pagoda with nine stories. In the early years, pagodas were made of wood and later developed to stone. In the Unified Silla period, the format changed to have two pagodas (二塔式) instead of one, the site was centralized not around the pagoda but on the main building where a Buddha statue was housed. Through this change it is possible to see that the transitions in religious beliefs were reflected simultaneously in the structure of temples. Bulguksa Temple (佛國寺) in Gyeongju is a prime example depicting this phenomenon, there are two pagodas in this Buddhist temple layout, the Dabatap Pagoda (多寶塔) and the Seokgatap pagodas (釋迦塔). <Fig. 2.20>

2. Dance

1) Dance of the Goguryeo Kingdom

The dance of Goguryeo (37 BC–668 AD), one of the three ancient Korean kingdoms, combined the magnanimous spirit of the culture of the northern states and the courageousness of its horse-riding tribe, showing its distinctive continental features in an open-hearted dance form. *Dongmaeng*, which was held in the 10th month, was a sort of thanksgiving rite to show gratitude and offer up prayer to heavenly gods and a holy ceremony to pay reverence to ancestors worshiped across the entire nation.

A record of Goguryeo dance can be found in tomb wall paintings and Chinese documents. The tomb wall paintings present the basic movements of the dance, costumes, the number of dancers, musical instruments etc., and providing detailed and realistic insight into the period. In particular, the wall paintings of the *Muyongchong* and *Dongsu* tombs clearly show that dancers and musicians were independent from one another.

One of the wall paintings shows a person dancing to the rhythm of instruments such as the *geomun-go* (six-stringed zither), *wanham* (similar to the sitar), and *tungso* (bamboo flute) while clapping their hands and twisting their legs into an X-shape. This shows that, at that time, ensemble music was already being performed to dance. Furthermore, from the movements of dance and the appearance of the dancers, it can be surmised that they were performances conducted by peoples of the lands west of China. Such evidences propped up the fact that Goguryeo not only established ties with China but carried out trade with other

| Fig. 2.21 Wall Painting of the Goguryeo *Muyongchong* Tomb

| Fig. 2.22 Women Dancers of Goguryeo

states from the west via the Silk Road.

(1) Types of Goguryeo Dance

Goguryeo dance can be examined based on the types depicted in the wall paintings of tombs and the types discussed in written documents. In particular, records in Chinese show that the dances including *jiseomu, hoseonmu,* and *goryeomu* were performed in royal banquets of the Tang Dynasty. Upon seeing a Goguryeo dance, Chinese poet Yi Baek praised the performance in a poem, "One male dancer, flutters his long sleeves dancing to a slow tune, appearing like a mystical large bird, *Daebung*, flying in the sky."

As for *jiseomu*, even though there are records stating "jiseo" referred to the name of song and dance, the original form of the dance cannot be found; it is only presumed that the dance was performed with a large instrumental orchestra.

Hoseonmu is a dance that originated from the countries to the west of China, and transformed into the Goguryeo style. This performance was a kind of acrobatic dance with performers stamping their feet on a circular carpet.

As shown in Yi Baek's poems, Goguryeo dance is presumed to have been lively and masculine. Later on, at the end of the Joseon Dynasty, this dance was re-introduced by Crown Prince Hyomyeong and continues to be performed to this day.

(2) The Characteristics of Goguryeo Dance

As observed above, the characteristics of Goguryeo dance, which achieved a lofty level of complexity through the spirit of the continent and the cultural exchange with China and the countries west of China, can be summarized as follows:

① The kinds of dance found in written records are the *hoseonmu, jiseomu* and *goguryeo-mu*. These dances have a continental spirit and technical artistry, and were popular in China as well.

② Goguryeo dance developed with the lively and masculine characteristics that reflected the people's energetic and progressive nature.

③ The dances were performed in garments with long and wide sleeves, providing an effect similar to that of today's *jangsam*, a Buddihist monk's clothing with long and broad sleeves.

④ The tomb wall paintings prove that there were professional dancers and orchestral musicians and they subsequently became the basis for court dance.

⑤ As presented in the *hoseonmu*, Goguryeo dance had acrobatic features.

2) Dance of the Baekje Kingdom

Among the main three kingdoms, Baekje (18 BC–660 AD) was located on the most fertile land south of the *Han* River and geographically it was a location with convenient marine transportation. Owing to this fact, it accepted the cultural influences of southern China and achieved great feats in art and culture. As the Baekje kingdom was established on the ancient Samhan lands, the traditions of Samhan's ritual for worshipping the heavens, such as ceremonies with song and dance, were continued for several days after the rites performed around seeding in the fifth month of the lunar calendar and harvests in the tenth month. In addition, there was custom in which people danced together carrying a percussion instrument similar to that of a monk's wooden gong, *moktak*. Again this has continued clearly to contemporary times in its original form as *nongak* (farmers' music) and *durae-gut* (commoners' folk music and dance).

In comparison to the Goguryeo kingdom, there are hardly any extant historical records on Baekje dance. Yet to our fortune, there are some precious facts recorded in Japanese. It dates back to the early 7th century when Mimaji, a citizen of the Baekje kingdom, learned the instrumental music of Wu Dynasty, in southern China and introduced it to the Korean Peninsula and even to Japan. The mask for this particular music is preserved at a temple named Dongdaesa in Japan and other places. The music was succeeded to be the *sandaenori*, a kind of masked theatrical dance of today in many regions across Korea. As Baekje was situated in the wide plains, the dance of the kingdom developed as the type of dance performed in famer's music, *nongak*, combining labor with religion into song and dance. In addition, based on cultural exchange with China and Japan, it imported song and music from China and transformed them into those of Baekje, and also introduced them to Japan, contributing to the prosperity of ancient Japanese art and culture.

(1) Types of Baekje Dance

Baekje dance is chiefly comprised of *kiakmu* (*kigaku*), a Buddhist mask dance; dances developed from folk dances such as the *nongakmu* (farmers' music and dance) and *Ganggangsullae* (female circle dance); *takmu*, dance with a percussion instrument similar to the monk's wooden gong, *moktak*; and Baekje *muak* (song and dance).

The written records state that the *kiakmu* "was introduced to Japan by the Baekje native Mimaji after he had acquired it from Wu, the southern China state." The *kiakmu* was a type of dance performed for memorial services. It was similar to *mukhee*, a kind of masked mime, and had elements of a comedy. *Kiak* means song and dance performed for memorial services; it is said that many children of the upper classes in Japan learned this dance, and it was widely performed for the purpose of promulgating Buddhism. Although the exact content and forms of the original dance are unknown today, it served as an important main branch of Japanese traditional dance and it is thought to be the predecessor of *sandaenori*, one of the masked plays with dance of Korea. Again, from this vantage, it can be said that Chinese *kiak*, introduced from central Asia, passed through Baekje, and was transmitted to Japan.

The *nongakmu* and *ganggangsullae*, which came from old customs of ancient Samhan, exhibited traces of dances performed in unison that reflect farming culture. In the Baekje kingdom, farming rites were held during the sowing season, the fifth month of the lunar calendar, and during harvest season, the tenth month, they were collectively referred to as *sodojae*. During these special times, people drank alcohol and kept up their singing and dancing all through the day and night. The *nongak* was a collaborative performance, with the objective of combining labor with entertainment, during the farming season. For the farmers, work and pleasure were not two separate things, for them, work was pleasure. For this reason, the *nongak* from the Korean farming culture grew into a highly developed genre. The *ganggangsullae* is a women's circle dance performed under a full moon. It boasts several amusing and playful characteristics.

Takmu danced with a *moktak* (wooden gong) can be assumed as an initial form of *nongakmu* considering Chinese records stating, "In Baekje, *takmu* similar to the court banquet dance was performed in the 5th and 10th month of the lunar calendar." The records stating that, "The instrument, similar to the *moktak* was played while dancing" can be interpreted to show this instrument was developed to become one of the *samul*, four percussion instruments played in *nongak*.

Finally, "Baekje-*muak*" denotes the music and dance of the Baekje kingdom out of all the music and dance transmitted to Japan from the three kingdoms. In records in Annals of Japan, Baekje instrumental orchestra is introduced in a form similar to that of Goguryeo's, with four performers of diverging roles: three musicians who played instruments called *hwaengjeok, gonghu, makmok,* respectively, and one dancer. Likewise, among all of the *samhanak*, which denotes the music of Baekje, Silla and Goguryeo, Baekje dance and music was the first to have reached Japan before AD 554. Furthermore, around the 6th century, Baekje music and dance was transmitted through the dispatch of Baekje musicians and dancers to Japan on a regular basis.

(2) The Characteristics of Baekje Dance

Baekje established a glorious culture and its influence outside of its own territory was monumental, yet there are limitations in tracing the exact forms and variations of music and dance that existed during the Baekje era due to the paucity of written documents on its antiquities and remnants. However, fragments of evidence show the existence of the Baekje-*muak*, which was transmitted to Japan, *nongakmu* (farmers' music and dance), *ganggangsullae* (female circle dance), *takmu* (dance performed with a Buddhist wooden gong), and *kiakmu* (Buddhist mask dance). The characteristics of such Baekje dance are as follows:

① Unlike Goguryeo, Baekje established its own dance culture with the influence of the music of southern China.

② Masked theatrical dances were developed and spread as far as Japan, leaving behind different types of masks.

③ The social rank of musicians and dancers was relatively high with nationally designated government positions.

④ There were many different folk dances that took the form of group dances including the farming dance and dance performed in unison related to farming culture. Additionally, folk dances like the *nongakmu, ganggangsullae* were performed in a complete form.

3) Dance of the Silla Kingdom

According to the *Samguk sagi,* a historical record of the Three Kingdoms of Korea, Goguryeo, Baekje and Silla, the dance of Silla prior to the unification of the three kingdoms, gradually developed from folk dances. Records state that in the 8th month of the lunar calendar, during the period of harvest, women sang a song called *hwoesogok* rhythmically in a sort of weaving competition known as *gilsamnaegi* and it can easily be supposed that they danced while they sang.

In this period, there were dances performed in courts to the instrumental accompaniment of the 12-stringed zither, *gayageum* along with songs. Some dances were performed only to *gayageum* music without songs such as namely *hangimu, mijimu, daegeummu.* Dance performed to *gayageum* accompaniment is one of the most distinctive characteristics of Silla Dance.

In the Silla dance and music, the roles of each participant were clearly delineated: there was a performer of music called *geumcheok,* dancer called *mucheok,* singer called *gacheok.* Dance, music, and song were divided and developed by professional experts in their respective fields. The types of dance were also diverse: *geommu*, *sangyeommu*, *muaemu* and *japhui*, is also known as Silla's *ohgi* (五伎, Five Amusements), were widely performed.

(1) Types of Silla Dance

Silla (57 BC–935 AD) was founded by amalgamating the states surrounding its kingdom and consequently inherited the ancient customs of Samhan. The amalgamation with the highly cultured state of Gaya allowed Gaya's dance to develop early on and spread widely in the Silla kingdom. Records show the strong influence of Gaya's art, particularly, a Gaya's citizen named Ureuk who "accepted an order from King Jinheung (in the 13th year of his reign, AD 552) to teach music and dance to Silla's citizens, Gyego, Beopji and Mandeok. Ureuk taught them at the national court. Ureuk taught Gyego the *gayageum*, and songs to Beopji and dance to Mandeok."

Silla dance can be classified as follows:

As the court dance for the ruling class, there were nine kinds diverted into two broad styles. The type of court songs and dances for special banquets that consisted of a *gayageum* performance, singing and dancing includes *hanshinyeolmu*, *sanaemu*, *sangshinyeolmu*, *sogyeongmu*, and *sanaegeummu*. Another type that consisted of *gayageum* and dance includes *hangimu*, *mijimu*, *daegeummu* and *gamu*. The composition and contents of these dances were not handed down to the present, however, they demonstrated distinct characteristics of the form of *geumgamu*, which denotes the combination of *gayageum*, song and dance,

| Fig. 2.23 *Geommu*

belonging solely to Silla.

The *geommu* is a kind of sword dance, and is also referred to as *geomgimu* or *hwangchangrangmu*. Stories said that *hwangchangrangmu* originated in a dance performed with a mask that bore the image of a boy named *hwangchang* who had killed the king of Baekje, to mourn the death of the young man. The dance is performed to this day and it is executed with two short daggers held in both hands and scores of buoyant and smooth movements. The characteristic of the dance is the diverse changes in movement and rhythm. Today this dance is performed without a mask and appears in the different forms of court dance and folk dance. <Fig. 2.23>

The *muaemu* is a dance performed to the *muaega* (*muae* song) composed for the purpose of spreading Buddhism. It is said that the dance developed by the great monk Wonhyo at the end of Silla.

The Silla *ohgi* was a playful acrobatic dance influenced by the western states bordering China.

There was another type of dance known as *gungjung jangnye* dance, which denotes dance performed in court funeral rites. The records on this dance are found in a Japanese document, which states: "In AD 453, 80 Silla dancers and musicians went across to Japan to pay tribute to the dead king and they wailed loudly at a place named Chukja of Daema-island of Japan, and when they resided in Nanpajin, they appeared at the king's grave wearing white clothes performing the *jangsonggamuak* (葬送歌舞樂, song and dance invoking the deceased to depart).

(2) The Characteristics of Silla Dance

As observed in the different types of Silla dance, there was a wide range of court and folk dances and entertainment performances of different types. In particular, in national ceremonies such as the *palgwanhwoe* (Festival of the Eight Vows) and *yeondeunghwoe* (Lotus Lantern Festival), influenced by Buddhism, music, dance and other forms of entertainment were performed and played important roles in such events.

The characteristics of Silla dance are as follows:

① The types of Silla dance include court dances which consisted of *gayageum*, song and dance, *geommu*, farming-folk dance and Silla *ohgi*, which was a kind of an acrobatic playful dance.

② Musicians and dancers were treated well in the court, as attested to by their high ranks.

③ The roles were divided into *mucheok* (dancer), *gacheok* (singer), *geumcheok* (musical player).

④ Court dance and music was so developed in terms of skills and scale that as many as 80 musicians and dancers were sent to the funeral of a Japanese king.

4) Dance of the Unified Silla Kingdom

Most of dances of Unified Silla were inherited from those of Silla period. The types of dance in this period include *cheoyongmu* (Cheoyong mask dance), *sangyeommu* (dance created by King Heongang), *seonyurak* (boat party dance) and the Silla *ohgi*, which focused largely on play.

Cheoyongmu developed from the tale of Cheoyong in the period of the 49th King Heongang (875–886). In this dance five people were placed in the five directional positions wearing the Cheoyong mask and garments symbolizing the five directions: the dancer to the

| Fig. 2.24 *Cheoyongmu*

east dressed in blue, the south in red, the center in yellow, the west in white and the north in black. Entering in the order of blue, red, yellow, white and black, five males perform an energetic and dazzling dance. This dance was performed in great court conventions held on the third month of the lunar calendar to dispel evil spirits and hail auspicious occasions and court banquets held when Chinese diplomatic envoys visited the kingdom. Later on, the dance developed into more sophisticated court dance and today it has settled as one of the most representative court dances. <Fig. 2.24>

The *sangyeommu* dance was said to have been created by King Heongang. It is said that he made this dance after seeing the Namsan mountain spirit dancing at the *poseokjeong*. According to the tale, the servants did not see the spirit and only the king could behold it.

The *seonyurak* (boat party dance) was a dance performed by several groups of female entertainers standing around a beautifully decorated boat called *Chaesun* dancing while rocking the boat. Inside the boat, two young apprentices stand at the front and rear side of the boat holding the anchor and the sail. The other female dancers hold the boat ropes, circulating both in and out of the boat singing and dancing to songs depicting the pleasure of fishermen. <Fig. 2.25>

Silla *ohgi* appears in five poems called *hyangakjapyeongohsu* (鄕樂雜詠五首, Five Poems of Five Entertainments) by a renowned writer of Silla, Choi Chi-won. It denotes five different types of playful entertainment in the style of the countries to the west of China. *Ohgi* includes *geumhwan*, *weoljeon*, *daemyeon*, *sokdok* and *sanyae*. *Geumhwan* was a type of acrobatic performance where the dancing was carried out while simultaneously throwing a golden ball into the air. Weoljeon was a kind of a mask dance originating from central Asia. *Daemyeon* was a slow and mysterious dance, performed while wearing a large mask. *Sokdok* was a group dance consisting of four to five dancers wearing blue colored masks. *Sanyae* is assumed to be a lion

| Fig. 2.25 *Seonyurak*

dance influenced by the countries to the west of China. Likewise, the dance of Silla developed with the unification of the three kingdoms inheriting the art forms of all three kingdoms including Goguryeo and Baekje. Different forms were accepted, along with the instruments, to develop a versatile variation of music to establish a large-scale dance form.

3. Music

The Three Kingdoms including Goguryeo, Baekje and Silla developed their own inherent royal court music through active international exchanges with neighboring countries, especially China and Japan. During this period, music represented the dignity of the royal court. In the royal court ceremonies, wind and string orchestra accompanied songs and dances, and string instruments took the central role as the symbol of the kingdoms. Among the Three Kingdoms, music of Goguryeo was the most developed and the largest numbers of historical materials on Goguryeo's music have been found.

In 668 AD, Silla unified the Three Kingdoms with the Tang Dynasty of China. Unified Silla accepted the music of Goguryeo and Baekje, and at the same time, imported the music of the Tang Dynasty. Buddhism became the main religion of Silla and Buddhist music spread and helped to establish a rich and diverse music culture in Silla. In the royal court of Unified Silla, both *dangak* (music of the Tang Dynasty) and *hyangak* (indigenous music) were practiced.

1) Music of the Goguryeo Kingdom

Aspect of the music culture of Goguryeo can be conjectured based on several extant mural paintings. In these paintings, scenes of several different musical genres including banquet music, processional music, and accompaniment music for acrobatic plays, are depicted. Banquet music of Goguryeo was an all-inclusive performing art, including singing and dancing with wind, string and percussion orchestras. For the banquet music, not many different kinds of musical instruments were employed, rather a chamber ensemble composed of a *wanham* (holding like Western mandolin), a *geomun-go* and one, two or three vertical flutes called *tungso* were used. <Fig. 2.26>

Processional music was performed for public processions, particularly for people of the highest status, such as the king, and was performed in a dignified manner with official attire, flags and arms.

| Fig. 2.26 Painting of Singing and Dancing from Goguryeo Anak Tomb No. 3

Wanham

In mural paintings, small and large scale processional music scenes are found. In the large scale processions, the paintings portray the images of musicians performing drums and metal percussion instruments on horseback along with musicians of wind instruments, making a total of approximately 60 musicians. In the small scale processions, three musicians play drums and one on a wind instrument. Consequently, as depicted in the paintings, it is possible to state that musical instruments of Goguryeo processional music include percussion and wind instruments whether conducted on a small or large scale. <Fig. 2.27>

Furthermore, music was always performed for different ceremonies in conjunction with special entertainments and acrobatics. The images of such acrobatics and accompanying musicians have been found in the mural paintings. These images show a group of musicians playing drums and trumpets for entertainment. The mural wall painting is a clear

| Fig. 2.27 Painting and Reproduction of Processional music from Goguryeo Anak Tomb No. 3

| Fig. 2.28 Painting of Musicians and Entertainers from Goguryeo Palcheong-ri Tomb

depiction of the ways in which music was incorporated into whole variety of ceremonies in Goguryeo. <Fig. 2.28>

In Goguryeo, diverse musical instruments including *ohyeon* (a string instrument with five strings), *geomun-go*, *wanham*, *hoengchi*, *go* drum, *piri* (bamboo flute), and *so* (a wind instrument with many bamboo pipes) were employed. Among these, *geomun-go* was the most representative instrument of Goguryeo and it is also found in mural paintings. The instrument in the painting has 4 strings with a rectangular sound box, but later it was modified into a six-string instrument by a musician Wang San-ak during the middle of the 6th century. This modified six-string *geomun-go* is still in use today. <Fig. 2.29>

| Fig. 2.29 *Geomun-go*

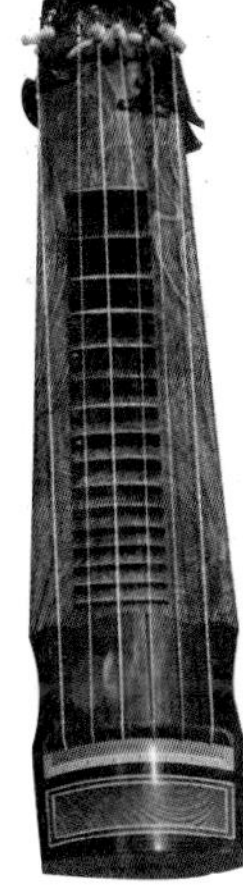

The *ohyeon* is the string instrument with five strings. Later in the Unified Silla period, *ohyeon* was called as *hyangbipa* and was played until the late Joseon period. <Fig. 2.30>

Hoengchi was a kind

of bamboo flute which played horizontally. As one of the representative instruments of Goguryeo and *hoengchi* is also found in tomb mural paintings. After the Unified Silla period, this instrument was known as the *daegeum* (a large transverse bamboo flute), which became the representative and important musical instrument in Korea today. <Fig. 2.31>

The *go* refers to a percussion instrument. Similarly the *go* of Goguryeo is an hourglass shaped drum and belongs to the *yogo* category. It is a miniature version of the present day *janggu*. <Fig. 2.32>

The *piri* is a double-reed oboe that is held vertically. Later it became known as the *hyangpiri* and is transmitted until the present day. The *piri* plays the main melody in several repertoires. <Fig. 2.33>

Since the kingdom of Goguryeo was located next to China, Chinese music began to be imported earlier than the 5th century and the music of central Asia was also imported through China. Goguryeo music, which was a combination of diverse foreign and native cultures, was performed at the Sui and Tang royal courts under the name of *Goryeogi*. Goguryeo music performed in China was an all-inclusive performing art, consisting of instrumental music, singing and dancing.

| Fig. 2.30 ***Hyangbipa***

Fifteen different instruments including string, wind and percussion instruments were used for these orchestras. Among these, twelve kinds of musical instruments were derived from central Asia through the northern states of China. Goguryeo music continued to be introduced in China until the 9th century.

Goguryeo music was also performed in Japan, including instrumental music, singing and

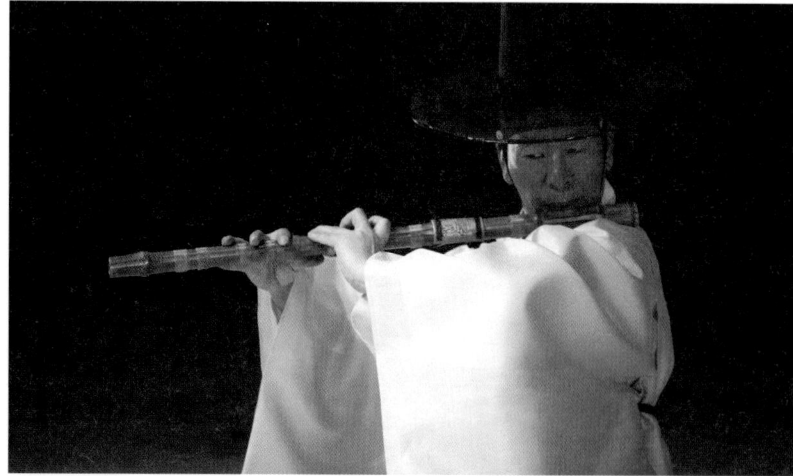

| Fig. 2.31 ***Daegeum***

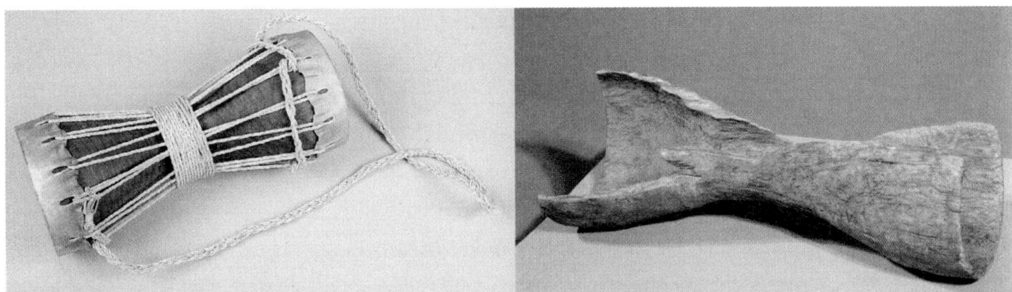

| Fig. 2.32 Body of *Yogo* excavated from Hanam City (Hanyang University Museum) and Its Reproduction (National Gugak Center)

dancing. Unlike the Goguryeo music performed in China, indigenous Goguryeo instruments including *hoengjeok*, *gunhu*, *mangmok* and *go* were used in Japan. Among these, *hoengjeok* refers to a transverse wind instrument *hoengchi*, *gunhu* refers to a string instrument, *geomun-go*, *mangmok* was the *piri* used in Goguryeo, and the *go* was a percussion instrument used in Goguryeo. Thus it can be said that Goguryeo music performed in Japan was indigenous Goguryeo music which was performed with Goguryeo indigenous musical instruments.

| Fig. 2.33 *Piri*

2) Music of the Baekje Kingdom

The ethnic composition of the Baekje people was the same as Goguryeo, therefore the two kingdoms, in terms of music, shared many similarities.

However, it is highly possible that the topographical differences between the two kingdoms could have influenced their musical tendencies. Goguryeo, located in mountainous area, produced bold and buoyant music relying largely on percussion instruments. On the contrary, Baekje's music was more lyrical with less emphasis on percussions since it was located in the plain area. Unfortunately, there are few extant records to give substantial knowledge on the music of Baekje as well as some archeological findings. Ancient forms of string instruments such as the *geomun-go*, *wanham*, and *bipa*, wind instruments like *jangjeok*, *baeso*, *hwoengjeok*, and *saeng* and percussion instrument *yogo* have been found. <Fig. 2.34>

Later than Goguryeo, Baekje began political, economic and cultural exchange with the southern states of China, which were located closer to Baekje. However, Baekje did not import central Asian music. Musical instruments from China were eight instruments including string, wind and percussion instruments. Five among the eight were from the southern states of China.

From a geographical point of view, Baekje was the closest kingdom to Japan among the Three Kingdoms, as a result the music of Baekje influenced that of Japan. As early as the 6th century, Baekje musicians were sent to Japan and their music, dance, and songs also were introduced under the name of *Baekje-ak*. After Baekje was taken over by Silla, many Baekje nobility fled to Japan and they took a central role in developing Japanese culture. Baekje music in Japan was performed with *hoengjeok*, *gunhu*, *mangmok* and *mu*, which are the same as those of Goguryeo music in Japan. Songs and dances with these musical instruments were all Baekje's.

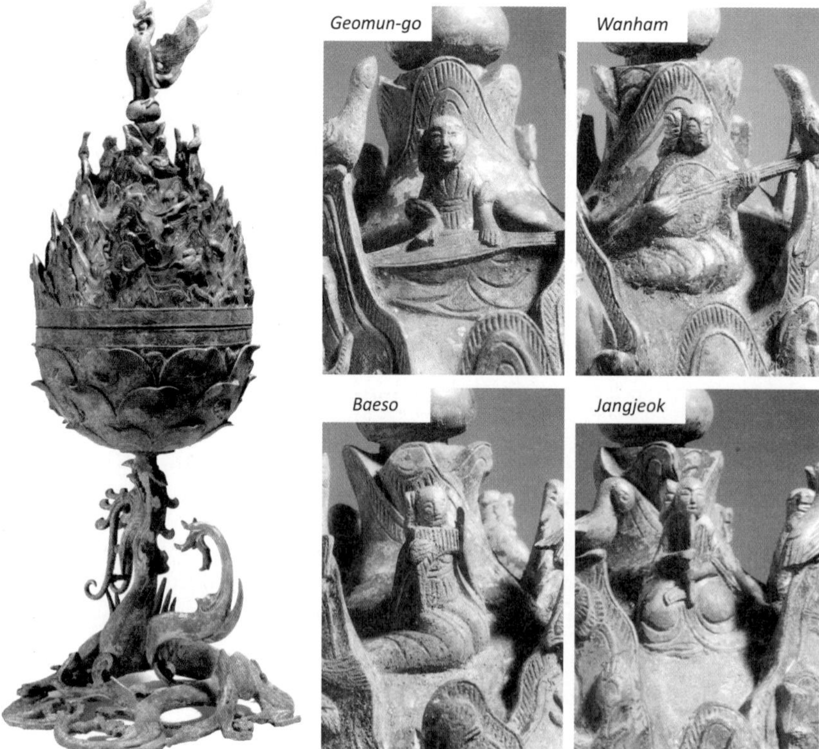

| Fig. 2.34 Baekje gilt- bronze incense burner, Buyeo National Museum

3) Music of the Silla Kingdom

Due to its geographical location, Silla did not import music from the outside, as a result, its musical culture was not diverse compared to those of Goguryeo and Baekje. In Silla royal court, music was performed along with singing and dancing accompanied by a string instrument.

The accompanied instrument refers to two different instruments, each of which existed before and after 551 AD. The string instrument before 551 AD is believed to be the ancient *gayageum*. And that after 551 AD is believed to be the Gaya's string instrument. Gaya was a tribal state in the southern part of the Korean peninsula, located adjacent to Silla. The instrument's name 'gaya' is from the nation Gaya. When Gaya was annexed by Silla in 551 AD., a musician Ureuk of Gaya fled to Silla with the instrument. This instrument, today's *gayageum*, was used for Silla court music and became the representative string instrument of Korea. <Fig. 2.35>

Silla music was relatively restrained rather than boldly expressing emotions, and the aesthetics of Silla court music later influenced the court music of Joseon.

Silla music transferred to Japan included song and dance with *gayageum* accompaniment. Silla music in Japan is the same as that in Silla court. But in Japan the *gayageum* was called *shiragi koto* (string instrument of Silla), because the *gayageum* was introduced to Japan from Silla. The *shiragi koto* is preserved at *shōsōin* repository of the Nara period (710–794) in Japan.

| Fig. 2.35 *Gayageum*

4) Music of the Unified Silla Kingdom

By unifying the three kingdoms with an alliance with the Tang Dynasty, Silla evidently imported diverse social systems, ceremonies and customs from China, including music. Hence the music in the Silla court got to consist of two categories, *hyangak* (indigenous music) and *dangak*. *Hyangak* is the music from former dynasty, while *dangak* is the music from the Tang Dynasty.

In the early stage of the Unified Silla, *hyangak* was performed with songs and dances accompanied by a *gayageum*. But later a diverse range of instruments such as *geomun-go*, *hyang bipa*, *daegeum*, *junggeum*, *sogeum*, *bakpan* and *daego* were also employed in *hyangak*. Among these, the *geomun-go* and *hyangbipa* were from Goguryeo while the string instrument *gayageum* was from Silla. The *daegeum*, *junggeum*, *sogeum* were similar instruments differing only in size, each of these was modified versions of Goguryeo's *hoengchi*. <Fig. 2.36> The *bakpan* and *daego* (large drum) belonged to *dangak*, but these were used for both *dangak* and *hyangak*. The *bakpan* was made with several pieces of wood together. This instrument is used to play to signal the beginning and ending of the phrases of the music.

A song genre without instrumental accompaniment was per-

| Fig. 2.36 *Samjuk (daegeum, junggeum, sogeum), Bakpan*

formed during the Unified Silla period. This genre was derived from a song type of Silla. Compared to folk songs, this song, called as *hyangga* or *sanoega*, was more sophisticated.

An incantatory song "Dosolga" was one of the famous *hyangga* repertoires. "Dosolga" was written by monk Wolmyeongsa, requested by King Gyeongdeok (760 AD). In his 19th year, suddenly two suns appeared in the sky for ten days and the King asked monk Wolmyeongsa to write a chant to end the heavenly calamity. As soon as when the monk sang the song, one of the suns disappeared. This song also falls into the category of Buddhist music, *beompae*.

Dangak of the Unified Silla refers to folk or popular music of China's Tang Dynasty. Because of the lack of historical records, detailed information about *dangak* in Unified Silla is not known. However, since music of all Three Kingdoms were intermingled together and it was categorized as *hyangak* as opposed to *dangak*, it can be conjectured that *dangak* was a totally new form of music. Perhaps it can be paralleled with today's *gugak* (Korean traditional music) as opposed to *yangak*, Western music.

Buddhist music refers to the music performed at Buddhist rituals and music for Buddhist propagation. During the Unified Silla period, music used for Buddhist ceremonies was called *beompae* and the music for propagation was known as *geosasori*. *Beompae* is the generic term to indicate Buddhist songs for sacrificial rituals. The origin of *beompae* was India and it was introduced to Korea and Japan through China. *Geosasori* was sung by the

| Fig. 2.37 ***Beompae***

great Buddhist monk Wonhyo to propagate Buddhism to the ordinary people. He sang in Silla text with familiar folk song-like melodies. It is similar to today's *hwacheong* and *hoesimgok* for popular propagation of folk song-like melodies with Buddhist teachings. <Fig. 2.37>

| Sound. 1 *Beompae* (Buddhist Ritual Music), "Hapjangge," Performed by Monk Yeong-Un

Goryeo Period

Ⅲ. Goryeo Period

The foundation of the Goryeo Dynasty (918–1392) signifies internal development in Korean history as the country shifted from ancient times to the middle ages. Established by powerful clan chiefs and intellects belonging to the highest official ranks of Silla (6 *dupum*), Goryeo was a more liberal society than Silla, which had been based on a strict hereditary class system (*golpum*: literally "bone rank"). The systems for rule were renovated through introduction of the state civil service exams and other measures designed to increase rationality and efficiency in governance. Confucianism was adopted as the ruling ideology, enabling the country to progress from an ancient state. In addition, the land and taxation systems were revised and the state took the lead in promoting industry by expanding available arable land and establishing handicraft and commercial systems, thereby laying the foundations for a strong economy. Goryeo began to trade actively, mostly with the Song and Yuan dynasties of China as well as the Kitans, Jurchens, and the Japanese. Byeongnando Harbor at the mouth of the Yeseonggang River (in North Korea today) served as a port of international trade, and was frequented by merchant ships from Song, Southeast Asia and Arabia.

The culture of Goryeo, corresponding to Korea's medieval culture, was a progression from the ancient culture built on the efforts and wisdom of the ancestors. With the adoption and application of Confucianism as the ruling ideology, popular recognition of Confucianism naturally spread, and in later Goryeo Neo-Confucianism was introduced as well. Meanwhile, Buddhism had a great influence on the everyday lives of the people, leading to more profound study of the faith and continued movements to join the doctrinal and meditation (*seon* or *zen*) sects. In the arts, aristocratic tastes were strongly reflected resulting in works of elegance and sophistication. Goryeo celadon and printing technology in particular were of world class.

While Goryeo was subject to frequent invasions, the people managed to resist and repel foreign forces. In the latter half of the 12th century the revolt of military officials (*Musin Jeongbyeon*) brought changes to society, which had been led by civil officials and the aristocracy, paving the way for those of low social status to enter officialdom. After a period of power by military officials and interference by the Yuan Dynasty of China, a new class of scholar officials emerged in the latter half of Goryeo who adopted Neo-Confucianism and sought social reform through the establishment of rational and people-centered politics. When the new literati, who dreamed of creating a new society, saw that Goryeo's days were numbered they lent their support to the General Yi Seong-gye to pursue reform. Yi was placed on the throne and the Joseon Dynasty was founded.

1. Art

1) Painting

In the Goryeo period (918–1392), Korean art grew more sophisticated, succeeding the ancient tradition that had flourished based on Buddhism. The highly refined style of Buddhist paintings which gained currency during the Unified Silla period continued to develop during the Goryeo period, as seen in the paintings of the Amitabha Buddha (Buddha of the Western Paradise), the Water-moon Avalokitesvara (Bodhisattva of Compassion) <Fig. 3.1>, and the Ksitigarbha Bodhisattva (Bodhisattva of Hell) in the latter half of the 13th century to the 14th century <Fig. 3.2>. Highly praised even in China for their finely detailed and richly colored images of Buddhas, Goryeo Buddhist paintings, along with blue celadon wares, were representative works showing the world-class excellence of Goryeo art. In this period, along with colorful painting in the Southern Song Academy style (*wonchepung*) including court paintings, paintings with non-religious themes gained popularity as well. Growing out of the literati tastes of the new scholar elites, such non-religious paintings exhibited new aesthetic attitudes. Development in this field had a great importance in forming the origin of a new Korean painting tradition, by laying the foundation for Joseon painting.

(1) Characteristics of Goryeo Buddhist Paintings

Except for Buddhist sutra illustrations, extant Goryeo Buddhist paintings are mostly from the 13th to 14th centuries. The disturbances of war during the dynasty and massive crackdown on temples under the anti-Buddhist policy of the ensuing Joseon Dynasty (1392–1910) destroyed nearly all Buddhist paintings in the country, while only some of those plundered by the Japanese and donated to temples in Japan in the late Goryeo period have

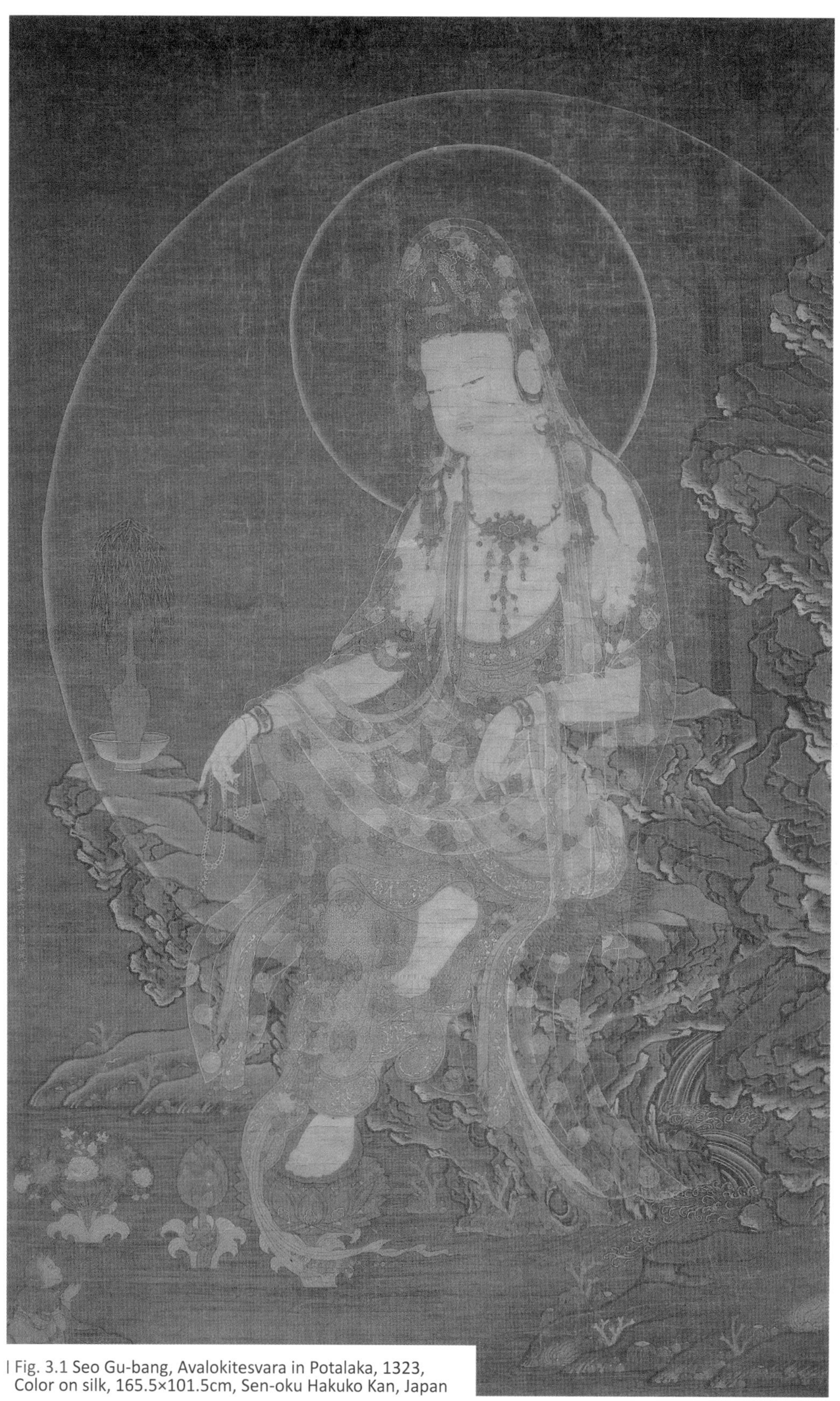

| Fig. 3.1 Seo Gu-bang, Avalokitesvara in Potalaka, 1323, Color on silk, 165.5×101.5cm, Sen-oku Hakuko Kan, Japan

| Fig. 3.2 Anonymous, Ksitigarbha, early 14th century, Color on silk, 106.7×45.3cm, Nezu Museum, Japan

remained. Some 160 hanging paintings are known to have survived, most featuring Amitabha, Avalokitesvara, and Kshitigarbha in iconography related to the (Western) Pure Land tradition.

Despite their stylistic link to the Song and Yuan periods, Goryeo Buddhist paintings feature unique iconography and techniques, including the Bodhisattva of Hell in a silk hempen hood, and the swastika (or srivatsalksana) pattern and impression of a thousand-spoked wheel found on the Buddha of Western Paradise. A representative work in the style of the naeyeongdo (Ch. laiying tu Illustration of Descent of Amitabha), which depicts the Amitabha Buddha and attendants descending from the heaven to greet the soul of the believer and taking him or her to the Western Paradise, is the painting "Buddha of the Western Paradise." This notable painting was commissioned in 1286 by Yeom Seung-ik (?–1302) from an influential family to pray for the longevity and happiness of the king and queen and his own admission to paradise. Occupying most of the canvas, Amitabha stretches out its arms to greet those who come, striking the benevolent "thrice-bent" (tribhanga) pose with the face, body and feet all turned to different directions. Characteristic of Goryeo Amitabha paintings, the swastika and thousand-spoked wheel patterns emblematic of great fortune and eternal life are prominent on the chest and palms of the saint. The face, arms and legs are depicted with thin, fluid lines while the folds are rendered with thick, powerful brushstrokes, to achieve a strong texture as well as changes and harmony through contrast. Pigments of bright colors including vermilion, verdigris, ultramarine and white are used on dark brown silk to exude a flamboyant, yet solemn ambience, while sophisticated color tones unique to Goguryeo Buddhist paintings are created through the mixed used of gold powder and the *ichae* ("painting from within") technique, that is, application of colors from the back. Different to that of Chinese or Japanese Buddhist paintings which use a great deal of yellow, ocher and cobalt, the color scheme shows the originality of Goryeo paintings. The delicate style of the large circular flower patterns depicted in gold powder on the red robes, and the three-dimensional expression of the lotuses painted in the aotufa (relief or embossing) technique also show the excellence of Goryeo Buddhist painting.

As discussed above, Goryeo Buddhist paintings are characterized by original iconography and composition; uniquely stylized floral patterns or lotus medallions adorning the robes; brilliance achieved through the use of original solid colors including vermillion, verdigris, navy blue and gold powder instead of mixing the pigments; profound harmony achieved through multi-layered depiction of elaborate patterns; the gentle, elegant body expressed with the "painting from within" technique, also called *baechae* ("painting from the back"), in which the colors are applied to the back of the silk to seep through to the front; and elaborate, fluid strokes rendered through the duplication of black ink and bright red lines.

A reflection of the mature aristocratic culture of Goryeo, the adornment and advanced artistic skills seen in Buddhist paintings are seen as a way to make up for the repetitiveness and simplicity of systematized iconography with increased detail. This painting style set the tradition for figure paintings and colored paintings and was transmitted to the 15th century to form the foundation of Joseon Buddhist paintings, before changing significantly to a more complicated and worldly style from around the 16th century.

(2) The Emergence of Non-Religious Painting

As the court and aristocratic culture developed in the Goryeo period, decorative court paintings and colored pictures in the Song Academy style were produced in great quantity. "Hwaguk" (Bureau of Painting) was set up to meet painting demand from the state, including the royal household, and was followed by the installation of "Dohwawon" (Office of Painting) and the emergence of professional painters in government employ (*hwawon*). The palace and places where the king went were adorned with a partition-style dragon folding screen (*yongui*) and painted folding screens (*chaebyeong*), while behind the king's throne in Daegwanjeon Hall at Yeongyeonggung Palace stood a folding screen illustrating a chapter from the Seogyeong (Ch. Shujing The Classic of History), titled "Muil" (Against Luxurious Ease), discussing Confucian governing techniques. At the royal shrine, *Jongmyo*, a folding screen depicting an axe (boui) was put up in each room respectively enshrining successive kings. As the Chinese considered yongui and boui as symbols exclusively use for their emperor, the Yuan court complained of Goryeo's use of them, especially the dragon folding screen, as imitation of Chinese protocol.

Besides the full-fledged development of decorative court paintings, a new philosophy of art began to appear in paintings, resulting in a qualitative difference from paintings of ancient times. With the formation of the literati class following implementation of the state examination in 958, the inclination for painting and writing grew and the theory of literati painting was introduced from Northern Song, leading to the emergence of paintings for appreciation. The emergence of new thoughts and ways regarding creation and appreciation of art facilitated the development of general paintings.

This new trend in Goryeo painting began to appear under the reign of King Munjong (r. 1046–1083) when respect for learning was actively promoted amid brisk cultural exchange with Northern Song. In particular, the rise of the elite literati class through the state examination system, well versed in literature, history and philosophy, led to the creation and appreciation of literati-style ink paintings, qualitatively different from previous paintings produced using many colors for practical or religious use. In other words, the literati enjoyed composing poems and practicing painting or calligraphy as a hobby based on East Asian medieval universalism, such as Chinese literature and Confucianism, creating a new environment for painting.

In the early Goryeo period around the 11th century, with the emergence of Confucian principles of rule by civil officials, the tradition of creating figure paintings or portraits as a means of edification was established as a way to improve and propagate the new dynasty's systems and ideology. In a style focusing on details and realism, portraits of the king and queen, meritorious subjects and sages were produced in great numbers from the early period for use at ancestral rites and to promote and enlighten the people on services for the state. Linked with the ideologies of *jaei sangseo* (Ch. zaiyi xiangrui "auspicious and inauspicious omens") or *pungsu* (Ch. fengshui geomancy), landscape paintings depicting real scenery also began to be produced.

From the mid-Goryeo period, around the 12th century, the literati took up such hobbies as the collection and appreciation of paintings. Literati artists also appeared and paintings began to deal with literary subject matters such as bamboo and plum blossoms rendered in ink, and a theory of literati painting emerged. In other words, the age of calligraphy and painting (K. *seohwa*, Ch. Shuhua) and the age of paintings for appreciation had arrived. Many images of illustrious monks and the portraits of scholar-officials were produced, and establishment of the Bureau of Painting in the early 12th century led to emergence of prominent portrait painters such as Yi Gi. The works of Guo Xi (1023–c. 1085), the greatest landscape artist from the Northern Song period, were introduced to Korea, and with the appearance of master painters such as Yi Nyeong, true-view landscape painting made such great progress that it was admired even by the artists of Northern Song.

Under the military rule of late Goryeo (late 12th to mid–13th centuries), development of general paintings was further expanded as general paintings came to be regarded by the literati and Buddhist masters as a medium to express inspiration or cultivate the mind. Through these two groups, the literati painting ideology of Northern Song, epitomized by the great painter Su Shi (1037–1101) and the critic Mi Fu (1051–1107), and a recreational style acceptable to the scholar-bureaucrats took root and flourished. Such tastes in painting and calligraphy deepened with the appearance of new art spaces, such as the scholar's study. Also, according to records, this period also saw the creation of standardized (or ideological) ink and brush landscape paintings such as "Eight Views of the Xiao and Xiang Rivers" (K. *Sosang palgyeong do*, Ch. Xiaoxiang bajing tu); the emergence of monks as artists and the rise of ink paintings themed on the Buddhist Zen sect; full-fledged development of figure paintings depicting a classical taste and episodes of the literati as recluses, such as Tao Yuan Ming (365–427), and adoption of uniquely Goryeo themes.

In the late period, from around 1250 to 1391, painting subjects became diversified through close relationship with the art circle of the Yuan Dynasty, and in regard to true-view landscapes, a painting of Mt. Geumgang attained fame as a painting for worship. The background landscape in "Bodhisattva Dharmodgata" (*Dammugal Bosal hyeonsin do*, <Fig. 3.3>) painted by Noh Yeong in1307 shows Mt. Geumgang in the area around Jeongyang-sa Temple. The techniques used to depict the chisel-shaped jagged crags and the earthly mountains hint at the origin of the painting style adopted by Joseon artists to paint the same subject. Also, the rendering of the rocks in "Water-moon Avalokitesvara," created in 1310, now in the collection of Kagami Shinto Shrine in Japan, and "Kstigarbha Bodhisattva Triad" (*Jijang samjon do*) from the same era at Engakuji Temple in Japan, provide insight into development of the landscape painting mode of the School of Guo Xi in late Goryeo and its influence on the formation of the early Joseon painter An Gyeon's landscape style in the 15th century. In the late period, portrait painting was so much in vogue that not only professional artists but also literati painters and even the king had a taste for this hobby. King Gongmin (r. 1351–1374), in particular, is said to have painted portraits of his queen, Princess Dachang of the state of Lu, vassals and even himself reflected in a mirror.

As discussed above, a diversity of paintings evolved through the Goryeo period, but

| Fig. 3.3 Noh Yeong, Bodhisattva Dharmodgata (detail), Screen of Amitabha with Eight Great Bodhisttvas (back side), 1307, Gold Pigment on Black Lacquered Wood, 21×12cm, National Museum of Korea

extant works from the late period only include the half-length portraits of An Hyang (1243–1306) <Fig. 3.4> and Yeom Je-shin (1304–1382), which are finely rendered with thin, fluid brushstrokes, as well as landscape paintings with human figures such as "Crossing the River on Horseback" (*Gima dogang do*) and "Hunting at the Northern End of Mt. Kunlun" (*Eunsan daeryeop do*), traditionally attributed to Yi Je-hyeon and King Gongmin respectively. While several other works are thought to be Goryeo landscape or figure paintings, their provenance and dates of production have not been confirmed.

Fig. 3.4 Anonymous, Portrait of An Hyang, 1318, Color on silk, 37×29cm, Sosu-Seowon, National Treasure No. 111

2) Buddhist Sculptures

During the Goryeo period (918–1391) Zen Buddhism (禪宗) established many temples in various regions. In addition, donations from powerful regional families allowed the production of Buddhist sculpture which reflected regional characteristics. Unlike the Unified Silla period when everything was centered around a single capital city, Gyeongju, during the Goryeo period influences and trends expanded through the Korean peninsula. Many of the change were brought over by new influences from neighboring Song (宋), Liao (遼) and Yuan (元) dynasty of China. At the beginning of this period, the influence of the late Unified Silla continued on, and consequently Buddha statues made from iron consumed in their popularity. This period produced statues like the monumental iron Buddha of Chungungri (春宮里) <Fig. 3.5> and those similar to the Sakyamuni Buddha. As with the Buddha at Soekguram Grotto (石窟庵), the Buddha with the robe draping from the left shoulder across the chest and under the right arm, leaving the right should bare and with the earth touching mudra (降魔觸地印) <Fig. 3.6>. In the Wouljeongsa Temple (月精寺) and Hansongsa Temples (寒松寺) in the Gangneung province, stone Bodhisattvas in the style of Liao (遼) wearing high-raised jeweled crowns <Fig. 3.7> and seated Sakyamuni Buddhas made from iron (鐵造) were popular. In the Nonsan region, a three stone Buddha statues of Gaetaesa Temple (開泰寺) and stone Bodhisattva were made in monumental sizes. <Fig. 3.8> Also in places such as Andong and Yangju, large Buddha statues were carved on

| Fig. 3.5 Seated Buddha, Iron, Chungung-ri, 10th century, 2.88m, National Museum of Korea, Treasure No. 332

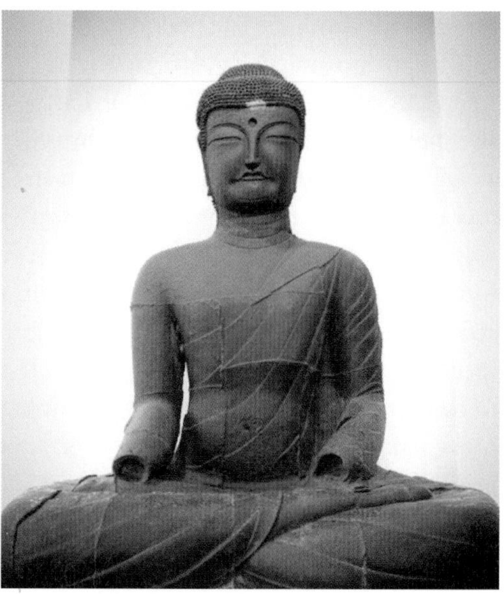

| Fig. 3.6 Seated Buddha, Iron, late Unified Silla-early Goryeo, Excavated from Unsan-myeon, Seosan, h. 2.59m, National Museum of Korea

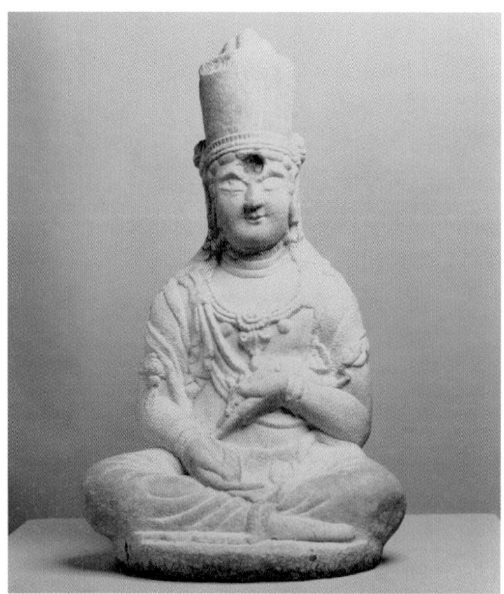

| Fig. 3.7 Seated Bodhisattva, Stone, from Hansongsa Temple Site, 10th century, 92.4cm, National Museum of Korea, National Treasure No. 124

| Fig. 3.8 Standing Maitreya, Stone, Gwanchoksa, 10th century, 18.12m, Gwanchoksa Temple, Nonsan, Treasure No. 218

| Fig. 3.9 Seated Buddha, Modeling, 2.78m, Buseoksa Temple, Yeongju, National Treasure No. 45

cliffs and rock mountains. Through these sculptures it is possible to understand that Buddhism and transformed to Korean traits. While the same time some statues show the attempt to accept new styles in sculpture coming from China. In the latter part of the Goryeo period, Munsusa Temple (文殊寺) in Chungcheong province and Janggoksa Temple (長谷寺) in Cheongyang, made bronze seated Buddha more serene, softer and kinder. During this time, Buddhism was focused more on the public, and the central power of Buddhism expanded from the capital to regional areas.

Buddhism expanded to the local provinces as movements arose where the mass populace became the central force in Buddhist activity. Thus, Buddhist statues came to reveal rigid facial expressions, thick drapery, and the omission of decorative jewelry; rendering the overall execution, local and rustic.

Particularly towards the end of the Goryeo period during the Mongol Intervention era, the central ruling area had close ties with the Mongols, and as a result, Tibetan Lama Buddha statues, which were popular among the Mongol royal court, influenced Goryeo. There were also plaster and wooden Buddha statues, the most important one being National Treasure No. 45 a seated Buddha made of clay at Buseoksa Temple (浮石寺), and Treasure No. 980 <Fig. 3.9>, a wooden seated Amita Buddha of Bonglimsa Temple (奉林寺).

3) Ceramics, Lacquerware, and Metal Craft

(1) Celadon and White Porcelain

The Goryeo period saw the production of celadon, and white porcelain for the first time on the Korean peninsula. Around the 10th century, celadon was produced primarily from areas near the capital such as Hwanghae and Gyeonggi provinces. When it came to the late 10th century and the early 11th century when the Tax Regulation and the central government were accomplished, it might know that the ceramic industry around the southwestern part were vitalized much. Most of these places such as Chungcheong and Jeolla Provinces towards the south-western parts of the peninsula were bound with the marine transportation road. As the ceramic making skills of the Yue Kiln [越州窯] in Zhejiang (浙江) Province of China were introduced in the early stages Korean artisans replicated the length of brick kilns (approximately 40m long), various types of implements for loading and stacking kilns, method of firing, working with clay, and even the forms themselves. After the 11th century, amicable exchanges with Khitan Liao [遼] re-invigorated the northern route to China; consequently the influence of the ceramic ware of northern China such as Ding ware (定窯), Ru ware (汝窯) and Cizhou ware (磁州窯) was felt, while at the same time Goryeo developed its own characteristics. Especially with the area of Gangjin (康津) rising as the center of pottery, between the end of the 11th century continuing on to the 12th century, Goryeo aesthetics and techniques developed to acclaim the reputation of perfecting East Asia's celadon green color (翡色). <Fig. 3.10>

The expansion and development of tea culture and the increased use of craft objects in everyday life allowed celadon to be made into a variety of objects other than those used

| Fig. 3.10 Celadon Melon-shaped Bottle, 12th century, Known to have been from In-jong-jang-roong (King In-jong's Tomb), h. 22.8cm, National Museum of Korea, National Treasure No. 96

| Fig. 3.11 Celadon Incense Burner with Lion-shaped Lid, h. 21.2cm, National Museum of Korea, Treasure No. 60

| Fig. 3.12 Celadon Mae-byeong with Inlaid Surface Decoration of Plum Tree and Bamboo, h. 29.2cm, National Museum of Kore

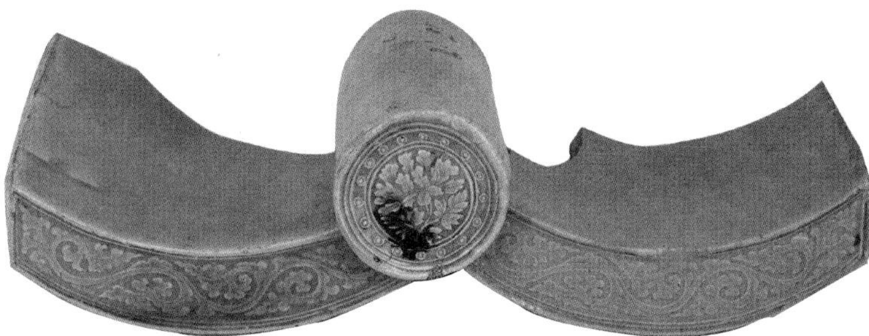

| Fig. 3.13 Celadon Roof Tile, Excavated from the kiln site of Gangjin Sa-dang-ri, 12th century, National Museum of Korea

only for food. Decorating methods on clay surfaces became diverse, including incising (陰刻, *eumgak*), relief (陽刻, *yanggak*), inlay (象嵌, *sanggam*), molding (象形, *sanghyeong*) <Fig. 3.11>, iron-brown underglaze (鐵畵, *cheolhwa*) and copper-red underglaze (辰砂, jinsa). Among these, the inlay was usually done in black or white, creating a contrast between the bluish-green color of celadon and the inlaid pattern.<Fig. 3.12>

The main potteries and kiln sites for producing celadon during its heyday were spread around Gangjin (康津) in the South Jeolla Province, and Buan (扶安) in the North Jeolla Province. Although the majority of the production was focused on those objects used for serving food, objects for every aspect of daily life such as stationary and cosmetic containers, as well as roof tiles and decorative architectural tiles were also made. According to 《The History of Goryeo (高麗史)》 written in the 11th year of King Euijong (毅宗, 1157), the roof of Yangeui Pavilion (養怡亭) of the Manwouldae (滿月臺) royal palace site, was covered with celadon roof tiles <Fig. 3.13>. In actuality, shards of celadon have been discovered from this particular site in Gaeseong.

After the invasion of the Mongols, a new form of ceramics began to appear following new preferences while new styles also infiltrated from China. From the latter part of the Goryeo period to the early Joseon period, production of celadon began to change in some aspects. Centralized potteries for production changed with an increase in smaller scale regional potteries begin to establish. Consequently regional characteristics became more predominant. Thus, decoration patterns became simpler and repetitive and less delicate.

(2) Lacquerware and Metalwork

Lacquerware refers to the techniques of cutting thin seashells into required shapes for inlaying (嵌入) or assembling them onto wooden surfaces. This method was used as early as the Unified Silla period for decorating copper mirrors, but the application onto wood, known as the Najeon technique (螺鈿技法) began in the Goryeo period. According to 《The History of Goryeo (高麗史)》, reveal that the craftsmen in charge of sketches and painting in

Joongsangseo (中尙署), Production Office for Official wares, were responsible for the original wood pieces for lacquer ware.

The 『Reference Document on Eastern Countries (東國文獻備考)』 states that the lacquerware of Liao royal court entered into Goryeo by diplomatic envoys and were given as gifts to King Munjong (文宗, r. 1046–1083). The diplomatic envoy Xu Jing (徐兢), who came Goryeo in 1123, wrote about Goryeo's najeon lacquerware in the 《*An illustrated description of the Chinese embassy to Korea during the Xuanhe period* (宣化奉使高麗圖經)》 and stated that, "the technique is so refined that it should be regarded as a precious object, even the horse saddle decorated with mother-of-pearl is of great finesse." In 1272, the Jeonhamjoseongdogam (鈿函造成都監), was installed to make furniture appropriate for storing the Tripitaka Koreana, a collection of all the sacred writings of Buddhism (大藏經). <Fig. 3.14> A container for storing the Buddhist rosary, decorated with tortoiseshell and inlaid with gold and silver (金銀) also remains.

The most notable aspects of metal work during the Goryeo period are the Buddhist altar fittings (佛具) and Buddhist bells (梵鐘). Moreover, because of the Buddhist ritual of lighting incense sticks for worship, many vessels were made, of which major types had a deep burner and wide open feet that look like a trumpet mouth and wide rim. There are some examples incised within the date of manufacture and the name of the maker. Examples include on the incense burner of Tongdosa Temple <Fig. 3.15>, a silver inlaid burner at the Pyochungsa Temple (表忠寺) made in 1177, a similar silver inlaid incense burner belonging

| Fig. 3.14 Lacquered Sutra Box Inlaid with Mother-of-Pearl, Chrysanthemums Design, 12th century, 26cm, Tokyo National Museum, Japan

| Fig. 3.15 Incense Burner with Silver Inlay, Bronze, h. 33cm, Tongdosa Temple, Yangsan

to Jungheungsa Temple (中興寺) made in 1344, and a bronze vessel with silver inlay made in 1346 Sangwonsa Temple (上院寺). There were also Kundikas (淨瓶) for everyday use and for ritualistic purposes to hold purifying water (淨水) <Fig. 3.16>, reliquaries for keeping sariras, incense burners and bronze drums (飯子, 金鼓) and bells (梵鐘) for Buddhist and Taoist rituals. The main method of decorating with metal were casting (鑄造), inlaying with silver or gold (入絲), and filigree (縷銀). Although materials differ between metal, ceramics and wood ware, the method in which decorations were applied and the use of shapes among these craft traits had a reciprocal connection. Depending on the rareness and quality of material, there existed a tendency for different ware to set the lead.

| Fig. 3.16 Kundika with Designs Depicting the Scene of Waterside, Bronze, h. 37.5cm, National Museum of Korea, National Treasure No. 92

4) Royal Palaces and Buddhist Temples

(1) Fortress and Royal Palace

Beginning from the Unified Silla period (7th–10th centuries), geomancy and the flow of good energy was already influencing in selection of land for establishing main capital settlements, land developments, and also for burial grounds. This notion had rooted itself firmly in the Goryeo period. The fortress capital settlement of Goryeo was Gaegyeong (開京) and it was established in 919 AD, the second year of King Taejo (太祖).

Other fortified cities besides Gaegyeong were Donggyeong (東京, present day, Gyeongju), Seogyeong (西京, present day, Pyeongyang) and Namgyeong (南京, present day, Seoul). In Gyegyeong, palaces like Manwoldae (滿月臺), Jangrak Palace (長樂宮), Suchang Palace (壽昌宮) were established. Unlike the north-south axis divide in city planning of the Three Kingdoms period, the geographical characteristics rendered these establishments to stand along the natural slope. Recent excavations on the Manwouldae palace site and the detailed descriptions on the structure and the layout of the architecture in 『Xuanhe Fengshi Gaoli Tujing (高麗圖經)』, an illustrated description of the Chinese embassy to Korea during the Xuanhe period, provide us with the understanding of the palace grounds of the Goryeo period.

In them there are detailed records regarding the structure, layout and architectural form of certain buildings. The Manwoldae was constructed in a comparatively confined space in a hill area; due to geographical constraints, it did not conform to the typical palace composition with the main axis facing the north and south. In gardens placed in the rear section of palaces, artificial hills for worshipping deities were created by assembling collected rocks. Waterways were installed to create ponds and streams with unusual flowers and trees to make the garden beautiful. 《The History of Goryeo (高麗史)》 record of detached palace in the east. There King Euijong (毅宗) built four pavilions in the compound, one of which was the Yangi-jong pavilion (養怡亭) covered with celadon roof tiles.

(2) Temple Architecture

In the capital Gaegyeong, along with the ten well known temples, many more were established. During this period, the two pagoda temple composition of the Silla period changed to a one pagoda style. Thus, the two methods alternated depending on the temple. In the early stages the pagoda form of Silla and Baekje were incorporated; as can be seen in 5 story pagoda of the Muryangsa Temple (無量寺)'s and the Iksan Wangguong-ri (王宮里) Temple. Towards the mid-Goryeo period, a more refined style was introduced and in the late Goryeo, variations in styles and levels were attempted until the style considered most typical of the period was est. The latter part of the Goryeo period saw influences from the Yuan (元) China and the pagodas took on a Lamaistic forms, as can be seen in Gyeongcheonsa Temple (敬天寺)'s ten story pagoda (National Treasure No. 68). In temple architecture, the single pagoda and double pagoda types co-existed. The Yeonboksa Temple (蓮福寺) of Gaeseong was erected with the main temple placed in the east, and the pagoda in the west (東殿西塔), in the same method as the Horyuji Temple (法隆寺) in Japan. Besides this method there were many others which coexisted at the time.

| Fig. 3.17 Geukrak-jeon, 12th century, Bongjeongsa Temple, Andong, National Treasure No. 15

| Fig. 3.18 Muryangsu-jeon, Rebuilt in Goryro Period, Buseoksa Temple, Yeongju

In addition, shrines worshipping the mountain gods or consecrated to the Big Dipper in Taoism were absorbed into Buddhism. Thus, temples housed not only shrines and sanctuaries such as Nahan for Buddhist disciples (羅漢殿), but also Ungjin-jeon (應眞殿), Youngsan-jeon (靈山殿), and other new types of buildings that brought about change from the original Buddhist temple layout.

At the beginning of the Goryeo period, the architectural styles of Unified Silla continued on until the mid Goryeo period. The use of supporting beams placed horizontally across the column bracket (*jushimpo*, 柱心包) was the main architectural form. Examples of this type extant today are the Geukrak-jeon (極樂殿, Hall of Paradise) at Bongjeongsa Temple (鳳停寺) in Andong (安東), North Gyeongsang province <Fig. 3.17>, and the Muryangsu-jeon (無量壽殿, Hall of Eternal Life) <Fig. 3.18>. Buseoksa Temple (浮石寺), also located in North Gyeongsang province. At the end of the Goryeo period, due to influence from the Yuan (元) Dynasty, the use of multi-bracket sets (*dapo*, 多包) developed. This *dapo* style not only had bracketing on the top section of the main pillars but also in the space between them. In order to install the brackets, a structure consisting of a cross-over and leveling of wooden beams was built. This type of wood construction is the most characteristic of Korean architecture. In Goryeo, beliefs in geomancy became popular. Therefore, most temples were established in auspicious locations so that they harmonized with the natural environment, following an organic arrangement by taking into consideration every detail of the natural landscape.

2. Dance

In the times of Goryeo, a golden age for the noble class culture in which Confucianism and Buddhism harmonized, not only the court dance and but also the magnificent and grand Buddhist ritualistic dance influenced by the national religion Buddhism flourished. *Palgwanhwoe* (八關會, Festival of the Eight Vows) and *Yeondeunghwoe* (燃燈會, Lotus Lantern Festival) which were carried on from the traditions of the Unified Silla period and were held with a variety of stage dramas called *Sandaejabgeuk*, took root as national festivals.

1) *Gungjung Jeongjae* (Court Song and Dance)

(1) The Acceptance of the *Dangak jeongjae* (唐樂呈才)

Dangak jeongjae (唐樂呈才, Tang Dynasty's Music and Dance) means a royal court

| Fig. 3.19 *Poguak*

| Fig. 3.20 *Yeonhwadae,* National Research Institute of Cultural Heritage

dance that originated in China. During the Unified Silla period and the Goryeo Dynasty, Tang Dynasty music had been imported, but there was a need to differentiate the authentic Korean music from the imported Chinese influences. For this reason, indigenous Korean music was referred to as *hyangak*, while the Tang Dynasty music was called *dangak*.

The first record about the introduction of *dangak jeongjae* is found in documents written in the 27th year of the reign of King Munjong (1073). According to the records of *gyobang* (敎坊, a school for training female entertainers in the Goryeo period), a female student, Choyoung (楚英) created a dance that consisted of 55 dancers and performed it in the court with the addition of four-character sayings such as "long-live the king" or "peace reign worldwide." From the Joseon period to the present day, this performance has been passed down as "Wangmodaegamu." Furthermore, according to the records concerning music in the *Goryeosa* (History of Goryeo), the *dangak jeongjae* of the Goryeo period includes "Pogurak" (抛毬樂, ball throwing dance), "Heonseondo" (獻仙桃, peach offering dance), "Suyeonjang" (壽延長, dance to wish for a long-life of a king), "Ohyangsun" (五羊仙, dance to wish for a good harvest) and "Yeonhwadae" (蓮花臺, lotus pedestal dance) among others.

The main characteristics of *dangak jeongjae* include the fact that it was a court dance imported from China, and that when the dance began and ended, two members carrying a dance prop made of bamboo called *jukganja* come out, leading the group of performers. Finally, the songs known as *changsa* (唱詞, song with lyrics), with lyrics in pure Classical Chinese, were sung. The "Pogurak" and "Yeonhwadae" was the most representative *dangak jeongjae* of the Goryeo period and their characteristics are as follows:

"Pogurak" (抛毬樂, ball throwing dance) was introduced to the Goryeo Dynasty in the 27th year of King Munjong (1046–1083) from the Song Dynasty, China. This was a dance created by Choyoung, a student of the *gyobang* (school for training female entertainers) and it was a female group dance consisting of 13 dancers. It was the only court dance that included a game-like aspect. This dance was composed in the style of a competition to put the *chaegu* (彩毬, wooden balls) inside the "Pungnyuan" (风流眼, hole in a cast). If the ball passed through the hole, the person who threw the ball was rewarded with flowers but if the ball did not make it through the hole the person was penalized by having a black ink spot painted on their face. <Fig. 3.19>

"Yeonhwadae" (蓮花台, lotus pedestal dance) was a dance in which two pretty young female entertainer apprentices danced while shaking two golden bells. The dance began as two *mudongs* (children dancers and singers for court performances) emerged as they opened the petals of lotus flowers in which they were hidden. The dance was passed down to the Joseon Dynasty as "Yeonhwadaemu," at times it was performed as a part of huge performance coupled with "Hakmu" (crane dance) and "Chyeoyongmu." <Fig. 3.20>

(2) The Development of *Hyangak jeongjae* (鄕樂呈才)

According to the records about music in the *Goryeosa*, the History of Goryeo, the *hyangak jeongjae* of the Goryeo includes "Mugo," "Dongdong" and "Muaemu." The characteristics of *hyangak jeongjae* is that it came from an authentic traditional Korean court dance created in Korea, *jukganja* (a dance prop made of bamboo) was not used, and all songs were sung in the Korean language, Its format was unrestricted compared to that of *dangak jeongjae*.

The origin of "Mugo" (舞鼓, drum dance) dates back to the period of the 25th Goryeo King Chungryeol (1274–1308), when a person named Yihon (李混) found a piece of wood on the seashore and fashioned it into a large drum while in exile. The sound of the drum boomed so loudly that people started to dance to the beat of the drum. Four people danced surrounding the drum while touching and hitting it in a form of *wonmu* (元舞, circle dance),

| Fig. 3.21 *Mugo*

and an additional four people danced at the four directions carrying flower sticks in both of their hands in a form of *hyeopmu* (挾舞, group dance). <Fig. 3.21>

"Dongdong" was a dance performed to the lyrics of "Dongdongsa," a song of Goryeo. In the Joseon Dynasty, the name changed to "Ahbakmu" (牙拍舞, ivory clappers dance). Performers hold *ahbak*, a kind of a percussion instrument, in their hands and dance face to face as they beat the instrument in the form of *daemu* (對舞, dance in symmetry).

2) The Development of Buddhist Ritualistic Dance

Palgwanhwoe and *Yeondeunghwoe* were the grandest Buddhist rituals of the Goryeo period. At the beginning of the establishment of the kingdom *Palgwanhwoe* and *Yeondeunghwoe* were restored as national ceremonies and were performed with song and dance containing features of the shaman and folk customs.

Palgwanhwoe was a ritual to pray for the well-being of the country and kingdom through song and dance. Carrying on the *Palgwanhwoe* of Silla, Goryeo added the custom of shamanism and folk culture, and developed it into an annual national ceremony. *Yeondeunghwoe* was a purely Buddhist-orientated service, meaning a lantern-lit memorial service for Buddha. This memorial service was performed to praise the virtues of Buddha and devote oneself to Buddha by brightening and correcting one's soul through lighting a candle in front of the Enlightened One. <Fig. 3.22>

Yeondeunghwoe and *Palgwanhwoe* were ceremonies related to Buddhism and at the same time the grandest integrated cultural events of this period with the religion being absorbed into existent folk customs. Another reason behind the importance of *Yeondeung-*

| Fig. 3.22 Stage Work about Offering Six Things (scent, lamp, tea, flower, fruit, rice) to Buddha, *Hunmudarae*

| Fig. 3.23 *Nabichum*, or the butterfly dance, National Research Institute of Cultural Heritage

| Fig. 3.24 *Barachum*, National Research Institute of Cultural Heritage

hwoe and *palgwanhwoe* is that Buddhist ceremonial dance was deviated from the events. The Buddhist dance was performed by monks as was the Buddhist music called *beompae*. Other Buddhist dances including *nabichum* (butterfly dance), *barachum* (cymbal dance), and *beopgochum* (dharma drum dance) are collectively referred to as *jakbeop*.

Nabichum or the butterfly dance, was one of the most significant Buddhist dances, its name was derived from the butterfly costume worn by dancers. Female Buddhist nuns were clad in a white Buddhist monk's robe (*jangsam*) and a sash wrapping the monk from the left shoulder down across the right armpit draped down to the ground (*gasa*) and conical head attire in the shape of a tower. They perform the dance carrying a peony flower and its blossoms in their hands. It is considered the most beautiful Buddhist ritualistic dance. The chief characteristic of this dance is that there are hardly any fast movements and even the shoulder and head movements were kept minimal with quiet, slow motions. <Fig. 3.23>

While the *nabichum* is serene and solemn, the *barachum* was more energetic. Performers dance forwards and backwards or turn around while holding a cymbal called *bara* in both hands. The dance was performed to cleanse the mind or the site of performance for cultivating oneself religiously by dispelling evil spirits. This dance is to be performed with a solemn heart. <Fig. 3.24>

| Fig. 3.25 *Beopgochum*, National Research Institute of Cultural Heritage

Beopgochum is a dance performed with beating drums meant to save the animals of the world. Without uniform rhythms or beat, this dance is performed to the chants of Buddhist scripture. It is usually performed quietly inside a Buddhist sermon hall and since it is a part of a ritual for Buddha using one's body, the dancer is to perform it without being conscious of the audience. <Fig. 3.25>

As observed above, since *jakbeop* are dances performed to purify one's heart towards Buddha, the forms of their solemn and somber movements are modest and mysterious. Such ritualistic dances for Buddhism are already extinct in their motherlands of India and China. However in Korea, the dances have been carried on as precious cultural traditions.

3) The Introduction of *Daeseong-aak* and the Development of Confucian Ritualistic Dance

Aak, the court music of China, was transmitted to Korea under the appellation *daeseong-aak* in the 11th reigning year of King Yejong (1105–1122), Goryeo. Starting with the introduction of new instruments and musical scores, tools used in court dances such as *munmu* (文舞, dance to praise virtues of scholars) and *mumu* (武舞, dance to praise virtues of military men) which were performed in the courts, 36 kinds of attire, dance costumes for each and other items were imported. After being transported into the country, such clothing and instruments were used for performances of *aak* along with *hyangak*, *dangak* during the court's morning meetings and other gatherings, but due to the loss or damage to the instruments, performances were on the decline. Likewise, the tradition of *daeseong-aak* seemed as though it was disappearing into the fog of history entirely, but later *aak* was restored by the great King Sejong (1418–1450) of Joseon Dynasty who had an excellent command of

| Fig. 3.26 *Mumu, Munmyo Jeryeak Ilmu*, Association for Research on *Jeongjae*

courtesy music when he adapted it by having instruments repaired, and producing it based on the original Chinese texts.

This *aak* passed through the Joseon Dynasty developing into *jeryeak* (music for the sacrificial rites commemorating deceased ancestors) of *jongmyo* (the Royal Ancestors' Shrine) and *munmyo* (a Confucian shrine). Today, the tradition continues through *munmyo jeryeak* (文廟祭禮, a sacrificial rite music paying tribute to several Confucian sages, including Confucius). In the *munmyo* sacrificial rite, *ilmu* was performed along with court music. *Ilmu* is a genre of dance performed by a group of people standing in several lines. This tradition disappeared long ago in China, but Korea kept up the tradition alive developing it into a precious cultural asset. <Fig. 3.26>

4) Dances based on Folk Religion

Folk religious dance fully express the spirit and culture of the non-ruling classes. Folk religious dances include not only folk dances enjoyed by the masses but also shamanistic ritual dances related to the religious life of ancestors. The special characteristic of the dances include the expression of emotions, such as joy, anger, sorrow, and pleasure without the strict forms and rules, which were found in royal court dances and Buddhist ritualistic dances.

The most representational folk dances of the Goryeo period were the *nongakmu* (farmers' music and dance), *ganggangsullae* (female circle dance), *notdaribalgi* (treading on brass bridge) and others. The *nongakmu* developed with the intention of encouraging the spirit of farmers and to free them from their laborious work so that they would become more productive. It began with heavenly rites for seeding and harvesting to express gratitude in the Samhan period, and gradually took on fixed forms. Throughout the Goryeo period to

| Fig. 3.27 *Jindo-ssitgimgut*, National Research Institute of Cultural Heritage

the twilight of the Joseon Dynasty, its beat, rhythm and movements of dance grew in refinement. There is saying that the *notdaribalgi* was developed during the time that King Gongmin (1351–1374) was taking shelter in the vicinity of Andong region following a revolt, and women of the region created it to console the princess.

Concerning the folk religious dance of the Goryeo period, there are records on the shaman ritual rain prayers in the 12th reigning year of King Hyeonjong (1021), and records on a gathering of shamans to pray for rain in the 6th reigning year of King Sukjong (1101) and the 16th reigning year of King Yejong (1162). <Fig. 3.27>

3. Music

Goryeo inherited the music of Unified Silla and also it actively incorporated imported music from the Song Dynasty of China. Especially in the year 1116, Goryeo imported Confucian music, *aak*, and subsequently the court music of Goryeo was categorized into *hyangak*, *dangak* and *aak*. *Hyangak* and *dangak* have been performed for various court ceremonies and state festivals and *aak* was performed at the Confucian sacrificial ritual. *Dangak* was replaced by the music of Song after the Song Dynasty was established in China. However, the music of Song was also called *dangak* and thus *dangak* became an inclusive term to indicate Chinese-derived music. Even some of the *dangak* instruments were included in the performance of *hyangak*, which expanded its boundary and developed into a new direction.

1) *Hyangak*, Indigenous Music

Hyangak of Goryeo was basically music of the Unified Silla. In the beginning, *hyangga* of Unified Silla, a song genre without instrumental accompaniment, was popular and new songs were composed in the *hyangga* form, but gradually new musical styles were developed. Early Goryeo songs included an exclamation phrase like *hyangga*, but such phrases were not found in the songs of late Goryeo. In general, the themes and lyrics of the song were mostly about filial piety, the righteousness of marriage, love, leaders confronting defensive situations, and the importance of the state. Most lyrics were written in Korean while some were written in classical Chinese characters.

A few Goryeo *hyangak* songs were documented in music compilation scores like the *Daeakhubo* and *Siyonghyangakbo*. A wide variety of songs were collected and written down in these manuscripts, from short and simple songs to long and complex ones. "Seogyeongbyeolgok" is one of the most representative songs. In this song, a simple melody is repeated several times. Following <Fig. 3.28> shows one melodic phrase of "Seogyeongbyeolgok."

The scales of Goryeo *hyangak* songs, written in the manuscripts mentioned above, are non-chromatic pentatonic scales. The melodic modes of these songs are *pyeongjo*, equivalent to the Western major scale, and *gyemyeonjo*, equivalent to the Western minor. Each continued in use throughout the Joseon Dynasty. <Fig. 3.29>

| Fig. 3.28 "Seogyeongbyeolgok"

| Fig. 3.29 *Pyeongjo* and *Gyemyeonjo* Modes

Instruments and musical implements of Goryeo include the *geomun-go*, *hyangbipa*, *gayageum*, *daegeum*, *janggu*, *abak*, *muae*, *mugo*, *haegeum*, *piri*, *junggeum*, *sogeum* and *bakpan*. Among them, the *geomun-go*, *hyangbipa*, *gayageum*, *daegeum*, *junggeum*, *sogeum* and *bakpan* were descended from the Unified Silla period, while the *piri* was a wind instrument from the Goguryeo period. *Abak*, *muae*, *mugo* were not instruments but props for indigenous court dance, *hyangak-jeongjae*. The *haegeum*, *piri*, *junggeum*, *sogeum* and *bakpan* accompanied court dance. The *haegeum* and the *janggu* were newly introduced from China. The *haegeum*, sometimes referred to as a fiddle, has two strings on a small resonate box, and it is played with a bow. It is related to the Chinese *erhu*; similar instruments can be found through Asia. The *janggu* is a two-headed hourglass shaped drum. The right side of the *janggu* drum is played with a thin stick made from bamboo while the left side is struck with performer's left palm, the two sides of drum head produce different tone colors.

| Fig. 3.30 *Haegeum, Janggu*

2) *Dangak*, Music of the Tang Dynasty

The *dangak* of Goryeo inherited its form from Unified Silla, but in the latter part of the 10th century Goryeo *dangak* was gradually replaced by *saak* from Song Dynasty. *Saak*, referring to song repertoires with Chinese lyrics, was popular among the intellectuals of Goryeo. Two repertoires of *saak* "Boheoja" and "Nakyangchun" were transmitted to present time

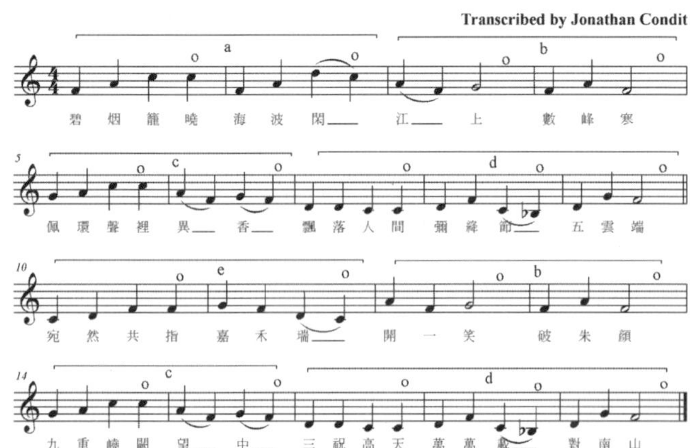

| Fig. 3.31 Goryeo *Dangak*, "Boheoja"

through various musical anthologies of the Joseon period. A single word of the text took one beat and the form of the song was the *hwandu* style, which literally means "changing the head" and indicates the beginning part of the song that changes while the rest of the parts are repeated. Thus, *hwandu* style can be written as A (a bcd) - A′ (e bcd) form. <Fig. 3.31>

| Fig. 3.32 Musical instruments for *Dangak* : *Ajaeng, Banghyang, Saenghwang, Dangbipa, Dangpiri, Taepyeongso*

The basic instruments used for Goryeo *dangak* were the *banghyang*, *tungso*, *dangjeok*, *dangpiri*, *dangbipa*, *ajaeng*, *daejaeng*, *gyobanggo*, and *bakpan*. Some other instruments like *saenghwang*, *janggu*, *haegeum*, and *taepyeongso* were added occasionally depending on the situation and conditions of the performance. The string instruments, *ajaeng* and *daejaeng* produce the lower tones. The *banghyang* is xylophone with several small metal plates. The *tungso* and the *dangpiri* are wind instruments played vertically while the *dangjeok* is played horizontally. Although *dangpiri* is considerably smaller than the *tungso*, it produces the loudest sounds, thus it usually plays the main melody. The *dangbipa* has a curved neck and four strings. The *gyobanggo*, a drum, is placed on a wooden stand enabling the upper head to be played. *Saenghwang* is a wind instrument made of gourd resonate box with several thin bamboo pipes of different sizes, it produces harmonic sounds by continuous inhaling and exhaling.

Dangak produces well-combined sonic dimensions with different kinds of instruments; continuous lower sounds produced by *ajaeng* and *daejaeng*, clear metallic sounds produced by xylophone-like *banghyang*, strong and deep sounds of *dangpiri* and high and soft sounds of *dangjeok*. <Fig. 3.32>

3) *Aak*, the Confucian Ritual Music

Aak originated from ancient Chinese rituals. *Aak* embodies the symbolic shapes of heaven, earth and nature. It is believed that *aak* nurtures one's heart, regulates heaven and earth, harmonizes god with man, and balances yin and yang. The lyrics of *aak* praise civil and

| Fig. 3.33 *Deungga* (Terrace Ensemble), *Heonga* (Courtyard Ensemble)

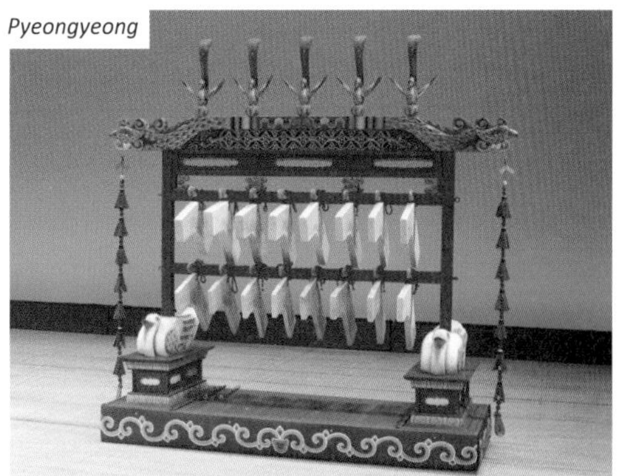

Jeok

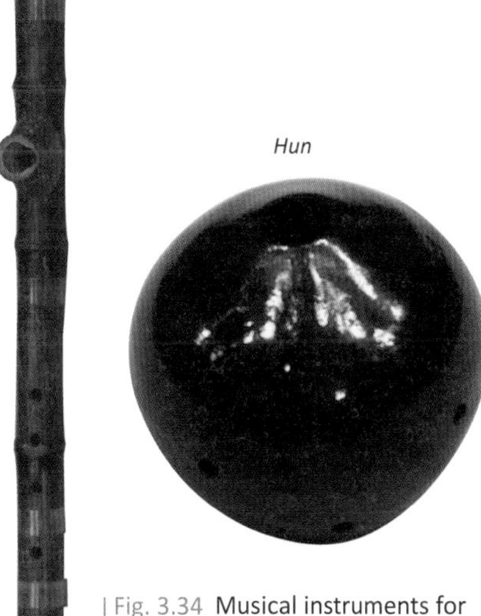

| Fig. 3.34 Musical instruments for *Aak* : *Pyeongyeong, Pyeonjong, Jeok, Geum, Seul, Chuk, Eo, Ji, Hun*

military achievements of ancestors and are visually expressed through dance.

Musical instruments for *aak* are all made from eight fundamental materials from nature called "eight materials" or *paleum* of East Asian cosmology, including metal, stone, silk, bamboo, gourd, earth, leather, and wood. *Pyeongjong* and *teukjong* are instruments that belong to the metal category; *pyeongyeong* and *teukgyeong* belong to the stone category; *geum* and *seul* are made of silk, *jeok* and *ji* are made of bamboo, *saenghwang* belongs to the gourd family, *hun* belongs to earth (soil) category, *chuk* and *eo* belong to the wood group. All these instruments are performed in two different ensembles, *deungga* (terrace ensemble) and *heonga* (courtyard ensemble).

Aak was first introduced to Goryeo in 1116, when King Hwijong of China (Song Dynasty) sent a number of instruments and ritual props, along with notations and written manuscripts of playing techniques. This early *aak*, called *daeseong aak*, was arranged by King Hwijong himself. *Daeseong aak* was performed at rituals such as *taemyo* (for royal ancestors), *wongu* (worshipping heavenly gods), *sajik* (worshipping earthly gods and gods of grain) and *munseonwangmyo* (dedicated to Confucius). *Aak* underwent many changes throughout Korean history. However, its tradition and music continued and sometimes indigenous instruments were used as replacements when the original instrument was unavailable or in disrepair.

Early Joseon Period

(14th–16th Century)

Ⅳ. Early Joseon Period (14th–16th Century)

Joseon was founded with the aim of addressing the ills of late Goryeo and building a new state. Establishing a system of rule centered on the king and a bureaucracy consisting of civil and military officials (*yangban*), Joseon instituted a social order based on a strict class system and patriarchal family system.

The Neo-Confucianism of late Goryeo was adopted as the ruling ideology, and in early Joseon, a new class of scholar officials based in the provinces became the ruling elite who dominated state affairs. From the mid–15th century, however, the *sarim* faction of scholars rose to prominence and eventually gained control of government. The *sarim* sought reform and as they expanded their presence in the court they clashed with the established *hungu* faction. This battle for power led to the massacre of scholars, and four literati purges occurred from the reigns of King Yeonsangun (r. 1494–1506) through King Myeongjong (r. 1545–1567). As a result of the purges, the *Sarim* were pushed out of government and many scholars were either killed or exiled. Having their base in the provinces, however, the *sarim*, even after being driven out of central government, continued to grow in force through means of educational institutes such as the *seowon* (private Confucian academies) and *hyangyak*, the "village contract" that enabled a degree of local government based on Confucian principles. When King Seonjo (r. 1567–1608) rose to the throne the *Sarim* returned to power, dominating government in the latter half of the 16th century. In the process, divisions occurred and the *sarim* split into smaller factions, resulting in factional politics where the two sides constantly criticized and kept a check on each other.

The ruling class of the Joseon Dynasty placed importance on practical learning and science and technology as the means to ensure the well-being of the people, national prosperity, and military strength. In the arts, early Joseon was a time when the simple, honest lives of the literati were reflected in paintings, calligraphy, pure white porcelain and other crafts. In addition, this was the period in which the Korean script, *Hangeul*, was invented, expanding the foundations for a people's culture and enabling culture and the arts to grow and flourish.

1. Art

1) Painting

With the objective of becoming a powerful Confucian country of East Asia, the Joseon Dynasty (1392–1910) made active use of paintings as a visual means of enlightening the people through the decoration of buildings, such as palaces and government offices, and the adornment of ritual halls. Accordingly, Joseon expanded the *Dohwaseo*, the Royal Bureau of Painting, in the early period for systematic training of artists, showing a more active approach to the cultivation of painters than any other Korean state. The scholar-officials (K. *sadaebu*, Ch. shidaifu), the ruling elite of the time, succeeded the tradition of the mid-Goryeo period, and considered paintings to have a function equal to poetry and calligraphy in expressing their wishes or emotions and as a medium for the cultivation of good character. They considered the ability to paint and appreciate art to be necessary for cultural and intellectual refinements. Through the efforts of these members of the elite who were both producers and consumers of art, the literati theory of painting as a means of realizing the virtue and principles of life ("the way") was established, which had the effect of increasing the number of art lovers.

In terms of philosophy or style, painting in the first half of Joseon can be divided into early and middle periods with the 16th century as the dividing line. Painting of the early period flourished with the assimilation of influences from Goryeo as well as the Song and Yuan dynasties of China. During the reign of King Sejong (r. 1418–1450) when the state made great efforts to study the systems and institutions of the preceding Goryeo dynasty to lay the foundations for the new nation, early Joseon painting further developed. In the middle period, bold and untrammeled ink and brush paintings in the style of the Zhejiang School of the Ming Dynasty grew popular under the literati's admiration for paintings of Xihu (West Lake) in Hangzhou, Zheijiang Province, and the growing influence of Neo-Confucianism, the ruling ideology, reflecting the rising power of the *Sarim* faction, a group of literati who upheld Neo-Confucian doctrine. This change likely came about when Koreans began to regard Ming Dynasty painting as the true Chinese painting from the time of King Jungjong (r. 1506–1544) and wide acceptance of the ideas found in Chinese and Korean literature in the period of King Seonjo's reign (r. 1567–1608).

(1) Landscape Painting

The Korean tradition of classical landscape painting was established through the work of An Gyeon (active ca. 1440–1470), a great painter during the reign of King Sejong. At

| Fig. 4.1 An Gyeon, Dream Journey to the Peach Blossom Land, 1447, Ink and light color on silk, 38.7×106.5cm, Tenri Central Library, Japan

the time the scholar-officials painted classical landscapes based on the Chinese model, at a time when China was pursuing a universal culture in the middle ages. An's masterpiece titled "Dream Journey to the Peach Blossom Land" (*Mongyu dowon do*, <Fig. 4.1>), painted in 1447, features Prince Anpyeong and scholars from the Jiphyeonjeon, the Hall of Worthies, in a dreamlike landscape filled with peach trees. Reflecting the style of the latter half of Goryeo, based on the Li Guo style of the Song and Yuan dynasties of China, the painting has the intellectual balance and order of Northern Song landscapes. But the manner in which the landscape forms and elements in "Dream Journey to the Peach Blossom Land" appear to overlap, one added onto the next, is closer to the Guo Xi style of the Yuan period. The stylized jagged rocks, marked with black dots, and the composition of the dreamland at the right with its overlapping ridges echo the expression of rocks and mountains found in Goryeo Buddhist landscapes of the 13th and 14th centuries.

In China, classical landscapes gradually shifted from the style of the Guo Xi school of the

| Fig. 4.2 Anonymous, Night Rain on Xiao and Xiang, Eight Views of the Xaio and Xiang Rivers (5th panel), Before 1539, Ink on paper, 98.3×49.9cm, Daigan-ji Temple, Japan

| Fig. 4.3 Anonymous, Gathering of Retired High Scholar-officials at the Pavilion of Reading (detail), circa 1531, Ink on silk, 91.5×62.3cm, Private collection, Japan

Northern Song toward the feeling of limitless space in the Ma-Xia school of the Southern Song. Through An Gyeon, these styles were fused together to create an eclectic Joseon style, recalling the stylistic hallmarks of Yuan dynasty painting. An's masterpiece features the strong natural forms with sharp undulations, the compositional contrast between high rugged scenes and broad distant spaces, and the sharp contrast between the background and ink forms, creating a dynamic landscape filled with vitality and mysterious change. "Dream Journey to the Peach Blossom Land" shows the infinite harmony and order of nature. When the Japanese Zen priest Sonkai visited Korea in 1539, he took back home the folding screen "Eight Views of the Xiao and Xiang Rivers" (*Sosang palgyeong do*, <Fig. 4.2>), which shows all the characteristics of An's work, such as the composition focused on one side and short and sharp brushstrokes and ink dots. Such landscapes, however, do not show nature as it is. But they are ideal images of nature, excluding direct communication between the artist and the viewer and being conventionally faithful to form and tone. As the Zhe style popular during the Ming dynasty, favoring large ornamental compositions was gradually assimilated into Korean landscape painting, the picture plane became flatter and the contrast between dark and light came to be stronger. The composition also showed overall decorativeness.

Paintings of scholars' gatherings (*gyehoe do*), popular during the 16th century, comprise a unique genre of Joseon painting that was inseparable from the rise of the scholar-official class and their taste for the arts. As a result, true-view paintings of famous scenic spots around Hanyang (today's Seoul), the capital city of the Joseon dynasty, were produced. "Gathering of Retired High Scholar-officials at the Pavilion of Reading" (*Dokseodang gyehoe do*, <Fig. 4.3>) from 1531 is a documentary painting, pictorially recording a social gathering of retired officials on a boat on the Han River. From the standing point of Apgujeong today, it depicts the scene of Oksu-dong across the river and even those of Mt. Bugak and Mt. Samgak in the far distance. This painting reflects both the styles of An Gyeon and true-view landscape painters of the time.

Landscapes continued to gain popularity in the 17th century under leading painters such as Kim Si (1524–1593), Yi Gyeong-yun (1545–1611), Yi Jeong (1541–1622), and Kim Myeong-guk (1600–?) set a new trend in landscape painting. Their works frequently show the scenes of figures enjoying nature posed against a landscape background. Their composition and brushwork were based on the styles of the late Zhe school of the Ming dynasty. But the features of even greater flatness became one of the most distinctive elements of Joseon Zhe-school-inspired paintings. In "Boy Pulling a Donkey" (*Dongja gyeol-lyeo do*, <Fig. 4.4>) by Kim Si, the main mountain peak soars up aslant. The scene of a boy struggling with a donkey refusing to cross the stream beneath a large pine tree constitutes the eye of the painting. There is a strong contrast between dark and light and black and white. Rough brushstrokes are used for the shading and modeling of rock and mountain forms.

| Fig. 4.4 Kim Si, Boy Pulling a Donkey, late 16th century, Ink and light color on silk, 111×46cm, Leeum, Samsung Museum of Art, Treasure No.783

(2) Portraiture

The portrait painting tradition, institutionally established in the Goryeo dynasty further developed during the Joseon period. Portraits served to glorify and enhance the rulership of Joseon kings and the political images of the new nation. In portraiture, the main subjects were the king and his high-ranking officials. For painters working at the Royal Bureau of Painting, it was the greatest honor and symbol of success to be selected to paint the king's portrait. The most famous royal portrait painters of the early Joseon era were Choi Gyeong, Yi Sang-jwa, Bae Ryeon, and Yi Heung-hyo who were granted high-ranking official positions.

For the sake of the likeness of the sitter's appearance, the court painters depicted him as accurately as possible. The brushwork was astonishingly fine. The meticulously painted por-

| Fig. 4.5 Anonymous, Portrait of Yu Geun, late 16th century, Color on silk, 180.5×103.5cm, Private collection, North Chungcheong Province, Treasure No. 566

traits show the high level of Joseon portraiture. In portraits of the king, they also managed to capture his character and spirit, displaying the greatest skill in the making of a portrait. In style, composition, and visual likeness, Joseon portraiture is the most distinguished in all of East Asian portrait paintings. As in the case of portraits of officials seated in a chair, in Joseon, the preference was for depicting the sitter in a three-quarter pose facing his right, unlike the trend in Goryeo or China. From the mid-Joseon period, as seen in the "Portrait of Yu Geun" <Fig. 4.5>, the curves of the face and the texture of the skin in portraiture are meticulously painted in countless fine lines that clearly show the physiognomy of the sitter. A colored mat is placed on the floor to create a luxurious atmosphere.

Along with portraits, paintings of Confucian sages, lofty scholars, and recluses were one of the most popular painting subjects in the early half of the Joseon dynasty. Joseon rulers made numerous efforts to create an ideal Confucian state. For the education of ordinary people in the virtues of Confucian ethics, they produced and distributed woodblock prints of model figures such as loyal subjects, filial sons, and virtuous women in order to inspire ethical thoughts and to cultivate morality. Meanwhile, the scholar-officials liked to paint and to collect nature-friendly paintings showing lofty scholars and recluses walking freely in the mountains and looking at the waterfalls while reciting poetry. "Lofty Scholar Contemplating Water" (*Gosa gwansu do*, <Fig. 4.6>) by Kang Hui-an (1417–1464), a major literati painter active during the reign of King Sejong, is one such painting. The latter half of the 16th century, however, saw the popularity of concise and small landscapes with figures, reflecting the influence of the Chinese Zhe school style.

In the case of paintings of Buddhist and Daoist subjects (*doseok hwa*), a radically new style emerged where the subject was rendered swiftly in a few bold strokes with minimal detail. Called *Seon* (Ch. Chan, Ja. Zen) paintings, such works were chiefly produced by court painters such as Kim Myeong-guk and Han Si-gak (1621–?), who had accompanied Korean envoys to Japan after the Japanese invasions of 1592–1598. Kim's "Bodhidharma" (*Dalma do*, <Fig. 4.7>), is one such painting that is distinguished by its bold and lively brushwork.

| Fig. 4.6 Kang Hui-an, Lofty Scholar Contemplating Water, 15th century, Ink on paper, 23.4×15.7cm, National Museum of Korea

| Fig. 4.7 Kim Myeong-guk, Bodhidharma, 1643, Ink on paper, 83×57cm, National Museum of Korea

This painting, representing the combination of the popular Japanese iconography and the innovative brushwork of Korea, features the bold, swift, and minimal brushstrokes. Kim's works left a deep impression on the Japanese clients in the early Edo period.

(3) Bird-and-Flower Painting

Both literati and court painters were as fond of bird-and-flower compositions (*hwajo do*) as they were of landscapes and figure paintings. Like other painting genres, bird and flower paintings developed systematically from the mid-Goryeo period and continued to flourish during the Joseon period. Realistic color paintings were officially promoted through the court painters based on demand inside the royal household. The major group interested in appreciating and collecting works of art along with members of the royal family was the class of scholar-officials who considered bird-and-flower paintings to be symbolic of escape from the mundane world into the harmonious world of nature. Painters expressed these

| Fig. 4.8 Yi Am, Blossoms, Birds and Puppies, mid-16th century, Color on paper, 86×44.9cm, Leeum, Samsung Museum of Art, Treasure No. 1392

ideas figuratively and allegorically, and bird-and-flower paintings were considered to be a means of cultivating one's innate nature.

Bird-and-flower paintings can be divided into two types: *daegyeong* or "large scenes" which typically feature a tree at the top and water or rocks at the bottom with different types of birds perched on either part of the picture, rendered with fine brushwork and coloring; and *sogyeong* or "small scenes," featuring simplified compositions with one or two birds rendered mostly in ink. If the former type in ink and colors combines the Goryeo tradition with the then popular Ming imperial court style, the latter brush and ink style was a new one reflecting the literary tastes of the scholar-officials.

The major example of the former style is Yi Am's (1507–1566) "Flowers, Birds and Puppies" (*Hwajo guja do*, <Fig. 4.8>). The top half shows a flowering tree treated by the outlines first and then filled in with colors, while the birds are rendered in the so-called "boneless (no outlines)" style. The painting is both decorative and natural at the same time, showing the purity and beauty of nature. Yi was gifted in painting hawks and dogs. He was considered the best artist in this field during his life. Japanese records say that his paintings define the unique Joseon style. The warmth and lyricism of Yi's works formed the foundation of Joseon bird-and-flower paintings.

Small-scene bird-and-flower paintings reached the height in the work of Jo Sok (1595–1668) who was famous as a loyal upright scholar. In the pictorial expression of the birds or the triangular leaves, Jo's paintings show the overall plain and dry brushwork with classical beauty. "Magpie Roosting in an Old Plum Tree" (*Gomae seojak do*, <Fig. 4.9>) features a

| Fig. 4.9 Jo Sok, Magpie Roosting in an Old Plum Tree, early 17th century, Ink on paper, 100.4×55.5cm, Kansong Art Museum

| Fig. 4.10 Yi Jing, Ducks among the Water Pepper Plants, early 17th century, Ink and light color on silk, 31×21cm, Kansong Art Museum

lonely magpie. In this painting, plum branches are rendered wonderfully in swift, dry brushstrokes using the "flying white" technique to reveal white streaks. In "Magpie Roosting in an Old Plum Tree" that best represents Jo's style; the magpie seems to be looking far into the distance, waiting patiently for the coming of spring. The vigorousness of the brushstrokes exemplifies the special character of mid-Joseon ink paintings. This painting reveals the painter's own patient wishes for the arrival of spring and the passing of troubles, which arose from his noble spirit after the Manchu invasion (*Byeongja horan*) of 1636.

Yi Jing's (1581–after 1645) "Ducks among the Water Pepper Plants" (*Yodang wonang do*, <Fig. 4.10>) shows a pair of ducks playing happily in the water below rocks where water pepper plants grow. This painting is filled with elements that define the spirit of the time: the angular, flat, and overlapping rock forms with the strong contrast of black and white, jutting out from one side, the decorative treatment of surfaces with light shading texture strokes, the depiction of the duck's feathers using the boneless technique, and the stylized flowers and reeds treated in ink dots. Along with the paintings of cows and horses, this harmonious mixture of a close-up subject, the unique expression of the ducks, and the beauty and calm atmosphere of the natural world represents a very Korean sense of aesthetics and emotion.

2) Sculpture

Sculpture of the Joseon period consisted mostly of stone guardians for burial tombs and decorative sculpture for the royal court. When we study the memorial services (for deceased ancestors held in front of the grave mounts) of the Joseon period, the royal tombs can be categorized strictly into three types namely *Neung* (陵), *Won* (園) and *Myo* (廟). There was a distinct hierarchical order in burial tombs. The *Neung* (陵) refers to the burial ground for the king and the queen, the *Won* (園) was for the king's close relations (parents, family, relatives, etc.), as well as the crown prince and his wife, and the *Myo* (廟) was for great princes, princesses, royal concubines, and nobilities. When preparing burial grounds for the royal family, stones were stacked around the grave to form supports and protection. Placed in the front of the graves were stone statues of a sheep (石羊) and stone statues of a tiger (石虎). <Fig. 4.11> A rectangular stone was also installed along with a pair of stone posts and stone lantern, placed in front of the stone statues. Finally a wall was built in the directions of the east, west and

| Fig. 4.11 Stone Statues (Animal), Yeongreung Royal Tomb, 15th century, Yeoju

| Fig. 4.12 Stone Figurines (left: Government Officials, right: Warrior), Yeongreung Royal Tomb, 15th century, Yeoju

| Fig. 4.13 Buddha, Gilt Bronze, from Sujongsa Temple stone Stupa, 1493, h. 13.8cm, Central Buddhist Museum

| Fig. 4.14 Seated Buddhist Goddess of Mercy, Dry lacquer, 1501, 91cm, Girimsa Temple, Wolseong, Treasure No. 415

north (3 sides) surrounding the grave itself. Beside the lantern, a pair or two pairs of stone figures stood facing each another to guard the grave while behind them stood stone horses. Below these, statues of warriors were also placed. <Fig. 4.12> The size and type of stone statues distinguished the hierarchical status of the deceased, and also represented the power of the royal court which followed the Confucian beliefs in ruling order and discipline.

As Joseon's main ideology was Confucianism (儒教), the production of Buddhist sculpture deteriorated, yet the statue of Buddha was still considered as a subject of worship and prayer. The period saw the production of smaller scale Buddha statues in bronze, wood, clay and so on. Diversity in form and style was less cultivated than in the previous times. Yet the tradition continued on throughout the entire Joseon period, with lavish reliquaries and the expression of eternal life placed all over the body of the Buddha. Representative of historical remains of period before the Japanese invasion of 1592 (*Imjinwoeran*) include the pagoda of the Sujongsa Temple (水鍾寺) as well as the gilt bronze Buddha (1493, 1628), <Fig. 4.13> the seated Buddhist Goddess of Mercy in dry lacquer (1501), <Fig. 4.14> from the Kirimsa Temple (祇林寺), and the wooden Amita Buddha (1492) that is now in a collection at the National Museum of Korea.

3) *Buncheong* Ware, White Porcelain and Wood Work

The term *Buncheong* ware (粉青沙器) began from the notion of decorating celadon clay with white liquefied slip. With the establishment of Joseon, government issues were being reformed and the government first developed a system of receiving provincially produced goods. As a result, ceramics with similar design and decoration came to be produce.

| Fig. 4.15 "*Deoknyeongbu* (德寧府)" Bowl with Stamped Pattern, Buncheong ware, 15th century, h. 6.1cm, d. 17.7cm, National Museum of Korea

The period saw an increase in the production of ceramic wares with inlay and impressed decoration originating from the Goryeo period. <Fig. 4.15> Additionally, the newly developed sgraffito (*bakji*, 剝地), incising (*eumgak*, 陰刻), iron-painting (*cheolhwa*, 鐵畵), slip-brushing (*gwi-yal*), were applied to *Buncheong* wares and developed a unique formative appeal. <Fig. 4.16> With the establishment of the official-kiln (官窯) in the second half of the 15th century, royal wares were provided mostly by the official-kiln in Gwangju (廣州), Gyeonggi Province. Thus, *Buncheong* ware production decreased, and it was produced for local consumption, gradually declining in quality and displaying strong local characteristics. In the 16th century, the production of ceramics in these regional potteries decreased. *Buncheong* ware was becoming less popular due to interest in porcelain and gradually diminished. The Japanese Invasion of 1592 did not help with this, the number of potters who could produce *Buncheong* ware also disappeared putting an end to the production of *Buncheong* wares.

| Fig. 4.16 Bottle with Under-glaze Iron-brown Fish Decoration, Buncheong ware, 15th century, h. 29.7cm, National Museum of Korea

The Joseon royal court restricted the production of high quality craft objects through a prohibition law. Moreover, plain but elegant and less finesse crafts were emphasized relating to the belief of humbleness (崇儉); such item were also emphasized, as the use was believed to promote notion of teaching and setting an example to others. Under such legislation, the use of white porcelain was institutionalized, and the production took on an active turn. Towards the latter part of the 15th century, the royal kilin (*Bunwon*, 分院) was established in Gwangju, Gyeonggi Province. The office in charge of producing white porcelain (*Saong-won*, 司饔院), was designated to supply and manage the utilitarian wares for the king's meals and banquets. Before the establishment of the *Bunwon*, in the 14th and 15th centuries, pure white porcelain <Fig. 4.17>, inlaid and blue and white porcelain types were developed. However, in the 15th and 16th centuries

| Fig. 4.17 White Porcelain Placenta Jar, 15th century, h. 45.5cm, Ewha Womans University Museum

| Fig. 4.18 White Porcelain Bottle with Under-glaze Cobalt Blue Decoration of a Scene with a Wise Elderly Person, 16th century, h. 47cm, Ewha Womans University Museum, Treasure No. 644

the quality and types varied depending on function and the class status of the people. While the Goryeo inlaid porcelain gradually decreased, blue and white porcelain became more and more popular. This was created by drawing patterns onto the bisque fired surface (after the first firing where the clay is made porous) with a natural blue color pigment used for porcelain, known as cobalt. Glaze was applied after the surface decoration was completed. The blue and white porcelain of the Joseon Dynasty received influences from *Yuan* and *Ming* Dynasties of China, later developed to have an authentic Korean character. <Fig. 4.18> Those made during the 15th and 16th centuries reflected the pattern and shapes made by the *Yuan* (元) and (明) *Ming* Dynasties. The cobalt was imported to Korea through China, and because painting with this material on fired clay required much skill, most of the blue and white porcelains were painted by skilled court painters. For the same reason production was on a small amount. The remaining blue and white porcelain today consists of bottles, plates, jars and many other pieces with interesting shapes. Patterns in blue and white include dragons (龍), floral scroll designs (寶相唐草), chrysanthemums (菊花), plum blossoms and bird (梅鳥), grass and flower (草花), pine and bamboo trees (松竹). In addition to piece of patterns, but sometimes poems were written on the clay surfaces.

Wood work also has its own special qualities. The artificial decorations and forms were reduced and simple lines and smooth surface presented harmony. The excellent execution of proportion allowed Joseon furniture to harmonize effectively within the natural architectural space. The wooden furniture had distinct qualities, simple and modest with stable decorations. <Fig. 4.19> Other than working with wood there were also the lacquer ware and burnt animal horns. <Fig. 4.20> According to historical documents, the different stages of working with wood required different skills from craftsmen, and division of labor was practiced. Among craftsmen, those who made small furniture and ornaments were treated important. Similar to Korean architecture, wood craft did not incorporate

| Fig. 4.19 *Gobi* (Letter Rack), Wood and Bamboo, late Joseon, h. 82.8cm, National Museum of Korea

| Fig. 4.20 Lacquered Boxs Inlaid with Mother-of-Pearl, *Sipjangsaeng* (ten symbols of longevity) Design, late Joseon, 25×14.5cm, Ewha Womans University Museum

the use of nails, instead pieces were either inter-locked or fitted together. Rather than having lavish decorations, the objects were decorated with the natural texture and structure of wood itself. Finally, to add a finishing touch black or reddish varnish was applied.

4) Architecture of Royal Palaces, *Seowons* (Private Academies) and Burial Tombs

Continuing with the traditions set by the Goryeo period, the architecture of Joseon consisted largely of the multi-bracket sets (*Dapo*, 多包) structure. As this method added grandeur to architectural structures, it was applied mostly to temples and royal palaces. Other styles included the integrated method of using both the brackets structure and the column bracket (*Jushimpo*, 柱心包). For less important architectural structure, the wing-like braket (*Ikgong*, 翼工) style was incorporated.

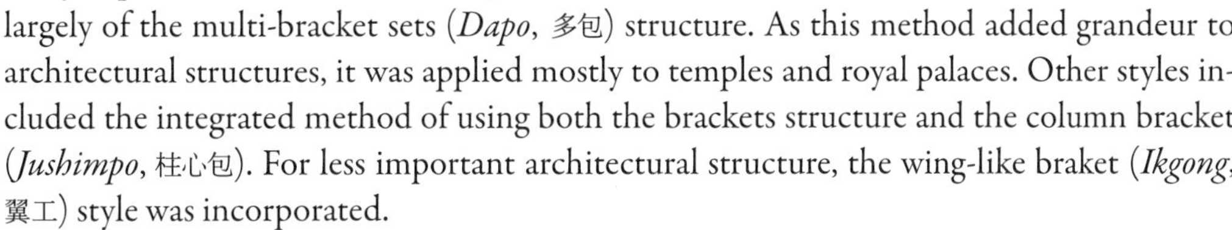

In 1392 with the establishment of Joseon, Hanyang (漢陽) became the royal residential settlement. King Taejo (Yi Seong-gye, 李成桂) in 1394, planned to build a royal palace in the beautiful natural environment of Hanyang, and he chose this location as the capital for the

| Fig. 4.21 Layout of East Palace (Changdeokgung Palace and Changgyeonggung Palace), 576×273cm, Korea University Museum, National Treasure No. 247

| Fig. 4.22 Geunjeongjeon Hall, Gyeongbokgung Palace, National Historical Monument No. 117

| Fig. 4.24 *Huwon* (Back garden), Chandeokgung Palace, National Historical Monument No. 122, World Heritage

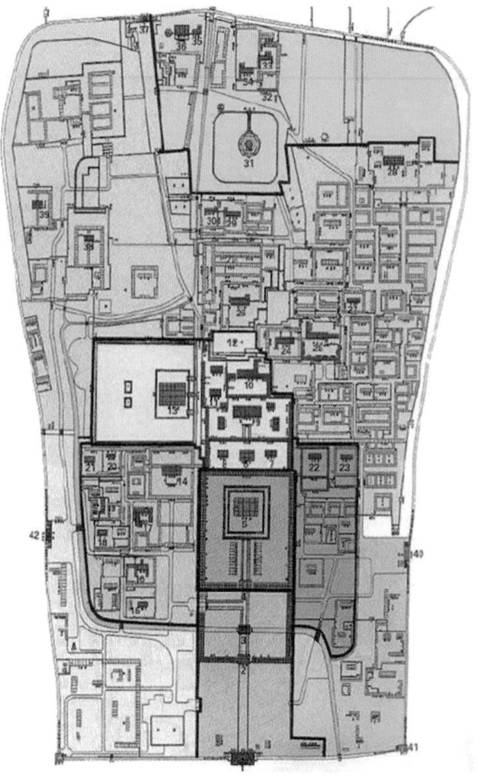

| Fig. 4.23 Arrangement Plan of Gyeongbokgung Palace

auspicious geomancy. <Fig. 4.21> Gyeongbokgung Palace (景福宮), Deoksugung Palace (昌德宮), Changgyeonggung Palace (昌慶宮) and Gyeongwungung Palace (慶運宮) were main palaces. Again there was a hierarchical order in the types of buildings, such as secondary palace (別宮), city fortress (邑城), government office (官衙) and others. <Fig. 4.22> The layout and composition of Joseon palaces differed slightly depending on the natural environment but in general, it consisted of government offices, king's working quarter and king's living chamber. <Fig. 4.23> The living section included the king's, queen's and the queen dowager's sleeping areas, in addition to the section that provided all kinds of facilities for the royal palace. The crown prince's living quarter was in the east and this was referred to as crown princess residence (*Dong-gung*, 東宮). Every palace had a rear garden which was used for recreation and education. In composition, they were often created in accordance with the natural environment. <Fig. 4.24>

The other side Confucianism was set as the main belief of the Joseon period and with this royal ancestral shrine (*Jongmyo,* 宗廟), private Confucian academy (*Seowon*, 書院), local

| Fig. 4.25 View of Jongmyo, Joseon, National Historical Monument No. 125, World Heritage

public school annexed to Confucian shrine (*Hyanggyo*, 鄕校) were established. The purpose of these was to perform ritual ceremonies (祭享) to ancestral sages and educate regional areas, by taking charge of important roles for education.

Among all of them, *Jongmyeo* enshrined the ancestral tablets of the Joseon royal family, more specifically those who were kings and queens. The royal ancestral shrine, comprised of the main hall and a subsidiary shrine. Among all the wood architecture of the time, this is considered to be the largest single unites space in the world. The appearance of this particular building is not lavish, lacking elaborate decorations yet it effectively represents the Confucian modesty. <Fig. 4.25>

Seowon was important institutions for teaching Confucian beliefs by scholars. The space was for lecturing and holding ancestral worship rituals. There was the study quarter and an area for worshipping past scholars. Within the *Seowon* itself, the shrine was located in the most secluded area, right at the rear of the complex. The shrine kept the tablets of great Confucian scholars. In the same shrine there was another section keeping the tablets of scholars who contributed to the development of neo-Confucianism, or raised the standard of studies on morality, achieved scholastic pursuits, or those who were extremely loyal. Ritual ceremonies were held in spring and autumn for these highly knowledgeable scholars.

In addition to the royal burial grounds were distinguished of the hierarchy of people. Royal tomb of the Joseon period was centered around *Seoul*. When the king passed away, government offices were established for the state funeral. According to geomancy, it is said that the auspicious site for a grave is facing the back to the mountains and the front to water (river, lake and so on; 背山臨水). The high mountain in the north is the main and on the left the mountain takes after the shape of a blue dragon, the right, a white tiger, and the *An-san* (案山, a hill facing the site of a house or grave) in the south. Within the boundaries of the grave, there should be existed a stream or a creek that flows to the east and collects somewhere. The auspicious site, the spot of fortune referred to as '*Hyeol*' (血) in Korean. The coffin was buried in this place and the tomb mound was constructed.

2. Dance

Throughout the entire Joseon Dynasty (1392–1897), there were two prominent kings who most heavily influenced the development of dance; namely King Sejong (1418–1450) and King Seongjong (1469–1494). King Sejong contributed to the establishment of creation of *aak* (court music) and *hyangak* (indigenous Korean music). King Seongjong published one of the largest music tomes from the Joseon period titled *Akhakgwebeom* (樂學軌範, A Guide to the Study of Music, Introduction), a documented text for learning music (learning to read and play music, writing compositions, and so on). It is an invaluable book containing comprehensive documents on music and dance.

1) Reorganization and Establishment of *Gungjung Jeongjae* (Court Song and Dance)

Early on in the Joseon Period, with the idea that courtesy and music should be established at the same time in order to shore up national order, a great deal of music and dance performed in the court were newly created. Such dances were created with content praising the founding of the kingdom and expressing the authority of dynasty rather than with artistic choreography. Personal emotions and religious worship were kept to a minimum and the instrumental accompaniment and rhythm were extremely slow and long, so the movements of dance evoked an elegant and sedate atmosphere. The number of dancers, costumes and formation in a space were based on the structure of Confucian philosophy, *Eumyang-Ohaeng* (Yin and Yang, and the Five Elements) rather than on the structure of choreography. The meanings of Eastern philosophy were woven into the dances.

(1) *Dangak jeongjae*

| Fig. 4.26 *"Monggeumcheok,"* Association for Research on *Jeongjae*

The *dangak jeongjae* of the Joseon period maintained within the main framework and developed without significant change from the Goryeo period. As the *dangak jeongjae* of this period had the purpose of advocating for the legitimacy of the foundation of Joseon, it is focused on touting the dynasty's accomplishments rather than aesthetic values.

"Monggeumcheok" (夢金尺, Dream of Golden Ruler Dance) was a dance with sacred connotations associated with the establishment of Joseon. It is said that the heavens gave Taejo, the first king of a dynasty, a *geumcheok* (Golden Ruler) to establish the kingdom. Jeong Do-jeon, one of the meritorious retainers at the founding of Joseon Dynasty wrote the movements of the music for the dance along with "Suborok" and "Mundeokgok." Through court dances, he sought to announce the legitimacy and morality of the Joseon Dynasty, which had ascended to power through revolution intent on a change of dynasty. <Fig. 4.26>

The "Hawangeun" (荷皇恩) dance was created under a directive of King Sejong to Byeon Gye-ryang and it was performed in festive ceremonies in which the king hosted visiting envoys from foreign countries. This dance was a joyful piece as it described the story of King Sejong accepting his heavenly destiny to take up the responsibility for the affairs of the kingdom, with a command from King Sejong's father, Buwang (King Taejong).

(2) *Hyangak jeongjae*

Representative *hyangak jeongjae* of the early Joseon period include "Bonglaeui," "Hyangbalmu," "Hak-yeonhwadae-cheoyongmu Hapseol" and so on. There was much *hyangak jeongjae* that still exists today created by King Sejong, who excelled in music and dance.

"Bonglaeui" (蓬萊儀, Phoenix Dance) was a court dance created by King Sejong to praise the merit and virtue of Taejo for establishing Joseon. This was an elaborate court dance centered on an epic poem in *Hangeul* (the Korean alphabet) from the rule of King Sejong titled the *Yongbiurcheonga*.

"Hak-yeonhwadae-cheoyongmu Hapseol" (鶴蓮花臺處容舞合設, combination of crane

| Fig. 4.27 *Hak-yeonhwadae-cheoyongmu Hapseol,* National Research Institute of Cultural Heritage

dance, lotus pedestal dance and Cheoyong dance) was a large-scale dance formed around the "Hakmu" (crane dance), "Yeonhwadaemu" (lotus pedestal dance) and "Cheoyongmu" (Cheoyong dance). Records state that dances were performed for the first time by being integrated together in this manner in the reign of King Sejong. Towards the middle of the 15th century, these developed into integrated song and dance performances on a grand scale. The court dance was divided into three sections: "Obang (quintet)-Cheoyongmu," crane dance and lotus pedestal dance and "Obang-Cheoyongmu." There were two dancers for "Hakmu," two for "Yeonhwadaemu" and five for "Cheoyongmu" for a total of nine dancers. <Fig. 4.27>

2) The Development of Confucian Ritualistic Dance

Unlike the Goryeo period, when Buddhist dance developed, the Joseon period's religious ritualistic dance was developed into *jongmyo jeryeak* and *munmyo jeryeak* under the influence of Confucianism. The *jongmyo jeryeak* was performed at the *jongmyosajik* (shrines) as a ritualistic ceremony to previous kings. During the ceremonies, dance and music were performed along with the strict discipline of ritual ceremonies. The dance performed to the *jongmyo jeryeak* was referred to as *ilmu* (佾舞, line formation dance) and it means literally "line dancing."

The *ilmu* came in many different forms: 8-*ilmu* (8 lines and 8 rows with a total of 64 dancers), 6-*ilmu* (6 lines and 6 rows with a total of 36 dancers), 4-*ilmu* (4 lines and 4 rows with a total of 16 dancers), 2-*ilmu* (2 lines and 2 rows with a total of 4 dancers) depending on the objective and status of the rites. *Jongmyo jeryeak* is one of Korea's most representative cultural assets and in 1964 it was designated as the first important intangible cultural asset (Important Intangible Cultural Property No. 1). Additionally, with its designation as a part of world cultural heritage under UNESCO in 1995, its historical and traditional contributions were recognized globally.

The original music for the *jongmyo jeryeak* was created by King Sejong, who excelled in music. After the creation of Korean alphabet *Hangeul*, he turned his efforts towards inventing new music to praise the accomplishment of the previous king, who had established Joseon. The result was the most outstanding achievement in music and dance in the early Joseon period. He left an unprecedentedly large number of new dances and music. *jongmyo jeryeak* was one of new pieces of music that he created at that time. In particular, he acted with the notion that the use of Chinese music at the rites for Joseon's ancestors had limits, thus, the music should be changed to something purely Korean, *hyangak* (the indigenous Korean music). However, the music was not immediately used for the *jongmyo jeryeak* – it was not used until the reign of King Sejo (1455–1468). Nevertheless, it laid the groundwork for the succession of *munmu* (civil dance) and *mumu* (military dance).

During the *jongmyo jerye* rows with a total of 36 dancers, this period, 36 dancers performed the 6-*ilmu* in lines. Since Joseon was not the imperial land of an emperor, the *8-ilmu* could not be performed. According to the principles of Confucianism, there were rules to restrict the number of dancers and formation. The *8-ilmu*, which was performed by 64 dancers, could be presented only by a nation ruled by an emperor. It was not until much later, when King Gojong (1863–1897) was conferred the title of emperor that the dance format changed to the 8-*ilmu* with 64 dancers and continued in this form to the present day.

The *ilmu* performed in *jongmyo jerye* was divided into *munmu* and *mumu*. *munmu* was performed with holding a wind instrument with three holes known as *yak* with the left

| Fig. 4.28 *Munmu, Jongmyo Jeryeak (Ilmu)*

| Fig. 4.29 *Mumu, Jongmyo Jeryeak (Ilmu)*, Association for Research on *Jeongjae*

hand and a long bow decorated with pheasant's feathers, jeok on the right. The *mumu* was performed with holding a wooden sword. The *ilmu* for *jongmyo jeryeak* is composed of more than 50 different dance movements that were very slow and simple and exude the beauty of control. <Fig. 4.28><Fig. 4.29>

3) Dance based on Folk Religion

The folk religion dances of the Joseon period were developed based on the manners and customs of the previous era. In particular, under the influence of the farming culture, dances for group amusement were widely performed in the villages. Group dances were a kind of communal dance invented and refined over a long period and enjoyed by everybody, male and female, old and young alike. Folk dance had developed in the manner closely related to the diverse aspects of the everyday lives of people, including labor, rituals, amusement, etc. Folk dance is mainly divided into three categories: recreational group dance that developed naturally in the lives of the commoners, artistic dance that was highly refined by professional artists, and masked dance that was conducted by performers wearing masks in the form of a play.

Recreational group dances included *nongakmu* (farmers' music and dance), *ganggangsullae* (female circle dance), and *dongraehakchum* (crane dance of Dongrae) among others as described previously. The dances in this category had a strong communal characteristic in which everyone could enjoy and participate.

Professional dances were performed by female entertainers known as *gisaeng*, clowns, acrobats from *gisaeng* school, and artists from promotional organizations for ordinary people. Professional dances were initially developed from folk and shaman dances or recreational group dances, and became more and more artistic and professional. The purpose of such was more for appreciation than for participation.

The masked dances had a strong theatrical character. Since they were spread all over the country and developed in diverse ways according to region, mask dances were categorized and given divergent names such as *sandaenori*, *yaryu*, *talchum* and others depending on the characteristics of each region. Masked dances, in particular, developed primarily in the latter period of the Joseon Dynasty as the commoners' consciousness grew.

Such folk dances advanced more towards the end of the Joseon period and they were succeeded by the "traditional dances" of today. Recreational group dances such as *nongakmu*, *ganggangsullae* and the *dongraehakchum*, which was developed in the early days of Joseon can be observed as follows:

From ancient times, agriculture was the fundamental industry and means of living for the Korean people and regarded highly as the major foundation for people living on the earth. *Nongak* can be considered one branch of the labor dances of Korean ancestors who sought to find pleasure in their painstaking farming work. It began as a performance with drum-like percussion and later developed to include more instruments like the *kwaenggwari* (small gong), *jing* (large gong), *janggu* (hourglass-shaped drum) and its rhythm became more polished. In the performance, the person who played *janggu* danced to the tune of the instrument with brilliant footwork. Also, a leader called *sangswe* danced *Bupochum* wearing a *bupo*, a sort of head attire with a rotating feathered end. The *sogochum* (tambour dance) was a dance for performers wearing *sangmo*, a hat with either a moveable feather or a long ribbon attached at the top, which is rotated by turning the head. With such flashy acrobatic movements, performers provide a spectacular sight. Since *nongakmu* became formalized throughout a long history and within different environments, it has succeeded maintaining different characteristic of each region, demonstrating the diversity of Korean folk culture.

Ganggangsullae was a communal song and dance performed by females, which originally developed in the southern coastal regions of Korea. It was a recreational combined both singing and dancing, usually taking place around the time of *Chuseok* (Korean Thanksgiving Day) under a full moon. The etymology of the term *ganggangsullae* originated from the dialect of Jeolla province, "*ganggang*" means circular and "*sullae*" means to turn or rotate. So the word *ganggangsullae* literally means rotating in a circle. The format of this particular group activity was structured to have one main singer perform a line of stanza of a song first, with the others following suit. On a *Chuseok* evening or full-moon night, women come out into a yard, waiting for the moon to emerge, and then rotate in a circle hand-in-hand and dance. <Fig. 4.30>

Dongraehakchum, as stated in the name, originated from the Dongrae region of Busan, in the southeast of Korea. Because of the beautiful landscape of the region, many idle youth of the gentry gathered there and often held dance events. On such occasions, the men who had a talent for dancing would step forward to perform. Their black head attire, *gat* (hat) and white robe with long sleeves looked like "a dancing crane." Hence

Fig. 4.30 *Ganggangsullae,* National Research Institute of Cultural Heritage

| Fig. 4.31 *Dongraehakchum*

the name of the dance, *dongraehakchum*. The dance itself derived from the Busan region's distinct *deotbaegi* dance, a kind of masked dance shown in Gyeongsang Province. Its coarse yet simple movements were polished into the crane dance with elegance and modesty. *Dongraehakchum* contains spontaneity and freedom of expression, which are typical features of folk dances. <Fig. 4.31>

3. Music

Joseon was a Confucian Dynasty and its primary belief was that of *ye* (moral order), which is the fundamental principle of the universe. One way to control *ye* was through music, and thus the Joseon government naturally emphasized all its musical occasions. This inspired the establishment of musical theories, publication of music manuscripts, and the invention of a musical notation that could specify pitch and rhythmic change. The new government called for restructuring of *hyangak*, *dangak*, and *aak*, composing new songs in praise of the new era. As time went on, *dangak* slowly began to lose its impact within court music, becoming more and more like indigenous *hyangak*.

Confucianism of Joseon emphasized strict division of man and woman. In the Goryeo Dynasty, most court musicians were male and the dancers were female. In the Joseon Dynasty, however, gender of performers for particular events was always pre-determined and strictly maintained.

1) Establishment of Music Theory

Music theory was firmly established during the reign of the fourth king, Sejong (1418–1450). King Sejong was keenly interested in music, immersing himself into music research along with many scholars. He also composed some musical pieces of *aak*, *dangak* and *hyangak*. King Sejong also invented *jeongganbo*, a notational system which notated rhythms that he used for his own compositions. The invention of *jeongganbo* notation inspired the invention of other notational systems as well.

He contributed greatly in establishing the basis for theory, which subsequently led to the publication of the first music theory book called *Akhakgwebeom* during the reign of Seongjong (1469–1494), the ninth king. This particular book played an important role for the next six hundred years. *Akhakgwebeom*, published with the aim of transmitting court music to future descendants, consists of nine chapters, which deal with music theory, performance order, instruments, instrumentation, dance order and methods, and dancers' costumes and props. It was fully illustrated to make points clear, and became the fundamental theory book for Joseon Dynasty. <Fig. 4.32>

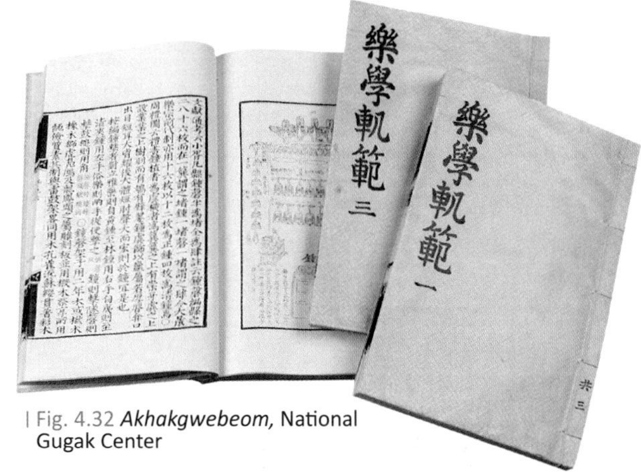

Fig. 4.32 *Akhakgwebeom*, National Gugak Center

During this period, rhythmic values were notated using the *jeongganbo*, while pitch was indicated using *yuljabo* (pitch notation), *oeumyakbo* (five-tones notation), and *hapjabo* (playing techniques notation). Unlike *aak* or *dangak* of Chinese origin, *hyangak* featured lots of rhythmic vitality, and therefore it became necessary for King Sejong to invent *jeongganbo*. His *jeongganbo* is a type of mensural notation, in which each vertical line was divided into smaller cells

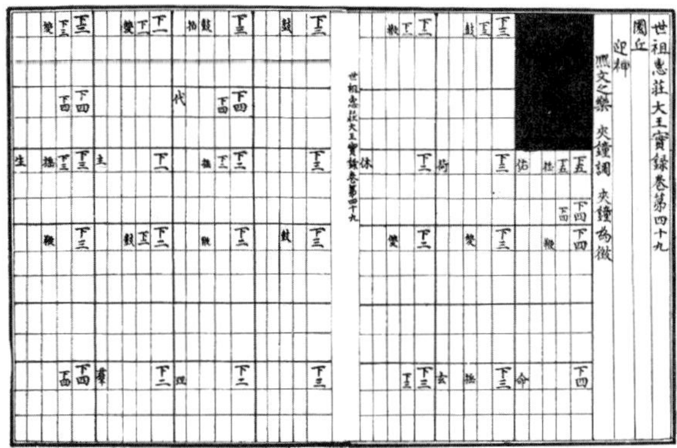

Fig. 4.33 Musical Score *Jeongganbo* recorded in the Annals of King Sejo

| Fig. 4.34 *Oeumyakbo*

| Fig. 4.35 *Yuljabo*

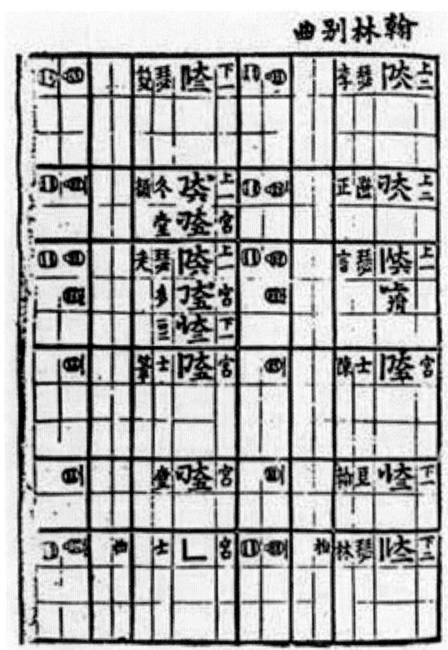

| Fig. 4.36 *Hapjabo* for *Geomun-go*

or squares called *jeonggan*. Pitch names are notated in each cell, while rhythmic value is determined by the number of cells (or parts of a cell) a note occupies. <Fig. 4.33> is a score with text attached, which shows the parts for melodic and percussive instruments, with five vertical lines forming one unit. <Fig. 4.33>

During the reign of King Sejo (1455–1468) a notation called *oeumyakbo* was introduced. It indicates the five main pitches of a melody and the system is apt for notating *hyangak*. The main pitch is indicated as *gung* (宮), with the higher or lower notes written using the *sang* (上) and the *ha* (下) symbols (meaning higher and lower tones respectively) <Fig. 4.34>. <Fig. 4.33> is notated with *oeumyakbo*.

During King Sejong's time the pitches were indicated by *yuljabo* instead of *oeumyakbo*. *Yulja* is the 12 names of the pitches in the octave scale and one *yulja* consists of two Chinese characters, such as *hwang-jong* (黃鐘; c), *tae-ju* (太簇; d), *go-seon* (姑洗; e), *jung-ryeo* (仲呂; f), *yim-jong* (林鐘; g), and *mu-yeok* (無射; a#). On the *yuljabo*, only the first character is notated. For indicating notes of the upper octave, '氵' is added to the original tone (黃=c), while adding '亻' for indicating notes of the lower octave (㒇–黃–潢; C-c-c').

During King Seonjong's time (1469–1494) a type of tablature for the *geomun-go* and the *bipa* was introduced. In here, specific performance methods such as fingering (ㄱ..), plucking (ㅣ..), string names (大..), and fret order (八, 六....) are indicated using abbreviated symbols. <Fig. 4.36>

2) Restructuring Court Music

At the beginning of the Joseon Dynasty, a number of songs were composed in praise of the new kings. The Chinese lyrics were accompanied mostly by *dangak* and *aak*, though sometimes also accompanied by *hyangak*. *Hyangak* was reserved for songs with Korean lyrics. From this period, court musicians discarded the age-old *daeseong aak*, a Goryeo heritage, and began composing new *aak* pieces based on their own research of ancient Chinese *aak*.

(1) *Aak*

Restructuring of court music began with *aak*. *Aak* is based on Confucius principles, chosen by the Joseon government as a national ideology. King Sejong was personally studied *aak* and ordered a thorough restructuring of the music. New instruments for the *aak* orchestra such as *pyeongjong* and *pyeongyeong* were reconstructed by Koreans, enabling new *aak* pieces to be composed. Since *aak* was now in full bloom, it came to be used not only for rituals but also banquets and national ceremonies.

Musically speaking, *aak* has a simple structure. The melody is based on a heptatonic scale, begins and ends on the main pitch. The lyrics are a fixed poem that has four syllables per phrase. One syllable is put to one pitch and all the pitches have the same time value, thus having no rhythmic variation. Since the melody is extremely formal and has no rhythmic interest, it came to be used only for ritual occasions.

| Sound. 2 *Munmyo Jeryeak* (Confucian Shrine Music), Performed by National Gugak Center

(2) *Hyangak*

The Joseon government also changed *hyangak*. For example, among the songs from Goryeo, those that dealt with moral values such as loyalty or fidelity were left untouched, while those with romantic contents underwent text alterations. King Sejong composed new compositions that praised the founders of the dynasty, such as "Jeongdaeeop," "Bota-

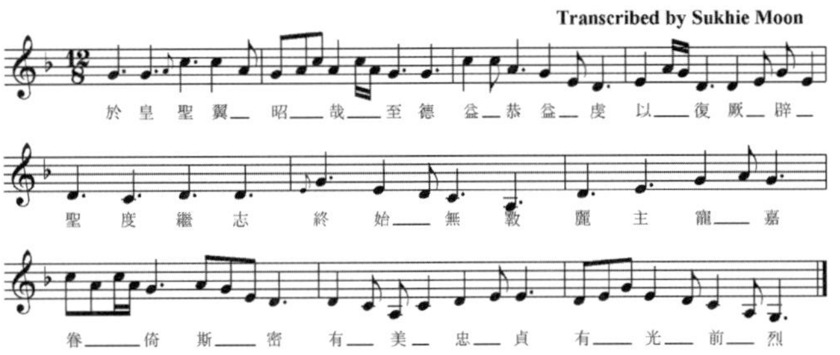

| Fig. 4.37 "Hyeonggwang" of "Botaepyeong" from Music Scores of Annals of King Sejong

epyeong" and "Bongnaeui." They were based on existing *hyangak* songs and processional music of *dangak* and required dance and singing as well as music. All three were used for court banquets and official ceremonies. "Botaepyeong" praises the civil achievements of the former kings, consisting of 15 pieces and requiring dance accompaniment. "Jeongdaeeop," with 11 pieces, praises military achievements, which also requires dancing. Both "Botaepyeong" and "Jeongdaeeop" used *hyangak* melodies and were mostly based on existing melodies from the Goryeo period. King Sejo designated both as official music for ancestral rituals, which are still played today. <Fig. 4.37>

In "Bongnaeui" performance, female dancers dancing and sing songs "Yeomillak," "Chihwapyeong" and "Chwipunghyeong." "Yeomillak" is the Sino-Korean version for "Yongbieocheonga (Praise Song for the Founding of the Nation)" and its melodies are in the style of *dangak*. "Chihwapyeong" and "Chwipunghyeong," on the other hand, is strictly Korean, using *hyangak* melodies.

"Bongnaeui" ceased to be performed at the end of Joseon Dynasty, however, the "Yeomillak" section from "Bongnaeui" later developed into four independent instrumental pieces and are still being performed today.

The instruments used for *hyangak* during the Joseon Dynasty include *geomun-go*, *gayageum*, *hyangbipa*, *daegeum*, *junggeum*, *sogeum*, *haegeum*, *dangbipa*, and *hyangpiri*. Compared to those of Goryeo, *dangpiri* was also added. Even though *dangbipa* was classified as a *dangak* instrument, it was indigenized and used for *hyangak* repertoires.

(3) *Dangak*

Like *hyangak*, *dangak* used in the beginning of the Joseon Dynasty borrowed from *dangak* of the prior dynasty. Although new pieces were composed for the new age, they were limited to processional music (*gochwiak*). However, during the first half of Joseon period, *dangak* slowly began to fade out, since no steady musical exchange with China was maintained.

Unlike the version imported during Goryeo period, Joseon's *gochwiak* has four syllables per phrase, with four phrases forming one movement. The melody starts and ends on the main pitch. Each syllable has two beats, which is maintained throughout the song without alteration. However, one syllable may have up to 4 pitches, which is very different from *aak* melodies (with one syllable taking only one pitch). In *gochwiak*, the melodic structure coincides with the text structure. <Fig. 4.38>

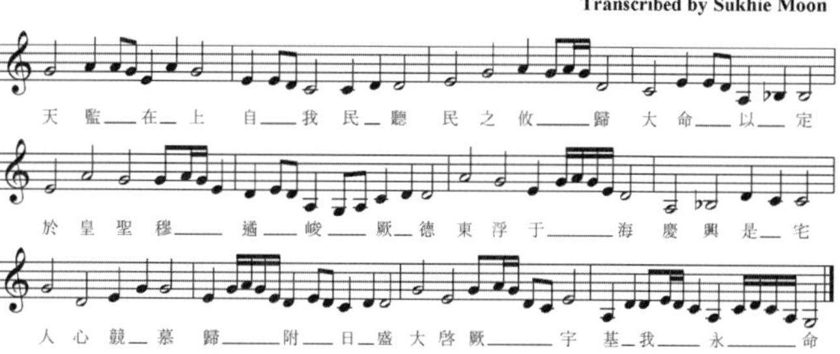
Gyewu of Botaepyeong
Transcribed by Sukhie Moon
天 監 在 上 自 我 民 聽 民 之 攸 歸 大 命 以 定
於 皇 聖 穆 遹 峻 厥 德 東 浮 于 海 慶 興 是 宅
人 心 競 慕 歸 附 日 盛 大 啓 厥 宇 基 我 永 命

| Fig. 4.38 *Gochwiak*, Music Scores from the Annals of King Sejong "Gyewu" of "Botaepyeong"

Score for Geomungo
Transcribed by Sukhie Moon
飄 落 人 間
彌 綸 節

| Fig. 4.39 *Hyangak* Style "Boheoja," 16th Century

The early Joseon period, many *dangak* repertoires from Goryeo were performed. However, these gradually reduced in number and the remaining pieces began to adopt *hyangak* style. The most distinctive difference between *dangak* and *hyangak* was in the rhythm. While most *dangak* melodies are syllabic, *hyangak* melodies are melismatic. Moreover, a single beat in *dangak* was duple, while *hyangak* was triple. "Boheoja," which was imported into Goryeo in the 13th century, featured one syllable per beat, and the time signature was 4/4. However, "Boheoja" in the 16th century, at the end of the first half of Joseon Dynasty, reflect the *hyangak* style in terms of rhythm. One syllable received up to 4 beats, one beat of which is divided into triplets. Such triple division is not found in original *dangak*, but is seen as being characteristically Korean. "Yeomillak," a type of *gochwiak* also shows similar rhythmic evolution, as is shown in <Fig. 4.39>. This particular score is for the *geomun-go* with one beat written as (♩.). <Fig. 4.39>

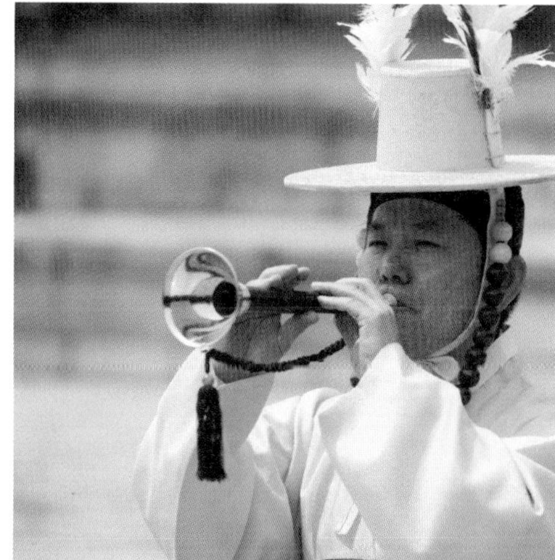

| Fig. 4.40 *Taepyeongso*

Instruments used for *dangak* at the beginning of the *Joseon* period were *dangbipa, ajaeng, daejaeng, dangpiri, dangjeok, tungso, janggu, gyobanggo, banghyang, bakpan, haegeum*, and *taepyeongso*. Most of the instruments were the same as those used during the Goryeo period. However many instruments used for *dangak* began to be used for *hyangak* repertoires. Among these, *dangbipa* was used for both *dangak* and *hyangak*. *Haegeum, ajaeng, janggu* and *taepyeongso* originally used for *dangak* in the beginning, were later used solely for *hyangak*. <Fig. 4.40>

3) Court Ceremonial Music

Since Joseon people believed that music had the power to harmonize society according to Confucian teachings, they actively used music for all types of court ceremonies. Music was heard during processions for the king or important officials. Performance and related duties of court music were conducted and organized by an institution called *Jangakwon*. At the same time, local government branches also had their own orchestras and dancers and branches were responsible for diverse local events. When a grand event took place in Seoul, the officials would bring their local musicians to the capital city in order to participate in the ceremony. This inspired musical exchange between the capital and the local cities.

Joseon court also held the following ritual ceremonies; *wongudan* for worshiping heavenly gods; *pungunnoewudan* for the gods of thunder, lightning, mountains, rivers, lands and villages; *jongmyo* for royal ancestors; *sajikdan* in worship of gods of lands and grains; and *munmyo* for Confucius and his disciples. Music played for these rituals was mostly *aak*. However, since King Sejo's reign, "Jeongdaeeop" and "Botaepyeong" were performed for *jongmyo jerye*, the ancestral ritual. <Fig. 4.41>

| Fig. 4.41 *Jongmyo jeryeak*

| Sound. 3 *Jongmyo jeryeak* (Royal Ancestral Shrine Music), “Jeuryeong,” provided by Moon Suk-hie

| Fig. 4.42 Court Banquet

Diverse banquets were held in the Joseon courts for celebrations, major memorial days and holidays. For these ceremonies, formalized *hyangak* and *dangak*, with strict rules, were performed along with *jeongjae*, court dances. Additionally, there were ceremonies for welcoming and sending off foreign ambassadors, as well as complementary feasts for heroes of wars. The events for foreign ambassadors were especially important and required special music and dance. <Fig. 4.42>

4) Court Musicians

Those who performed music and dance in Joseon's court were *aksaeng* musicians, *akgong* musicians, blind musicians, children dancers, and female entertainers. *Aksaeng* and *akgong* were male musicians. *Aksaeng* musicians were chosen among the commoners, called the *yangmin* class and took charge of ritual music. However, the rest of the musicians were selected from *cheonmin*, the lowest class in Joseon society. The *akgong* musicians performed *hyangak* and *dangak* at banquets, while blind musicians played in women's gatherings, located behind a curtain. Children dancers were employed for *jeongjae* in banquets. This was because Joseon people were under the strict gender segregation rules on public occasions. However these restrictions were not observed thoroughly during the 600 years of the dynasty. The roles of *aksaeng* musicians and *akgong* musicians were handed down to their descendants, until the titles were abolished in 1894.

Late Joseon Period

(17th–19th Century)

Ⅴ. Late Joseon Period (17th–19th Century)

Following the Japanese invasions of 1592–1598 and the second Manchu invasion in 1636, Joseon set out on a program of wide reform and reconstruction in order to stabilize the lives of the people and address social ills. Under such widespread social changes, a shift occurred in culture also, previously led by members of the ruling class, the *jungin* class of skilled professionals and commoners rose to prominence. Technological advances in all fields such as astronomy and medicine achieved from the early half of the Joseon Dynasty promoted development in industry, including agriculture and commerce, while the introduction of Western culture accelerated the effect. An individual's economic power came to play an important role in determining social status, causing changes to the class system of late Joseon and subsequent social unrest. Thanks to efforts to reestablish the authority of the throne, productivity increased and silver was used as currency for a flourishing trade, bringing about economic growth. The capital, Hanyang (Seoul today) and other big cities increased in population and experienced unprecedented prosperity. On these foundations, a new cultured class called the *gyeonghwasajok*, based in Hanyang and Gyeonggi Province, arose and created a new cultural and artistic environment by assimilating the evolutionary critical thinking of late Ming and the unworldly tastes of the literati and their pursuit of beauty. They changed the trend of thought, seeking to achieve quantitative growth and qualitative change. A new class of artists rose to lead the cultural scene, including court painters and literary figures of the commoner class. Such changes, which accompanied the restoration of royal authority, the rise of the new literati, and the spread of Western learning in East Asia, served to bring traditional Korean culture to maturity and laid the foundations for the shift to the modern era.

1. Art

1) Painting

The late Joseon period was a time when new and diverse artistic movements took place in all fields in order to reform society as a whole after the country had been devastated by two wars, the Japanese invasions of 1592–1598 and the second Manchu invasion of 1636. With the reconstruction efforts designed to put the royal court back on a solid founding, the increased agricultural productivity increased and active trade led to economic growth. The capital city of Hanyang and other large cities grew in population and experienced unprecedented prosperity. On these foundations, a unique group of rich and cultured scholar-officials called *gyeonghwasajok* (splendid rich and powerful clan of residents of the capital), comprised of noble families living in the capital city of Hanyang and the Gyeonggi Province area, played a central role in the development of a new cultural environment. They enjoyed literati pastimes that encouraged freedom from worldly affairs and aesthetic appreciation. They made efforts to emulate the intellectual culture of the late Ming literati, bringing about major changes in art. This newly introduced late Ming cultural spirit also spread widely through the efforts of court painters and literati who were not of the *yangban* class. Such changes, which accompanied the revival of the royal court, the new literati movement, and the rise of Western cultural influence in East Asia, pushed Korea's medieval culture toward its final days and prepared the ground for shift to modern times. Rapid progress was seen in the formation of a uniquely Korean style culture (Hong, 1999). In line with such revival of the royal court and the renewal of culture, the new activities and trends in art were clearly different from those of the preceding era. It was particularly evident in the field of painting. The new trend in art began to appear during the time of King Sukjong (r. 1675–1720).

(1) Changing Attitudes towards the Production and Consumption of Painting

The late 16th century (reign of King Seonjo) saw the rise of new activities and hobbies for literati culture, including prevalence for collecting antiques. By the second half of the 17th century the collecting fever had spread among the *gyeonghwasajok* families, promoting and enhancing the value of appreciating and collecting art works and antiques. This trend then spread to scholars of the "middle people" class (*jungin*) and finally to the merchants and commoners, resulting in the active production and consumption of paintings. Accordingly, the collecting and appreciating culture of art works flourished and many writings about art criticism were produced during this time.

The collecting fever of paintings, in particular, spread through the members of the literati of the western faction (*seoin*) and by the latter half of the 17th century, as mentioned above, it began to transcend the political affiliation and social class to catch on among the common people. The collecting and appreciating of art works and the love of painting were considered to be a "chronic disease" and enthusiastic collectors known to "concentrate on art works in their collection, forgetting hunger and thirst" grew in number. During the reigns of King Sukjong and King Yeongjo, this trend came to be led by the leading *noron* (old doctrine) and *soron* (young doctrine) factions who lived in the northern part of Hanyang. From the latter part of the reign of King Yeongjo and the early reign of King Jeongjo, the collecting culture of art works reached the new height as it grew popular across a wider spectrum of social classes in society including secondary sons, intellectuals of illegitimate birth (*seoeol*), skilled professionals, such as doctors and interpreters among the middle people (*jungin*), low ranking officials such as petty officials in the provinces, and wealthy members of the merchant class. This resulted in the quantitative expansion of painting collections.

The perception of painting and the approach to creative activity also changed. The increased painting activities due to the demand of art lovers gave rise to new professional fields such as art appreciation and art criticism. And clear progress was made in theoretical criticism and real criticism of paintings. Painting developed into a field of endeavor that almost rivaled the study of Confucian classics in terms of professional zeal and debate over its values. The rise in theoretical writings about painting fell in line with the people's desire for the reform of the society and culture of the late Joseon period. The critical outlook that analyzed and reflected on the spirit of the time became widespread. Such critical thinking not only changed ideas about painting including the outlook on painting and theories on creative activities, but also acted as an important factor in the development of new trends in theme and style.

Literati painters, in particular, made efforts to express the nature of heaven in painting and to pursue a dualistic path: in re-creating the truth and spirit of the subject, a complementary relationship existed between the value of classicism, or antiquity, and the power of direct observation. The important thing was to re-create the appearance of an object in a form that conveyed the "real spirit," a trend that led creative artistic activities during the 18th century. In the case of classicism, the object was considered one with nature and was expressed as an image cherished in the heart of the artist, transcending the external form to extract the "spirit." Thus the meaning of the object lies in the realm far beyond its appearance. 19th century art followed this path with more emphasis on the value of classicism.

(2) The Dominance of the Southern School and the Introduction of Western-Style Painting

As for the method of expression, the techniques of the Southern school which were based on the idea of the supremacy of literati painting and gained orthodoxy in the late Ming period were actively adopted and served to reform the existing painting styles in the late Joseon era. To enhance the realism of the object, Western painting techniques were also introduced for a modified style. Ink dots and brushstrokes for texturing and shading, elements used by the Southern school, had been partially used in generic paintings of the late Goryeo and the early Joseon periods. But the Southern school style was not fully introduced until the latter half of the 16th century. The works of the Four Great Masters of the late Yuan period—Huang Gongwang, Wu Zhen and Wang Meng, and Ni Zan (1301–1374), Dong Qichang (1555–1636), and the Wu school were introduced during the reign of King Seonjo (r. 1567–1608).

The reception of the Southern school, however, began during the reign of King Sukjong (r. 1674–1720) when artists with a strong consciousness of their identity as literati painters emerged. Yoon Du-seo (1668–1715) was one of these pioneering new-style literati artists. Yoon mastered the Southern school style through painting manuals such as the Gushi huapu, a picture album published in 1603 by a Ming court artist named Gu Bing and the Tangshi huapu, an album of *Tang* poetry and paintings. His painting "Thatched Pavilion in Sparse Forest" (*Sorim mojeong do*, <Fig. 5.1>) is a composition in the style of Ni Zan, using dry, slanted brushstrokes and sparse lines. It exemplifies the early aspects of the Southern school painting in Korea. The literati painting style was carried on in the works of Jeong Seon (1676–1759) and

Fig. 5.1 Yoon Du-seo, Thatched Pavilion in Sparse Forest, early 18th century, Ink and light color on paper, 24.6×23cm, The Head House of Yoon in Haenam

Sim Sa-jeong (1707–1769) and ultimately evolved into the Joseon Southern school style, replacing the painting styles of the previous period characterized by a combination of the traditional style of An Gyeon and the Zhe school.

The Southern school style spread during the reign of King Sukjong through Yoon's close friend and art connoisseur, Yi Ha-gon (1677–1724), Yoon's son Yoon Deok-hui (1685–1766), and artists such as Jeong Seon and Jo Yeong-seok (1686–1761) who were friends of Yi's. The reception and popularity of the Southern school style was closely tied to the widespread reverence for the literati painting tradition and the sympathy with Dong Qichang's criticism of the formalism of the Northern school, the school of professional and court painters. The introduction of many Ming paintings and painting manuals also played an important role in the development of the Southern school in late Joseon Korea. Among those painting manuals was the Mustard Seed Garden Painting Manual (*Gaejawon hwajeon*) which served as a kind of textbook in disseminating the Southern school style throughout East Asia. As a color woodblock-print book, it also promoted the shift to ink and light color paintings, which was different from the existing monochrome ink and brush paintings. Jo Yeong-seok discussed both the difference between the literati style and the style of professional artists and the split between the Southern and Northern schools. As a literati painter, Jo later showed an avant gardeattitude in employing the new style of the Anhui school of the Qing dynasty artist Hongren (1610–1663).

The Southern school style formed the mainstream during the reign of Yeongjo (1724–1776) thanks to Yoon Du-seo and others and was handed down to the next generation of literati painters such as Sim Sa-jeong, Heo Pil (1709–1768), Yi In-sang (1710–1760) and Kang Se-hwang (1713–1791), and even non-literati painters such as Choe Buk (1712–1786) who hailed from the class of skilled professional painters. At this time, Korean literati painters made efforts to emulate the lofty minds and painting styles of the Four Great Masters of the late Yuan and painters of the Wu school of the Ming by copying the Chinese painters' works and learning their techniques. In addition, they began to adopt the new style of the Qing dynasty literati artists. The late Joseon literati painting trend could be divided into two main streams, one seeking the beauty of form as seen in the work of Sim Sa-jeong who combined various styles of the Southern school masters and created a composite style, and the other seeking the beauty of content as found in the work of Yi In-sang and Kang Se-hwang who regarded their art as a means of expressing the self.

During the reign of King Jeongjo (r. 1777–1800) the Southern school style took on the aspect of a state-endorsed or academy style through the efforts of such court painters as Kim Eung-hwan (1742–1789), Kim Hong-do (1745–1806), and Yi In-mun (1745–1821). The Southern school style continued to the 19th century. Professional and court painters such as Yi Han-cheol (1808–1880), Yu Suk (1827–1873), and Jang Seung-eop (1843–1897) pur-

| Fig. 5.2 Kim Su-cheol, Pavilion among Pine Tree Covered with Snow, mid-19th century, Ink and light color on paper, 23.1×45cm, Kansong Art Museum

sued the beauty of form in literati painting. In contrast, literati painters of nobility such as Yoon Je-hong (1764–?), Sin Wi (1769–1845), and Kim Jeong-hui (1786–1856), and those of the lower class such as Yi Yu-sin (active late 18th century), Yi Jae-gwan (1783–1837), Jo Hui-ryong (1789–1866), Huh Ryeon (1809–1892), Jeon Gi (1825–1854), and Kim Su-cheol (active mid–19th century) <Fig. 5.2> sought to represent the beauty of content in literati painting by following the calligraphic brushwork of Yi In-sang and Kang Se-hwang. Some painters also created unconventional, eye-provoking works, using new compositions and rich and pretty colors. The new trend among these literati painters was also reflected in a new style of flower paintings. The late Joseon literati painters sought to paint the true form of the subject and to use their art as a means of expressing their thoughts and ideas. By rejecting and transcending the formal likeness of an object in painting, they made great achievements in painting and calligraphy. In addition, new decorative style paintings emerged with the urbanization of Hanyang and the increase in demand for art works. As such changes took place with the enlightenment movement toward the end of the 19th century and the

| Fig. 5.3 Anonymous, Bookshelf and Various Utensils (detail), early 19th century, Color on paper, 68.5×342.4cm, Leeum, Samsung Museum of Art

late Joseon art world's close relations with the Shanghai school then popular in China, a new generation of painters emerged. Among them, Jang Seung-eop was the most distinguished painter. Jang developed his own style known as the Owon style (after his pen name), and took traditional painting into the modern era along with Jo Seok-jin (1853–1920) and Ahn Jung-sik (1861–1919).

Western painting techniques were first adopted during the reign of King Sukjong in the late 17th century. As King Hyojong's (r. 1649–1659) plan to invade the Qing dynasty failed, the political tension between Korea and China began to ease. As a result, the trade and cultural exchange between Korea and China rapidly increased. Western painting techniques were known to Korea through the introduction of Westernized Chinese paintings <Fig. 5.3>. The techniques of perspective, shading, and depth was experimented by court painters such as Kim Jin-yeo (active ca. 1710s) from the later part of King Sukjong's reign. During the time of King Jeongjo, Western painting style became one of the major components of court painting. Under the leadership of Kim Hong-do, court painters used Western painting techniques in the making of portraits, documentary paintings of court processions and ceremonies. With the help of Western painting techniques, they achieved visual realism in painting. In addition, paintings of bookcases from a scholar's study were produced by the use of Western perspective.

In the 19th century, while the trend for literati painting was strong, Western painting techniques such as the depiction of shadows came to be used in the making of pictures. Furthermore, Western learning gained popularity among scholars. From around 1880, Western painting techniques began to be utilized in Buddhist paintings. Western painting technique was used, however, without proper understanding of the modern system of visual expression that sought to recreate the world scientifically with human beings at the center of the world.

It was applied only as a painting skill to enhance the reality of a painted object, as a visual aid to make something look real. The true understanding of the spirit of Western painting was only understood and adopted after the beginning of the enlightenment period (late 19th–early 20th century).

(3) True-View Landscapes

True-view, or realistic, landscapes of famous mountains and natural scenery suddenly arose as a new trend, qualitatively different to the practical, functional paintings resembling topographical maps produced since the Goryeo dynasty. They became objects for appreciation in the 17th century, and gained enormous popularity in the early 18th century. Jeong Seon played a pivotal role in the development of true-view landscapes. Jeong's true-view landscapes were created through a self awareness and desire to break away from the old habits of ignoring the real shape of natural features and relying only on formula, which resulted so often in stylized and conventional paintings. He mastered the Southern school painting styles and visited frequently famous scenic spots around Yeongdong, Yeongnam and Hanyang to experience the spirit and energy of those places for himself. He made great efforts to perfect his painting skills and painted so many true-view landscapes during his lifetime to the degree that his worn out brushes would have formed a mound.

| Fig. 5.4 Jeong Seon, Bakyeon Falls, early 18th century, Ink on paper, 119.1×52cm, Private collection, Seoul

Jeong painted all sorts of subjects in the true-view landscape style including scenic spots, country villas, outdoor gatherings, and government offices, but mostly he concentrated on famous scenic spots in the vicinity of Hanyang and those in Mt. *Geumgang* and the Yeongnam region. Depending on the nature of his subject or the intended use of the painting, Jeong used multiple perspectives in his work, looking down from above, looking up

| Fig. 5.5 Jeong Seon, After Rain at Mt. Inwang, 1751, Ink on paper, 79.2×138.2cm, Leeum, Samsung Museum of Art, National Treasure No. 216

from below, rendering his subject through the contrast of vigorous brushstrokes and strokes made with the brush pointed and flat, the active use of ink dots large and small, and the mixture of dark bold brushstrokes and light elegant coloring. Paintings epitomizing Jeong's style such as "Bakyeon Falls" (*Bakyeon pokpo do*, <Fig. 5.4>) and "After Rain on Mt. Inwang" (*Inwang jesaek do*, <Fig. 5.5>) are grounded in knowledge of the cosmic forces and laws behind the harmony of yin and yang, and the workings of nature uncovered by the legendary Fu Xi of ancient China who studied the heaven to work out astronomy and the earth to work out geography.

Jeong's true-view landscape style was carried on and spread through his son and grandson as well as court painters during the reign of Yeongjo such as Choe Buk, Kim Yu-seong (1725–?), Yi Seong-lin (1718–1777), Kim Eung-hwan, Kim Hui-gyeom (active late 18th century), Jang Si-heung (active late 18th century), and Kim Seok-sin (1758–?). However, literati artists of the time such as Sim Sa-jeong, Kang Se-hwang, Huh Pil, Kim Yun-gyeom (1711–1775), Yi In-sang, Yi Yun-yeong (1714–1759), and Yun Je-hong (1764–?) overlooked Jeong's style in preference for the styles of the Wu and Anhui schools of China, or other new styles. Kang Se-hwang was particularly critical of Jeong's true-view landscape style; he was a proponent for the exact, faithful depiction of the subject as in portraits, considering Jeong Seon's style to be too manneristic. The true-view style of literati painters as

| Fig. 5.6 Jeong Su-yeong, Guryong Falls, 1799, Ink and light color on paper, 30.8×33.8cm, National Museum of Korea

advocated by Kang further developed during the reigns of King Jeongjo and King Sunjo (r. 1800–1834). Kang Se-hwang, Kim Hong-do, and Jeong Su-yeong, incorporated Western painting techniques and rising new styles into realistic landscapes based on Western perspective <Fig. 5.6>. Realistic landscapes were in constant demand. They were favored by the royal court and scholar-officials. The tradition of realistic landscapes continued into the 19th century. Such court painters as Uhm Chi-uk (active 19th century), Jo Jeong-gyu (1791–?), Kim Ha-jong (1793–?), and Yu Suk played a key role in the further development of realistic landscapes. In the case of landscapes of Mt. *Geumgang* or landscapes of the eight scenes of Guandong, expansion in demand for realistic landscapes led to the creation of decorative folk paintings following the tradition of realism.

(4) Popularity of Genre Paintings

Genre paintings focused on the lives of the four classes of people—the scholars, farmers, technicians and merchants—therefore portraying scenes of agriculture, the city, government offices, and seasonal customs gained popularity during the late Joseon period. Such paintings of everyday life emerged during the time of King Sukjong under the name *sokhwa* meaning "vulgar paintings" and were also called *isokdo* (rustic vulgar paintings). According to the request of envoys from the Qing dynasty, genre paintings at this time were produced as a kind of national project. Yoon Du-seo and members of his family lay the foundation of genre paintings. Their paintings of rural communities busily going about their work in the "small scene" style began to develop within the traditional genre painting context. This kind of subject matter and the method of composition were carried on by such painters as Kim Du-ryang (1696–1763) and Sim Sa-jeong with a little bit more emphasis on the Southern school painting techniques.

Around this time, Jo Yeong-seok began to produce fresh, lively scenes of the lives of

| Fig. 5.7 Jo Yeong-seok, Sewing, early 18th century, Ink and light color on paper, 22.5×27cm, Private collection, Seoul

all sorts of people and all sorts of situations, including women and monks, with simple yet precisely captured drawings in ink and light color, breaking new ground in genre painting. As his subjects were captured from first-hand observation, his paintings have the conciseness of line drawings, as seen in "Sewing" (*Baneujil*, <Fig. 5.7>) and "Snack in the Fields" (*Saecham*) where the outlines are executed in charcoal first and painted over in ink. They are mostly small vertical scenes with a tree in the background or feature the new type of composition with no background. In the latter case, the figures are central to the composition, a trend that was succeeded by Kim Hong-do as seen in his Album of Genre Paintings (*Pungsok hwacheop*). Also, as found in "Visiting a Friend in the Snow" (*Seoljung bang'u do*), which portrays a scholar's visit to a close friend on a snowy day; Jo also produced many elegant pictures featuring fine brushstrokes and seasonal atmosphere. This kind of style was carried on by Kang Hui-eon (1710–1784) in *Sain samgyeong cheop* (Album of Three Views of the Scholars).

Under the reign of King Jeongjo genre paintings were more actively produced by court painters and became so popular that scholars used them to decorate their study rooms. According to the poem "Hangyeongsa (Poems of the Capital City of Hanyang)," written around 1790 by Kang I-cheon (?–1801) about the paintings sold in downtown Hanyang, the genre paintings produced by the court painters were so realistic that many people cov-

| Fig. 5.8 Kim Hong-do, Dancing Boy, Album of Genre Paintings by Danwon, late 18th century, Ink and light color on paper, 27×22.7cm, National Museum of Korea, Treasure No. 527

Fig. 5.9 Sin Yun-bok, A Rendezvous, Album of Transmitting the Spirit of Hyewon, early 19th century, Ink and light color on paper, 28.2×38.2cm, Kansong Art Museum, National Treasure No. 135

eted them. Under the reigns of King Jeongjo and King Sunjo, genre painting became one of the major themes for painting examinations designed to select the *jabidaeryeong hwawon*, or stand-by court painters or court painters in attendance who worked at the *Gyujanggak*, the royal library. This shows the increase in demand for such paintings at the government level.

The genre painting trend was led by Kim Hong-do (pen name Danwon) who was a favorite of King Jeongjo and received the patronage of scholar officials and wealthy commoners. The acknowledged leader in his field by the time he was in his late 20s, Kim's paintings are characterized by rhythmic brushstrokes, free and easy, and that result in lively, droll expression of the lives of the people <Fig. 5.8>. His genre paintings from albums and folding screens served as a model for court painters and his legacy was carried on by artists such as Kim Deuk-sin (1754–1822), Kim Yang-gi (active 19th century), Sin Yun-bok (1758–?), Kim Hu-sin (active 19th century), and Yu Suk, and even influenced folk painting.

Sin Yun-bok was the son of the court painter and royal portrait artist Sin Han-pyeong (1726–?). While partially influenced by his father and Kim Hong-do, in terms of the theme, composition, depiction of figures, and method of coloring, Sin Yun-bok developed his own individual style. As seen in Album of Transmitting the Spirit of Hyewon (*Hyewon jeonsin-cheop*), now in the collection of Kansong Museum of Art, Sin painted sensual scenes from the *gisaeng* houses and the wealthy people who frequented them. Sin was successful in eye-witnessing and pictorially recording the pleasure culture of the time. The suggestive genre scenes featuring women clearly show the social and cultural change of the time <Fig. 5.9>. Though partially influenced by the popular novels of the late Ming and Qing dynasties of China, Sin's work has a special quality that comes from the fine brushstrokes, the contrast of beautiful clear reds and blues, the sensuous beauty of the figures, which are depicted with truth and affection. The romantic way of life in the city is represented with his artistic sensibility.

(5) Types and Characteristics of Decorative Court Paintings

Decorative court paintings were used in the royal palaces of the Joseon Dynasty including the Gyeongbokgung Palace and the Changdeokgung Palace. Some of them were used for the decoration of official spaces such as the throne hall and halls of administration where rites were held. Others were used for residential quarters and bedchambers, all sorts of gate pavilions, and living quarters (Hong, forthcoming). The throne hall, as the central building of the palace and the seat of the king, had a niche in the middle of the ceiling that was decorated with two colorfully painted wooden dragons. The throne, where the king sat facing the south, was installed on a platform reached by stairs and had a canopy overhead. Installed behind the throne was a folding screen of the "Sun and Moon and Five Peaks." Such screens featuring the sun and moon symbolizing the heaven, the mountains representing the earth, and the red pines and waves indicating the water, are painted in bright, deep colors in stylized, archaic fashion, emphasizing the beauty of form.

The palace administration hall, where the king and his ministers took care of state affairs and discussed the Confucian classics, usually featured a folding screen with thought-provoking subject matters, such as farming scenes from everyday life, or paintings of ancient figures such as sages or wise kings from Chinese history, including the "Nine Elders of Fragrant Mountain [Xiangshan]," "Three Visits to the Thatched Cottage" and "Greeting King Wen [ruler of Zhou]." To enhance the awareness of the importance of learning and to encourage study, King Jeongjo always placed paintings of bookcases on either side of the hall.

The residential part of the palace, or the inner palace (naejeon), and the bedchambers were where the women of the royal family slept and rested. But to ensure that they did not forget their duty for even a moment and to stop them from becoming complacent, under the spirit of "non-ease, "folding screens bearing maxims and depicting the activities of respected Chinese kings or queens or state events and ceremonies were placed here and there. King Sejo's (r. 1455–1468) queen hung on a wall a painting of the four classes of society. In the crown prince's bedchamber was displayed a folding screen depicting a scene of filial piety. King Myeongjong (r. 1545–1567) was an admirer of the Neo-Confucian scholar Yi Hwang (1501–1574, pen name Toegye) and a folding screen titled *Dosan do* (Mount *Dosan*), where the scholar lived in retirement, was placed in his bedchamber so that he could look upon it continuously.

Various decorative paintings were found in the bedchambers and other palace buildings that were official but private at the same time. King Sunjo's bedchamber featured a folding screen of "Banquet at Yaochi Palace," where Xiwangmu (Queen Mother of the West) held a feast for King Mu of Zhou when he visited her at the Yaochi Palace in the Kunlun Mountains. On the southwestern wall was a landscape painting, used to create an auspicious and other-worldly atmosphere. In the ritual room, a folding screen of peonies was placed on the eastern wall, and a painting of nine mountain peaks on the northern wall, and in the bedroom there were folding screens of plum blossoms or bamboo as well as paintings of plum blossoms and bamboo together. The side rooms flanking the bedroom are said to have been decorated with paintings of varied subjects such as seven cranes, Daoist immortals, flying dragons, and birds and flowers.

Pictures of gate guardian gods, or door gods, were stuck on many gates of the palace at the New Year's rites to ward off evil spirits, a custom dating back to the Three Kingdoms period. Originally the images used were the Chinese god Zhong Kui who exorcises ghosts and evil spirits, and Cheoyong, the Korean guardian against smallpox dating to the Silla Kingdom, but by the late Joseon period theyhad changed to General Wei Chigong and General Qin Qiong of the *Tang* Dynasty in China, who had been incorporated into Chinese folk religion as door gods.

Paintings were also used to decorate court events. For weddings, a large folding screen 3m high featuring the ten symbols of longevity was used along with other screens depicting peonies and lotuses. Folding screens used from the late Joseon period featured young boys playing, or General Guo Ziyi from *Tang*, who was immortalized as the God of wealth and happiness, to symbolize a happy life and many sons. Banquets for the queen or queen dowager were decorated with screens of the ten symbols of longevity or birds and flowers. At funerals, a screen featuring peonies in five colors or covered in plain white paper, was used. The same kind of peony screen was used on the third anniversary of death held at the mortuary shrine (honjeon), and a screen of the sun and moon and five peaks was placed where the portrait of the deceased king was enshrined. While the five-peak screen was used to symbolize the seat of the king, peony folding screens were widely used around the palace for all kinds of court events including funerals, weddings, and coronations. They were also found in the royal bedchamber. Both the five peaks and peony folding screens are highly stylized, executed in the royal court painting style which has a handicraft feel. Folding screens featuring Guo Ziyi were executed in the gongbi technique, a meticulous, detailed method of using rich colors and layers of color washes characteristic of the Chinese court painting style known as yuanti.

(6) Boom in Folk Painting

In latter half of the Joseon period, the social atmosphere of extravagance and praying for good fortune led to a sudden increase in folk paintings used for the decoration of homes and social and personal events to pray for financial security and success and defend against evils. The economic growth and prosperity of cities gave rise to the social atmosphere of luxury and extravagance during the reign of King Sukjong. Excessive spending on festive events among wealthy people, especially the *jungin* and merchant classes, aggravated the general mood. Influenced by the custom of the royal court and the gentry to decorate the palace and their homes with paintings, wealthy people began to do the same. Coupled with the trend of praying for good fortune, this led to a sudden rise in the production of folk paintings, which were used as talismans on festive and holiday occasions to bring peace and prosperity to the family and to ward off evil spirits. The surfeit of folk paintings at this time was also influenced by the mass production of New Year's woodblock prints (nianhua) in China during the late Ming and early Qing periods to decorate homes in celebration of the New Year.

| Fig. 5.10 Anonymous, Tiger and Magpie, 19th century, Ink and light color on paper, 91.7×54.8cm, Leeum, Samsung Museum of Art

Though the folk paintings that have

been handed down to the present are diverse, they originated in the custom of decorating front gates, windows, and kitchen doors on New Year's Day with pictures as talismans against bad luck. Doors and gates were decorated with pictures of door gods and auspicious animals such as magpies, cocks, tigers, and dogs. Tigers were often depicted with magpies, but in the 19th century such paintings gradually grew more stylized so that the tiger's face often ended up resembling a cat <Fig. 5.10>. This may have resulted from the belief at the time that cholera, which had hit the capital, was carried by the mouse spirit, or because as enemies of mice, cats were considered to be a symbol of longevity.

| Fig. 5.11 Anonymous, Pictorial Depictions of the Chinese Characters for "Hyo (filial piety)" (detail), 19th century, Color on paper, 48×28.2cm, Private collection, Seoul

Most of the extant folk paintings were used to decorate interiors. Pictures were pasted on walls between rooms and inside closet doors, while folding screens and hanging scrolls were used inside the room itself. Folding screens were widely used as a barrier against the cold and they were also used as ornamental items at various ceremonies and rites of passage. It is said that inside *gisaeng* houses even the ceilings were decorated with paintings. The room occupied by the lady of the house (*anbang*) usually featured paintings of birds and flowers, flowers, or plants and insects, while a newly-wed's room usually had a folding screen painted with young boys as a symbol of fecundity, brought as one of the bride's marriage articles. Children's rooms often featured a folding screen with pictorial depictions of the Chinese characters for filial piety and other virtues <Fig. 5.11>. The room occupied by the master of the house (*sarangbang*) was decorated with landscapes on folding screens or hanging scrolls, and folding screens of various subjects such as Confucian sages, Daoist immortals, Mt. *Geumgang*, hunting scenes, scholarly implements, and bookcases. In the capital, decoration of homes with paintings spread from the wealthy upper class to the ordinary people in the late Joseon period, and then spread nationwide, a trend that continued in to the 1930s.

According to the sudden increase in demand for paintings, stores specializing in paper and folding screens formed a market around Gwangtonggyo Bridge (near Jongno today) in the center of Hanyang. In response to seasonal demand for paintings, a temporary market appeared near Jonggak at year end. The paintings used to decorate the royal palace and the homes of the gentry and the wealthy *jungin* class and merchants were produced by court painters or artists who had once worked there. They were high quality works executed in the royal palace painting style using the meticulous gongbi technique. On the other hand, folk paintings used in ordinary homes were low quality works produced by people known as *hwanjaengi*, a derogatory term for "artist." In the mid–19th century, Yi Gyu-gyeong (1788–1856), in his encyclopedic book Random Expiations of Master Oju (*Ojuyeon munjang jeon-sango*), mentioned the works produced by such artists as follows: "Paintings whose meaning is hard to know are conventionally placed on folding screens and on the walls of ordinary commoner homes." These folk paintings were also known as *sokhwa*, meaning "vulgar paintings."

The repetitive, exaggerated forms and radical compositions of folk painting are not the result of the grassroots spirit of the lower class's resistance against the authoritarian order of the court, or the primitivism-based spirit of Western modern art. As the popularity of paintings spread among the common people, folk painting resulted from an overheated desire to ward off evil and bring good luck through magical means. These have many similarities to those found on ceramic goods made at private kilns in Jingdezhen at the end of the Ming dynasty. As the popularity of folk painting became nationwide, regional characteristics began to emerge.

2) Sculpture

The change in the social atmosphere of the late Joseon period reflected on sculpture. The phenomenon brought about a new change in the style. The demand on art expanded, it was no longer restricted to the noble class, but also to merchants and to all levels of society. People who accumulated wealth began to demand new art types favorable to their own tastes. In painting, images related to the *Nahan* (羅漢, Arahan), boy monk,

| Fig. 5.12 Right: Standing Statue (Judge), Wood, 18-19th century, Left: Standing Statue (Girl), Wood, 18-19th century, Horim Museum

animals, and so on, began to express well-defined character of the sculptor <Fig. 5.12>. Along this, consistency in sculpture styles for royal tomb, mounds, broke free, taking on a variety of forms. Among the ordinary people, sculptures of either *Buksu* (deity guarding a village or a burial ground <Fig. 5.13>) or shaman were produced considerably. In the royal palaces and among ordinary houses, various small statues were depicted and executed on roof tiles. Characters of those sculptures, the monk, the monkey and so on, were mainly originated from the Hsi-yu Chi (Journey to the West, 西遊記). These moved away from existing models and took on a freer aesthetics. The sculpture of the late Joseon period was more human in expression, presenting emotions of joy, happiness and sorrow. Expressions were refined with liveliness and tranquility, while also showing extreme omission and courage in transformed shapes adding humor and a variety of formative effects.

The remaining Buddhist sculptures from the Joseon period are mainly from the late period. It appears that there were no great changes in style during this time. After the Japanese Invasion of 1592, the proportion of the figure collapsed and statues became formalized. Thus, the Buddha became

| Fig. 5.13 Right: *Jangseung* (Tutelary Post), Stone, Namjang-ri, Sangju, North Gyeongsang Provice, Left: *Jangseung* (Tutelary Post), Stone, Sunhwa-ri, Sunchang, North Jeonna Provice

| Fig. 5.14 *Mokgaktaeng*, late 19th century, 176×177cm, Gyeonggguksa Temple, Seoul

short and small, without capturing any of the curves of the upper body. The face is also lifeless without expression almost like reflecting on the circumstances of Buddhism in society during this period. The *Mokgaktaeng* (Buddhist illustration sculpted in relief on wood, 木刻幀), made after the 17th century is one of the most prominent of late Joseon Buddhist sculptures. <Fig. 5.14> In the 17th century, some groups of sculptors and scholars took interest in the arts. They were from local districts, and it was only within that sculptor groups created statues of Buddha. On the other hand, statues of officials and animals placed in front of the royal tombs and statues of the 12 zodiac animals and four deities were made around the palace. Such examples reveal that sculpture in the second part of Joseon period became simpler with folk-like characteristics.

3) Versatility in White Porcelain, Wood and Metal Work

(1) White Porcelain

From the 17th to the mid 18th century, the Japanese Invasion of 1592 left a great mark in the production of ceramics. The production of blue-and-white ware, although temporary, provoked upheaval in the official kiln, due to the halt in the import of cobalt into the country. Yet the production of this particular ware soon increased. <Fig. 5.15> After the late 17th century with the recovery of economical and social stability, the blue-and-white porcelain was again popularized among the royal family and gradually among ordinary people, Joseon was unfamiliar with the techniques involved in making polychrome wares, the blue-and-white ware techniques was experimented to the full. The royal Joseon court considered modesty and humbleness to be the ultimate virtues

| Fig 5.15 White Porcelain Jar with Grapevine Decoration in Underglaze Iron-brown, 18th century, h. 53.8cm, Ewha Womans University Museum, National Treasure No. 107

for gaining fortune and blessing. As a result, the blue-and-white porcelain was considered too lavish, and the literati class continued to issue petitions stating that the elaborate nature of this ware needed to be suppressed. However, in the royal kiln (官窯) the production and demand for blue-and-white porcelain increased, and towards the late Joseon period, this particular ware was produced from different parts of the country. <Fig. 5.16> There was an increase in daily wares in this particular form, and some were colored with entirely blue by adding cobalt. In order to meet the growing demands and also to reduce the production cost, cheap cobalt was brought into Korea from Beijing's markets. The patterns were painted by a specialist known as the "Hwacheon-gjang (畵靑匠)." With the increased popularity of blue-and-white porcelain, even ordinary people began to have their preferences. Objects for stationary were considered extravagant possessions for those people. Besides the cobalt-blue painted on the surface, methods of decorating white porcelain became diverse; *Cheongchae* (靑彩, decorating with blue color pigment), *Cheo-hwa* (鐵畵, painted with iron-based underglazed), *Cheolchae* (鐵彩, iron-based underglazed technique), *Cheolyu* (鐵釉) iron-based glaze, *Sang-hyeong* (象形, molding technique), *Tugak* (透刻, Openwork), *Yanggak* (陽刻, relief technique), *Jinsa* (辰砂, underglaze copper-red). <Fig. 5.17> However in 1883, the privatization of the *Bunwon*, official kilin, inflicted a break in the consolidation of techniques and people. Newly introduced foreign ceramic pieces infiltrated in large quantities. The descended tradition was severed as Joseon was about to enter into the modern period.

| Fig. 5.16 White Porcelain Ink Dropper in the Shape of a Mountain, 19th century, h. 21cm, National Museum of Korea

| Fig. 5.17 White Porcelain Circular Ink Dropper with embossed carving, 19th century, h. 5cm, National Museum of Korea

(2) Wood work, Metal work and the Craft of Burnt Animal Bones (*Hwagak*)

In the Joseon period, wood work differed from those of Goryeo period in type, form and pattern. Everyday wares predominated production. Elaborate decorations were avoided, and natural textures were kept by simply adding a transparent coating. The structure of the forms was stable with excellent functional qualities. Newly attempted aesthetics were sought by adding refined linear qualities, clean treatment of the surface and so on. Such qualities were based on Confucian naturalism, which embraces with modesty and humbleness, typifying an indigenous Korean aesthetics. Furniture of this period reflected the conception of time. Moreover, the distinct gender difference is also apparent. Furniture for the men centered around the *Sarangbang* (scholar's studio) life while female objects focused on the inner living quarters and the kitchen. The earlier lacquer wares retained influences from the Goryeo period in the execution of patterns-floral scrolls patterns. But the shape and forms were highly functional, and in the second half of the Joseon period, lower ordinary class also could use lacquer wares.

In metal work, silver inlay, lacquer ware and *Hwagak* (華角) techniques (ox-horn craft

| Fig. 5.18 Incense Burner (left, h. 25.3cm) and Paper Holder (right, h. 17.6cm) with silver Inlay, 19th century, National Museum of Korea

work) were highly developed. Silver inlay descended from the Goryeo period, and it later developed into chiseled inlay, and then to gilt inlay and so on. In general, silver was commonly used and the main objects for this type of decoration consisted of incense burners, braziers, scientific tools, stationary objects, iron *piri* (flute), candlesticks, cigarette holders, weapons, saddles, locks, etc.. These were decorated with patterns of good fortune and longevity such as dragon, phoenix, giraffe, turtle, demon mask, and twelve zodiac signs and so on. <Fig. 5.18> The lacquer technique was used for decorating furniture and small ornamental objects. The lacquer technique of creating geometric patterns on furniture and objects coincided with the silver inlay technique used on bronze wares.

Ox horn shaved into thin plains almost as thin as a piece of paper were painted with colored and decorated. These were then assembled onto wooden surfaces-furniture. The technique originated from the Tang (唐), China where tortoise shells were colored in red or added with a fine color and texture. It was first introduced to the Joseon court during the second half of the Joseon period using red, blue, yellow, black and white based on the five fundamental colors. Patterns such as the twelve zodiac signs, cloud and dragon, pine tree and tiger, flower and bird, sky and peach tree, flower and grass, and Four Gracious Plants (四君子) were used. The images were depicted freely. If ceramics and wood craft showed a more disciplined use of color and form, compositions were more versatile with lavish decorations. Thus, *Hwagak* objects mostly belonged to the inner female quarters.

4) Wood Architecture

The multi-bracket sets (*Dapo*, 多包) structure became the main form of architecture by the second half of the Joseon period. The layering of the support beams added grandeur to the exterior of temples and palace buildings. However, in government office buildings and ordinary houses, the Goryeo bracketing methods were continued in a simplified way, introducing the wing-like bracket (*Ikgong*, 翼工) style form where the roofing was elevated on either ends. After the 15th century, complex flower and plants patterns were engraved on the interior of buildings, particularly those of temples and palaces. <Fig. 5.19> However, the Japanese Invasion of 1592 destroyed many important buildings. Moreover, during the reign of King Injo (r. 1623–1649), the Qing China invaded, and architecture began to deteriorate. This inflicted considerable change in architectural tendencies. Overall artistic elements became delicate with detailed lay outs, and structures became dispersed and complicated.

On the other hand, houses belonging to the upper class had separate section for the male and the female; the outer section of the house was for men while the inner section was for women. The female quarter belonged to the mistress of the house and it was customary

| Fig. 5.19 Daewoongbojeon, Naesosa, 16th century, Dapo Style Condstruction, Buan, North Jeolla Province, Treasure No. 291

for it to be located far north from the main entrance, in the innermost part of the entire house. The location of the women's quarter was intentionally planned so that women were kept inside the house, restricting them from going out. It deliberates the social condition of the period. Contrary to the female quarter, the male space, known as the *sarangchae*, was a place for conducting social meetings, studying, recreation and for holding discussions with people. Therefore it was located in the front section of the house. The space was structured specifically for the master and the eldest son of the house.

Besides, upper middle class houses kept ancestral shrines, ancestral shrine (*sadang*, 祠堂) for worship. These were kept in the innermost quarters, far away from the main entrance; either behind the *Daecheong* (a hall with a wooden floor) or on the highest altitude of the compound, behind the *Sarangchae* (scholar's studio).

2. Dance

1) The Golden Age of *Gungjung Jeongjae* (Court Music and Dance)

The policies for music and dance advanced with King Yeongjo (r. 1724–1776) and Jeongjo's (r. 1776–1800) plans to reform culture towards the end of the Joseon period. Along with these reforms, music and dance were developed and by the time of King Seonjo

(r. 1800–1834) many *gungjung jeongjae* (court dances) had been created. According to the *Seonjosilrok* (Documents on the Reign of King Seonjo), Crown Prince Hyomyeong (孝明世子) was given the role of representing King Seonjo, and one of his achievements was reforming policies for dance culture. He aggressively pushed ahead with policies concerning dance, rectifying problems related to Confucius ritual dance *ilmu* and encouraged dancers and musicians to practice dance. Such policies were executed with assistance from Kim Chang-ha. Kim, who was favored by Crown Prince Hyomyeong, assisted in holding a court banquet commemorating the 30th reigning year of King Sunjo by choreographing several *jeongjae*.

(1) *Dangak jeongjae*

No distinct changes were visible in the contents of *jeongjae* during the late Joseon period as it simply continued in the forms of early Joseon. However, in the twilight years of Joseon, the differences between *dangak jeongjae* and *hyangak jeongjae* grew hard to define and the two seemed to mix.

However, there was a new *dangak jeongjae* created by Crown Prince Hyomyeong during the reign of King Sunjo. "Jangsaengboyeunjimu" was composed of two dancers with *jukganja* (a dance prop made of bamboo) and five dancers who performed circle dance. It is considered the court dance with the largest number of variations in formation. "Yonbaekbokjimu" was created to celebrate the 30th reigning year of King Sunjo in 1829. The lyrics of this *jeongjae* were written by the Crown Prince Hyomyeong. The dance consisted of two dancers with *jukganja*, one *sunmo*, who dances at the center of circle and four other dancers who perform a group dance.

(2) *Hyangak jeongjae*

Hyangak jeongjae flourished around the latter part of the Joseon Dynasty thanks to Crown Prince Hyomyeong who made new *jeongjae* and dedicates it to his father the king at court banquet celebration to please him.

"Chunaengjeon" (春鶯囀, Dance of the Spring Nightingale) was created by Crown Prince Hyomyeong to celebrate the 40th birthday of his mother the queen *Sunwonsuk-hwanghu* (純元肅皇后). The dance,

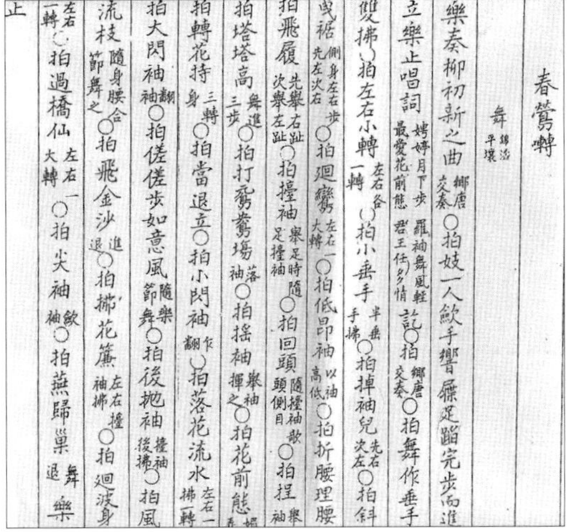
春鶯囀
舞
樂奏柳初新之曲 鄉唐交奏 ○拍 妓一人斂手響屧趾蹈完步而進
立 樂止唱詞 娉婷月下步 羅袖舞風輕 最愛花前態 君王任多情 訖○拍 鄉唐交奏 ○拍 舞作垂手
雙拂○拍 左右小轉 左右各一轉 ○拍 小垂手 半垂手拂 ○拍 掉袖兒 先右次左 ○拍 斜
裀 側身左右步 先左次右 ○拍 廻鸞 左右一大轉 ○拍 低昂袖 以袖高低 ○拍 折腰理腰
拍 飛履 先舉右趾次舉左趾 ○拍 撞袖 舉足時隨足撞袖 ○拍 回頭 隨撞袖斂頭側目 ○拍 捏 舉袖
拍 塔塔高 舞進三步 ○拍 打鸞鶯塲 落袖 ○拍 搖袖 舉袖揮之 ○拍 花前態
拍 轉花持身 三轉 ○拍 當退立 ○拍 小閃袖 乍翻 ○拍 落花流水 左右一拂一轉
拍 大閃袖 翻袖 ○拍 傞傞步 如意風 隨樂節舞 ○拍 後拋袖 撞袖後拂 ○拍 風
流 枝 隨身腰合節舞之 ○拍 飛金沙 進退 ○拍 拂花簾 左右撞袖拂 ○拍 廻波身
左右一轉 ○拍 過橋仙 左右一大轉 ○拍 尖袖 斂袖 ○拍 燕歸巢 舞退 樂
止

| Fig. 5.20 Chunaengjeon Mubo (code and pictorial documentation of dance movements, similar to music scores)

meaning a "nightingale on a spring day," depicted a nightingale sitting on a tree branch, singing on an early spring morning. To symbolize the nightingale, a yellow costume, *aengsam* (an outer coat with yellow sleeves), was worn with floral head attire. Both hands were dressed in multi-colored long strips of cloth known as *hansam* and the dancer performed on a floral bamboo mat, *hwamunseok*. It is a dance of immense grace and beauty with great diversity in movement. It is also the only *jeongjae* in which a dancer performs alone on a 6-foot floral bamboo mat, and considered one of the preeminent *gungjung jeongjae*. The lyrics for "Chunaengjeon" are as follows:

娉婷月下步 As fine refined features walk beneath the moon,
羅袖舞风轻 the wind that dances in silk sleeves, appears lighter than ever.
最爱花前态 poised in front of the loveliest flower,
君王任多情 the king entrusts his most tender heart.

"Musanhyang" (舞山香, Fragrance of Dancing Mountain Dance) was created in the 28th year of the reign of King Sunjo and it is similar to "Chunaengjeon," in its single-dancer execution, but differs in that it is performed on a mobile stage that resembles a bed called *daemoban*. While the "Chunaengjeon" portrayed feminine elegance, the movements of "Musanhyang" are more powerful and masculine power. <Fig. 5.21>

| Fig. 5.21 "Musanhyang," Kim Yeong-sook

"Gainjeonmokdan" (佳人剪牧丹, a beautiful person picking a peony flower) was a dance created by Crown Prince Hyomy-

| Fig. 5.22 "Gainjeonmokdan"

| Fig. 5.23 "Chundaeokcheok," Kim Myung-sook, Nulhui Dance Company

eong in the 28th year of King Sunjo. It is performed with the act of enjoying oneself by picking peony flowers in a vase and it was a form of court dance consisting of only women. Ten to 12 dancers take part in the performance. <Fig. 5.22>

"Chundaeokchok" (春台玉燭, Jade Candle on the Spring Table) was created by King Sunjo at the height of the *gungjung jeongjae* and it was the only *hyangak jeongjae* beautifully performed on top of a temporary stage holding a lantern. The dance performed on the stage being set up with sculpted red banisters and stairs on all four sides, and its movements were elegant and graceful. <Fig. 5.23>

2) The Development of Folk Dance

Folk dance is dance that has developed organically out of certain aspects in the everyday lives of people, labor, rituals, and amusement. The characteristics of Korean folk dance can be summarized as follows:

① The content of dances expresses the emotion and communal mind connoted with the modest life of the common people.

② There is plenty of room for improvisation expressed according to individual characteristics rather than focusing on the formalities of dance.

③ There is no elaborate stage decoration or costumes, unlike court dances.

In such folk dances, the sorrow, taste and energy of ordinary people are at all times palpable.

Folk dances have succeeded by developing closely with the diverse lifestyles of ordinary people, however, from time to time, dances were performed for the sole purpose of enjoying the energy and style of dance. In this process, some folk dances developed into professionalized performances due to their inherent artistic qualities. They were cultivated independently to become specialized dances for the performing arts and they were called *yein* (artist) dance. The dances which fell into this category were *seungmu*, *salpurichum*, *taepyeongmu*, *geommu* danced by female entertainers known as *gisaeng* from *gyobang* (a school for training female entertainers) or *gwonbeon* (劵番, *gisaeng* association). Additionally there were masked dances which became specialized by organizations associated with performers and traveling entertainers.

(1) Dance of Professional Performers

The *yein* (artist) dances were performed by performers, who worked professionally, not by ordinary people. The dances were polished with sophisticated techniques and they were more tailored to the artistic appreciation of the audience. The dances were performed mainly indoors, such as in the inner quarter's of house, guest room, or pavilion, rather than outdoors. The dances were primarily performed by individuals to showcase their artistic talents.

| Fig. 5.24 *Seungmu*, Lee Mae-bang

① *Seungmu* (Buddhist Monk Dance) <Fig. 5.24>

The Buddhist Monk dance, *seungmu* is recognized as the core of folk dance and it is perhaps the most aesthetically sublimated artwork. The charm of this dance lies in solemn movements of waving the long sleeves of the garment, *jangsam*, and in the final drum beating. The monk's costume includes a white *jangsam*, cone-shaped head attire and a red sash worn around the shoulders. The atmosphere of the dance is well depicted in the Jo Chi-hun poem "*Seungmu*." Particularly the introduction in which the monk's appearance is described as wearing, "The light silk, white peaked hat / Gently fold and float / Hiding one's blue-tinted shaved head in a peaked hood...", evokes the image of a delicate woman concealing her sorrow (a kind of pent-up emotion called *han* in Korean) deep down in her heart only to unfold the monk's guise. The dance composition unfolds with various rhythms. This particular dance received national guardianship when it was designated as Important Intangible Cultural Property No. 27 and two representative styles remain today: the Lee Mae-bang style and the Han Young-sook style.

| Fig. 5.25 *Salpurichum*, Kim Myung-sook

② *Salpurichum* (Dance of Exorcism) <Fig. 5.25>

The *salpurichum* was part of the shaman ritualistic dance, meaning "undoing misfortunes (*aek* in Korean)." It was performed to cast away bad spirits and evil. Originally, the *salpurichum* was conducted at the end of a shaman *gut* (exorcism ritual) and this was further revised and reconstructed by the *gisaeng* (female entertainers) to cultivate it into a more artistic and technical form. It was performed in the *gibang* (pleasure houses) as an improvisatorial dance. The *salpurichum* was performed while wearing a white skirt and top with white Korean socks, holding a long white draping silk cloth in the hands. The hair of the performer was pulled back in a bun with a hairpin through it. This dance with its images of white reveals *han*, one of representative aesthetic concepts of Korean art, in a most striking way. The sorrowful movements of the dance and the flowing lines of the white silk cloth in space create a beautiful harmony. The *salpurichum* was designated Important Intangible Cultural Property No. 97 and it includes the Lee Mae-bang style, Han Young-sook style and Kim Sook-ja style of *dosalpurichum*, which was developed from *dodang-gut* of Gyeonggi Province.

③ *Taepyeongmu* (Dance for National Prosperity and Peace) <Fig. 5.26>

Taepyeongmu was a dance wishing for a "tranquil and peaceful reign" and was created by Han Seong-jun (1874–1941). The accompanying music was influenced by Gyeonggi Province's *dodang-gut* and the dance was performed to various rhythms. The dress for this dance is the attire of king and queen. Due to the royal garb, it is often mistaken as a court dance but it is in fact a folk *yein* (artist) dance with a strong shamanistic features and highly developed artistic and technical skills. The most distinguishing feature of this dance is the fast and elaborate foot movements following the rapid swirling beats created by the white socks and subtly revealed red under skirt beneath the slightly raised indigo blue skirt. Kang Sun-young's *taepyeongmu* style was designated as Important Intangible Cultural Property No. 92.

| Fig. 5.26 *Taepyeongmu*, Kim Myung-sook

(2) Mask Dance

The characteristic feature of the mask dance, which grew popular among the masses towards the end of the Joseon period, was that the spectator and the performer enjoy the dance together in the same sphere, without differentiation. The mask dance can be interpreted as behavior that releases the participant's pent-up *han* through the farcical and humorous acts they carry out behind the veil of their masks. In such mask dances, the non-ruling ordinary

| Fig. 5.27 *Songpasandaenori*, National Research Institute of Cultural Heritage

classes delightedly released their suppressed resentment and sorrow through laughter. Such traditional dances were widely performed later on during the 1980s, combined with the democratic movement, which spread among university students.

The mask dance was performed by males and compared to other folk dances, the energy and liveliness of the performance was strongly felt. Especially, the movement of pulling and then boisterously releasing the sleeves of *hansam* (long cloths held in the hand) with song added a buoyant sense to the dance. When watching mask dance combining excitement and exhilaration, the spectators naturally find themselves muttering cheerful comments like "*eolsso*," "that's great!" or "very good," which adds more enthusiasm and momentum to the dance, eventually encouraging more audience participation. The mask dance was called with different names such as *sandaenori, talchum, yaryu, ohgwangdae* depending on the region of origin.

Songpasandaenori (Songpa mask dance) was a mask dance that developed and passed down in the Songpa region. The name *sandaenori* refers to the mask dance of the central part of Korea. *Songpasandaenori* was a branch of *sandaedogamgeuk*, which was a theatrical mask dance enjoyed by the people of the Seoul-Gyeonggi region, and was performed annually on the first full moon day of a new year, at *Dano*, the 5th day of the 5th month (lunar calendar), and on *Chuseok* and on other festive holidays. The entertainers in masks hold theatrical performances evolved around wit, dance, song and acting. <Fig. 5.27>

Bongsantalchum (the masked dance of Bongsan), a mask dance that originated from Bongsan of Hwanghae Province became representative among the area at the end of the 19th century. It consisted of seven acts and five chapters. The first act is *sasangjwae* (四上佐, a ritual dance dedicated to gods of four directions), the second *palmeokjung* (dance of the eight

I Fig. 5.28 *Bongsantalchum*, Bongsan Mask Dance-Drama Preservation Society

I Fig. 5.29 *Bukcheong Lion Mask Dance,* National Research Institute of Cultural Heritage

unworthy monks), the third *sadangchum* (dance of *sadang*, professional performers), the fourth *nojangchum* (dance of an old general), the fifth *sajachum* (lion mask dance) depicting a scene in which a lion leads an old veteran general to transgress and punishes apostatized monks. The sixth act is the *yangbanchum* (dance of a nobleman) and the seventh is the *miyalchum* (dance of Miyal). The seventh act consists of a story about the intertwined love-triangle among an old man, his wife Miyal, and his mistress, in which the old woman Miyal was beaten to death by her husband. The performance ends with a shaman *gut* to pacify the vindictive spirit of the Miyal. *Bongsantalchum* is the most masculine and dynamic among the mask dances of other regions and is considered one of the archetypal mask dances of Korea. <Fig. 5.28>

The *bukcheong lion mask dance* from the Bukcheong region of Hamgyeong Province is an illustrative example that Lion mask Dance, developed with influences from the continent and the northern provinces of China and took on a more folk-like character. Among the many lion dances of Korea, the *bukcheong lion mask dance* stands out because its movements are refined and diverse and an array of performers adds variety to the dance. <Fig. 5.29>

3. Music

Joseon court music declined after two major wars: Japanese Invasion of the *Yimjin-*

woeran (1592) and the Manchurian Invasion of the *Byeongjahoran* (1636). These two wars caused great financial difficulty and many of the court instruments were destroyed as well as the number of musicians declined. Meanwhile, during late Joseon period, as the economic power of the country shifted from the court to the literati, the latter's music (*pungnyu* music) and folk music (*minsokak*) began to rise and develop.

1) Decline of Court Music

After the war with China, *aak* ceased to be performed in court rituals. It was reconstructed after 10 years, but the number of musicians in the orchestra reduced from 200 to 40. In order to revitalize *aak*, King Yeongjo (1724–1776), based on the study of *Akhakgwebeom*, tried to reconstruct many of the former *aak* instruments as well as train more *akgong* and *aksaeng* musicians. However *aak* never regained its former glory. Compared to *aak*, *hyangak* showed less deterioration. However, most of repertoires from Goryeo and early Joseon period ceased to be played and new repertoires of *gagok*, "Yeongsanhoesang," "Yeomillak" and "Boheoja" were performed for court banquets. "Yeomillak," "Boheoja," "Jeongeup" and "Dongdong" were formerly vocal music but turned into instrumental dance music during this time. Both *gagok* and "Yeongsanhoesang" were originally court *hyangak*, but became established as *pungnyu* music developed by the middle class, *jungin*. At the same time, "Boheoja" and "Yeomillak" became more and more indigenized as they were played by the middle class, from which many instrumental pieces were born.

Dangak from the Goryeo Dynasty, actively performed during the first half of Joseon Dynasty, virtually disappeared, with only "Boheoja" and "Nakyangchun" remaining. Both pieces were performed during in and out of processions of the King and during court dances. Of the two, "Boheoja" gave birth to instrumental variations. It was originally imported from China in the 13th century and is still being played today. After its introduction, its rhythms became more diverse. "Yeomillak," originally composed as a processional music, was still being performed, giving birth to many other instrumental variations.

2) Establishment of *Pungnyu* Music

Joseon was a class-based society, with strictly differentiated *yangban* (aristocrats), *yangmin* (commoners), and *cheonmin* (the lowly) classes. However, during late Joseon period, a new middle class, called *jungin*, appeared. They were rich commoners and those who aspired to become *yangban*. They were the main patrons for the performing arts. Being amateurs

| Fig. 5.30 *Gagok* Performance, Performed by Kim Yeong-gi

themselves, they developed a new musical style called *pungnyu* music.

Pungnyu music can be considered a branch of court music tradition, in that it emphasized restraining emotions. Its early performers were *akgong* and *gisaeng*, female entertainers from the court. The repertoire was originally quite limited, only including court music. However, a new repertoire for *pungnyu* music began to be constructed, not caused by an intentional act of composition, but naturally springing from private social gatherings for musical activities. In order to aid memory music, musicians began to transcribe their music using their own notational systems. Based on this, they published certain music scores, which are mostly scores for *geomun-go*. Today these scores constitute important sources for studying the music of the late Joseon period. Musical instruments for *pungnyu* music included *geomun-go*, *gayageum*, *bipa*, *daegeum*, *danso*, *yanggeum*, and *saenghwang*, which were performed as solo, duet and ensemble form.

The vocal genres for *pungnyu* music includ *gagok* (long lyric songs), *gasa* (na rrative songs) and *sijo* (short lyric songs). *Gagok* and *sijo* are songs with three lines *sijo* lyrics, but *gagok* divides the three lines of *sijo* poetry into five lines. *Gagok* song is accompanied by a chamber ensemble and *gagok* song cycles are sung alternatively by both female and male singers. <Fig. 5.30> On the contrary, *sijo* is only accompanied by a single instrument such as a *janggu* or a *daegeum*, and is sung either by a male or a female singer. *Gasa* is sung with long narrative *gasa* poems in a similar vocal style with *gagok* or *sijo* and sung without any instrumental accompaniment. Since the lyrics of *gasa* are not standardized, musical style is not also standardized.

| Sound. 4 Female *Gagok* (Long Lyric Song), "Urak," Performed by Kim Yeong-gi

The most representative *pungnyu's* instrumental repertoires include "Yeongsanhoesang," "Boheoja," "Yeomillak" and "Jajinhanip." "Yeongsanhoesang" is the most representa-

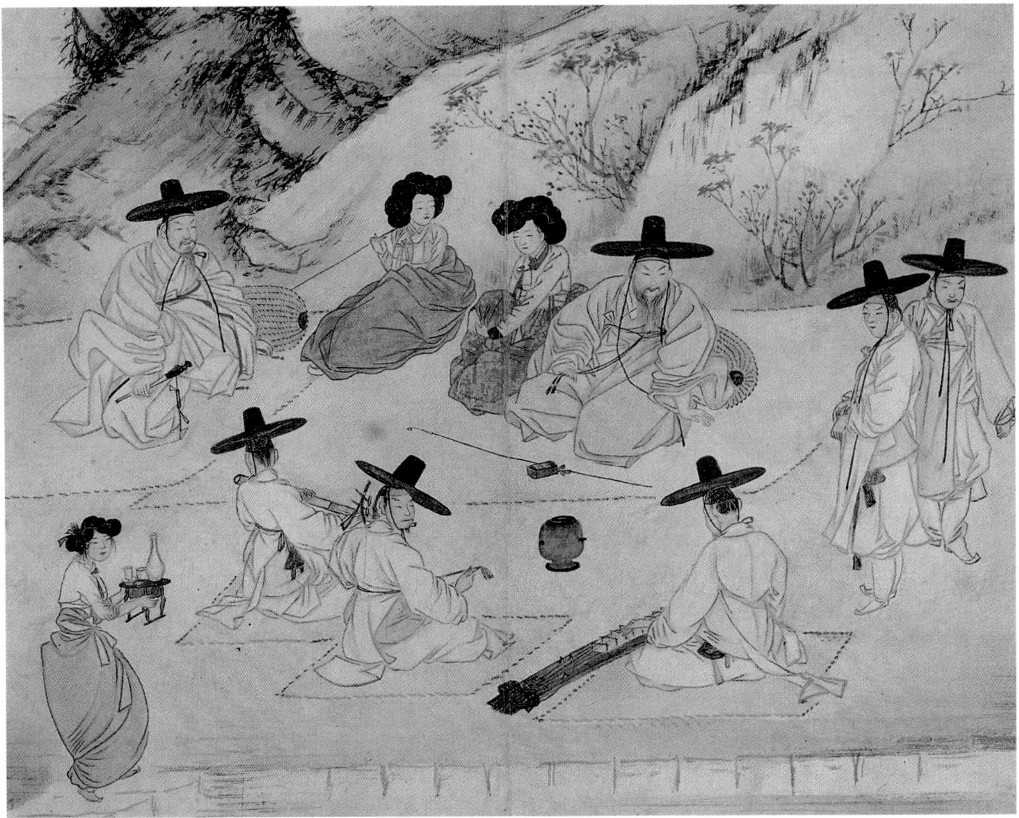

| Fig. 5.31 Painting of Performance of *Pungnyu* Music by Sin Yun-bok, Kansong Art Museum

tive *pungnyu* repertoire. Originally '"Yeongsanhoesang" was a piece of Buddhist vocal music that was performed for court dance. Instrumental ensembles performed while female entertainers sang seven Chinese syllables of the first line of a Buddhist sutra *yeong san hoe sang bul bo sal* (Mass to the Buddha on the Spiritual Mountain). Currently "Yeongsanhoesang" is an instrumental suite which consists of nine short pieces. These short pieces are either variants of the original melody or newly created. "Yeongsanhoesang" begins slowly and speeds up gradually through its nine pieces to a fast pace at the end, lasting about fifty minutes in total. Three versions of "Yeongsanhoesang" are performed. "Hyeonak Yeongsanhoesang" is the longest version and combines string instruments like *geomun-go* and *gayageum* with soft wind instruments. "Gwanak Yeongsanhoesang" is performed by a wind ensemble with winds and bowed strings. "Pyeongjohoesang" has a melody that is transposed down a fourth compared to the original version.

"Jajinhanip" has developed from the accompanying music for a vocal piece *gagok*.

Compared to instrumentation for *gagok* accompaniment, in which soft *sepiri* and *daegeum* are employed, "Jajinhanip" uses the loud *hyangpiri*, *daegeum*, *haegeum* and *janggu* without singing. Often "Jajinhanip" is played as a solo piece for the *daegeum* or *piri* and *danso* and *saenghwang* duet. <Fig. 5.31>

| Sound. 5 *Pungnyu*, "Taryeong" from "Yeongsanhoesang," Performed by National Gugak Center

| Sound. 6 *Pungnyu*, *Daegeum* Solo, "Sangyeongsan" from "Yeongsanhoesang," Performed by Yim Jae-won

3) Rise of Folk Music

Folk music, which is called *minsokak*, was mostly performed by professional musicians. They were of the lowest class in the society, but unlike the *jungin* amateur musicians of *pungnyu* music they were more artistically accomplished. The most famous and beloved genres that sprung from the folk tradition were *pansori*, *sinawi*, and *sanjo*. Unlike the court

Pansori Performance

| Fig. 5.32 Painting of *Pansori* performance, Anonymous, Seoul National University Museum

or *pungnyu* music traditions, folk music was more liberal in its emotional expression. *Minyo* (folk song) and *nongak* (farmer's music) genres were also performed and enjoyed by not only professional musicians but also commoners.

Pansori is a theatrical music wherein a singer delivers a long dramatic story with a drummer (*gosu*). *Pansori* is a compounded musical works with songs (*sori*), narration (*aniri*), and gestures (*ballim*). The drummer accompanies the singer on the barrel drum, *buk*, by playing *jangdan* (rhythmic patterns) and also makes calls of encouragement (*chuimsae*) at appropriate phrase endings. The role of the singer was not only to sing the song well but also to transmit the story effectively in order to make the audience laugh and cry.

Traditionally twelve repertoires (stories) were sung in *pansori*, only five of which were passed down to the present day, their themes coincide with the five cardinal principles of Confucian ethics as follows. The theme of "Heungboga (The Song of Heungbo)" is brotherhood. The theme of "Chunhyangga (The Song of Chunhyang)" is a wife's loyalty to her husband. The themes of "Sugungga (The Song of the Underwater Palace)" and "Simcheongga (The Song of Simcheong)" are loyalty to the king and filial piety respectively. "Jeokbyeokga (The Song of Red Cliff)" delivers the classical story of the battle of Red Cliff from the novel *Sanguochi* of China. Currently more stories are sung in *pansori* form including some episodes from the Bible or famous historical figures in Korean history. *Pansori* today was designated as a Masterpiece of the Oral and Intangible Heritage of Humanity by the UNESCO. <Fig. 5.32>

| Sound. 7 *Pansori*, "Simcheongga (The Song of Simcheong)," Performed by National Gugak Center

Sinawi is a type of instrumental ensemble with improvisation derived from shaman music, originally an accompanimental music for songs or dances during a shaman ritual. Several musical instruments perform heterophonic melodies together based on two basic rhythmic cycles, slow and fast respectively. *Sinawi* permits individual variations and improvisation, solo melodies of each instrument are also performed during the course of a performance.

Today *sinawi* accompanies *salpuri*, folk dance. *Sinawi* is often described as improvisational music, however it is now transmitted through scores and beginning to loose its improvisational nature. *Sinawi* features heterophonic harmony of several musical instruments. Originally *sinawi* was performed by the *hyangpiri*, *daegeum*, *haegeum*, *ajaeng*, *janggu* and *jing*, but today *gayageum* and *geomun-go* are also added to a *sinawi* ensemble.

Gayageum sanjo is a solo instrumental piece accompanied by a *janggu* or *buk* drum. Since the music of *sanjo* has been crystallized through several generations of musicians, it is often referred to as the most artistic genre in Korean music. The most expressive and artis-

Photo of Lee Chae-suk's *Gayageum Sanjo* Performance

| Fig. 5.33 Painting of *Gayageum* Performance by Sin Yun-bok, Kansong Art Museum

tic techniques of each musical instrument are accomplished in the *sanjo* form, thus *sanjo* is the highest level of performance genre of each instrument. Similar to "Yeongsanhoesang," *sanjo* begins in a slow tempo and speeds up towards the end. In *gayageum sanjo*, melodies are manipulated and embellished by bending and vibrating the strings with the left hand, the right hand produces complex and diverse rhythmical sounds by plucking and flicking the strings. Producing diverse microtonal sounds is the most unique feature of the *gayageum sanjo*. Rhythms and modes used in *sanjo* are borrowed from those of *pansori*. <Fig. 5.33>

| Sound. 8 *Gayageum Sanjo*, "Jinyangjo," Performed by Park Hyun-sook

Farmers' music, called *nongak* or *pungmul*, is one of the oldest music in Korea. It is performing art and religious ritual, and developed into a totalistic art consisting of ritual, procession, work, and play. The sounds are mostly produced by percussive instruments such as *kkwaenggwari* (a small brass gong), *jing* (a large brass gong), *janggu*, and *buk*. The *taepyeongso* (a double-reed oboe) is the only melodic instrument in a *nongak* band. A typical *nongak* procession consisted of percussionists with flags in the front, followed by dancers and entertainers in costumes. Its musical aspects can be described as the harmonization of contrasting timbers. A modern adaptation of *nongak* for the contemporary stage is called *samulnori*. A *samulnori* ensemble consists of the four main rhythmic instruments, usually omitting the *taepyeongso*. A typical movement proceeds from slower sections to faster sec-

| Fig. 5.34 *Samulnori, Nongak*

tions, in which contrast between tension and release is featured. *Samulnori* began in 1978 when four instrumentalists (Kim Deok-su, Kim Yong-bae, Choe Tae-hyun and Yi Jong-dae) performed it on stage for the first time. It is now established as a major musical genre in Korean traditional music. Today *samulnori* is receiving international acclaim, delivering the beauty of Korean music all over the world. <Fig. 5.34>

| Sound. 9 *Samulnori* (Percussion Quartet), Performed by National Gugak Center

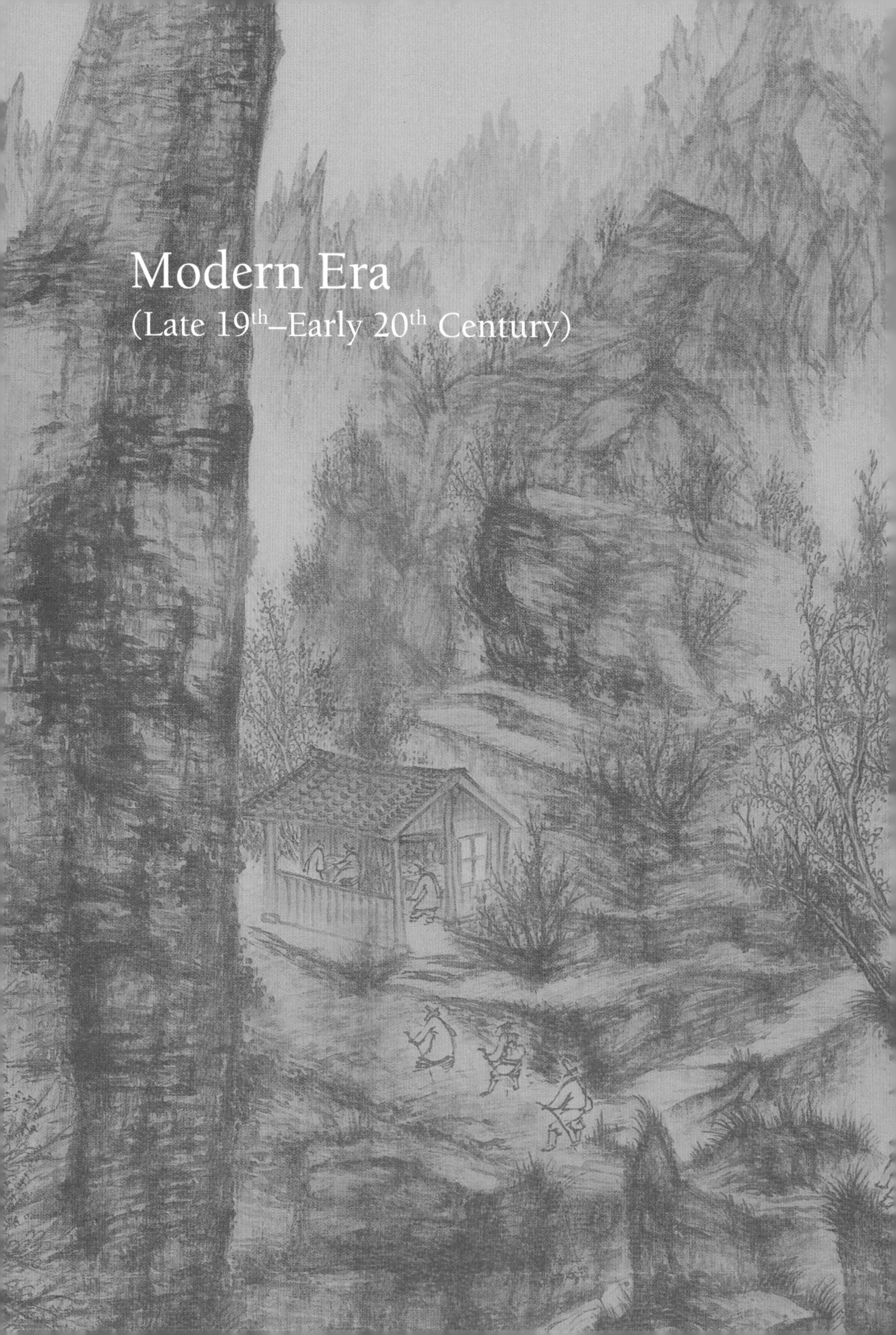

Modern Era
(Late 19th–Early 20th Century)

VI. Modern Era (Late 19th–Early 20th Century)

As Western learning spread through East Asia, Joseon maintained a closed door policy under traditional systems and from a sense of the strength of Western culture. When it was finally forced to open its ports by the Japanese, it played on the peripheries of the world capitalist market and took its first steps on the road to modernization. With the collapse of the medieval "emperor" system as a result of the Sino-Japanese war, in 1894 Gojong declared Korea's independence from China and proceeded with the historical task of reforming the country into a modern nation-state. But before Joseon society was able to develop internal capacity for modernization, when its doors were opened to imperialist powers the battle between Japan and other countries for their interests in the country escalated, dashing Joseon's efforts to modernize the country on its own strength.

After forcibly annexing Korea in 1910, Japan began a period of oppressive colonial rule of the Korean peninsula. Pursuing a dual policy of discrimination and assimilation, it sought to make Koreans bow down to the Japanese emperor and deliberately distorted Korean culture and history to destroy the people's will for independence. In response, Koreans fought hard for independence both inside and outside the country, undertaking diplomatic efforts and working to increase the capabilities of the Korean people. Thanks to these efforts and the victory of the UN allied forces in the Pacific War, Korea country gained independence in August 1945.

Though independence was restored with the Japanese surrender to the allied forces on August 15, 1945, and the end of WWII, the US and Soviet forces jointly occupied the Korean peninsula on the grounds of disarming the Japanese military, instigating a split between left and right. In the end conflict between the two sides led to the division of Korea into North and South, which was further reinforced by the Korean War (1950–1953).

1. Art

1) Painting

Under the growing influence of Western civilization, the Joseon dynasty that had chosen a closed-door policy finally joined the world market. The Joseon court was later forced to open its ports under Japanese pressure. The monarchial system broke down and the country began to move toward the modern era. In particular, as the emperor system of China faced its crisis in the aftermath of the Sino-Japanese war, in 1894 King Gojong (r. 1863–1907) proclaimed that Joseon's independence from the tributary relationship with Qing China and began the historical task of turning Korea into a modern nation-state. King Gojong also ushered in the age of enlightenment, by dealing with political issues of Joseon's responses to the West and Japan.

As the country pursued modernization based on eastern values and western technology, the art of painting and calligraphy, led by the Kim Jeong-hui school, which thrived in the 19th century came to have the task of maintaining and preserving eastern values in the age of enlightenment. Under the cultural policy of the Japanese colonial government, painting in Korea came to be reorganized under the broad title of "misul," a general term created by the Meiji government of Japan as an equivalent to the Western concept of "art." Under the public of this term, a separation was made between *seoyanghwa*, or Western painting, and *dongyanghwa*, or Eastern painting, and efforts were made to establish a modern national art exhibition that would feature both. Painting flourished and further developed even more with the establishment of the Joseon Art Exhibition (*Joseon Misul Jeollamhoe*) in the 1920s, a time dominated by theories studying art in relation to culture and society and plein-air realism. Around the 1930s, modernist painting began to emerge, following the footsteps of late Impressionism. And under the influence of the Pan-Asianmovement, native Korean themes became popular. Eastern art, which had declined under heavy Western influence, came to be seen in a new light as a form of subjectivism or spiritualism in the context of Western expressionism. Under the name of "new Eastern painting" (*sin-dongyanghwa*), traditional art took on an international sensibility. Eastern modernism, as a combination of modernism and nationalism, developed rapidly in the 1950s after passing through the turmoil of the late 1940s following Korea's liberation from Japan.

(1) Eastern Painting

When the Joseon Art Exhibition (*Joseon Misul Jeollamhoe*) was established in 1922, calligraphy and painting, previously known by the collective term *seohwa*, were separated with calligraphy treated as an independent category in the exhibition. Painting was divided into Eastern painting and Western painting, which formed the mainstream of art until the late 1920s. Western art then began to take predominance, accelerating the transition to modern art. In the field of traditional colored painting, the coexistence of Korean and Japanese art became an issue, and under the new name of Eastern painting other traditional genres such as landscapes as a vicarious method of travel (*wayu*), edification paintings, and ornamental paintings were recreated as genres suited to a modern exhibition.

The first generation of Eastern painting artists belonged to the *Seohwa* Art Association, and genres were divided into ink and wash landscapes, figure paintings, and bird-and-flower paintings. The earliest efforts to reform traditional painting under the name of Eastern painting were made in early 1923 after the first Joseon Art Exhibition. In March 1923, Lee Sang-beom (1897–1972), Noh Su-hyeon (1899–1978), Byeon Kwan-sik (1899–1976), and Lee Yong-u (1898–1930) formed the *Dongyeonsa* (Society for Collective Studies). In their art, they sought a compromise or fusion between Western and Eastern painting and took the lead as modern reformers of landscape painting.

Lee Sang-beom's "After Sunset" (*Haejin dui*), which only remains in photographs, and Byeon Kwan-sik's "An Alley" (*Eoneu golmok*) depicts scenes from everyday life. They are therefore radically different both in title and theme from preceding landscapes. Moving away from literati depictions of natural scenery embodying the ideals of cosmic harmony and separation from the mundane world, artists began to focus on the real world where people make their living, and on ordinary scenes showing the aesthetics and sensibilities of ordinary life. The new realistic ink and wash landscapes developed under the influence

Fig. 6.1 Lee Sang-beom, High Mountain and Long River, 1966, Ink and light color on paper, 56.5×128cm, Private collection, Seoul

| Fig. 6.2 Byeon, Kwan-sik, Autumn Light at Samseonam in Outer Mt. Geumgang, 1959, Ink and light color on paper, 150×117cm, Private collection, Seoul

of Japan's new Southern school of realism, and while the tradition of classical landscapes, the mainstream of the *seohwa* era, was continued by artists in the Honam region such as Huh Baek-ryeon, reformed ink and wash landscape painting increased greatly through the Joseon Art Exhibition, and eventually became the mainstream.

Korean-style realistic ink and wash landscapes developed in the latter half of the 1950s, in accord with efforts to distinguish "what is ours and what is not" as a consequence of increased consciousness of Korean identity. Lee Sang-beom's "High Mountain and Long River" (*Sango sujang*, <Fig. 6.1>) features low hills and simple farmers living without greed, exuding simplicity and a peaceful harmony created with subtle color and dark ink dots. Byeon Kwan-sik's "Autumn Light at Samseonam in Outer Mt. Geumgang" (*Woegeumgang samseonam chusaek*, <Fig. 6.2>) shows a very lively, individual style, expressing the grand beauty of the country's mountains and rivers in the layered ink technique and broken lines using powerful brushstrokes.

Colored figure paintings and bird-and-flower paintings also developed in new ways as seen in the work of Kim Eun-ho (1892–1979), Choe U-seok (1899–1965), and Lee Yeong-il (1894–1953). If realistic landscapes at the time were categorized as "southern painting" (*namhwa*), colored figure paintings, and bird-and-flower paintings were so popular in Japan and dominant in the Eastern painting section of the Joseon Art Exhibition that they came to be called "Japanese painting" (*ilbonhwa*). Paintings of beautiful women called miindo and new style bird-and-flower paintings had emerged a few years earlier than the new realistic landscapes, fully reflecting the Japanese style from 1923.

Kim Eun-ho had gained fame as a portrait painter from his days as a student at the *Seohwa* Art Association. Keen to his success as a modern painter, Kim generally submitted paintings of beautiful women or birds and flowers, which concurred with aesthetic issues discussed in Meiji Japan and the ideals of beauty at the time. His 1923 work "Lost in Thought" (*Eungsa*, <Fig. 6.3>) features an image of the "new woman" with her hair in the modern Japanese *hisashigami* style (like a low pompadour) and dressed in a semi-transparent white jacket, a white shawl, a short skirt, and white shoes with heels. This image echoed the "student style" that was popular among the *gisaeng*. The pure and innocent image, static yet beautiful, represented a new style and sensibility, and was an image that long dominated the national art exhibition.

In the 1930s, artists producing colored paintings added a touch of the decorative court style of the traditional Northern school to achieve a meticulous, detailed method of painting, and in the 1950s the second generation of Eastern style painters, namely those producing colored figure paintings, started the "new Eastern painting" movement in an attempt to break away from Japanese influence. These artists criticized the ink and wash landscape painters, who dominated the national exhibition, as old school artists who were simply following traditional forms. Against criticisms of this nature, the landscape artists sought subjectivism in literati painting using the language

| Fig. 6.3 Kim Eun-ho, Lost in Thought, 1923, Color on silk, 130×40cm, Private collection, Seoul

of modern Western art and combined ink and wash with color techniques. Kim Ki-chang (1913–2001) and Park Re-hyun (1920–1976) succeeded in treating classical Korean style subjects and earthy, ordinary subjects in a constructive semi-abstract style founded on cubism. Lee Ung-no (1904–1989) treated realistic themes relating to the ordinary people in thick, rapid and powerful brushstrokes, achieving a highly expressive style developed in the context of fauvism.

(2) Western-Style Oil Painting

One of the most significant events in the history of painting during the early Japanese colonial period was the emergence of painters working in the style of Western painting. Koreans who had studied oil painting at the Tokyo School of Fine Arts returned home and became the first real Western-style painters in Korea. In the late 1920s, great quantitative and qualitative development in Western painting was achieved as the number of students returning home from Japan grew. In addition, while only the techniques of Western art had been adopted in the late Joseon dynasty, the philosophies began to be accepted also, and Western painting became the leading genre of art in Korea, a trend which continues to the present.

| Fig. 6.4 Ko Hei-tong, Self Portrait with Fan, 1915, Oil on canvas, 61×46cm, National Museum of Contemporary Art, Korea

The first Korean to study Western painting was Ko Hei-tong (1886–1965), who entered the Department of Western painting at the Tokyo School of Fine Arts in 1909. After graduating in 1915, he returned to work in Korea but in the late 1920s he switched to Eastern painting, or traditional Korean painting. Three of Koh's oil paintings remain extant. They are all self portraits painted around 1915. The technique reflects the style of the Japanese plein-air school. This school was started by Kuroda Seiki (1866–1924) who had studied in Paris, and his style can be described as academy style impressionism, based on neo-classicism flavored with impressionism, or an impressionistic academy style. "Self Portrait with Fan" (*Buchaeleul deun jahwasang*, <Fig. 6.4>), one of Koh's oil paintings from 1915, is signed in alphabets and represents his everyday life. The framed oil painting and the books bound in Western style seen in the background give us an insight into the artist's sense of self as a Western style painter and new intellectual.

| Fig. 6.5 Kim Gwan-ho, Sunset, 1916, Oil on canvas, 127.5×127.5cm, The University Art Museum, Tokyo University of the Arts, Japan

Kim Gwan-ho (1890–1959) entered the Tokyo School of Fine Arts in 1911, two years after Koh, and graduated at the top of his class. He was the first Korean Western style painter to hold a solo exhibition. "Sunset" (*Haejilnyeok*, <Fig. 6.5>), which won a special mention in Munjeon, an art exhibition organized by the Japanese government-general, holds a special place in Korean art history as the country's first nude painting. The figure is an idealistic portrayal of a nude scene from the back, in a pose of both relaxation and tension. Bathed in the light of sunset, the painting has a lyrical mood. This modern Japanese-style academism spread through Korea and formed the basis of Western style painting in the country. In the spring of 1918, Ra Hye-seok (1896–1948) graduated from Tokyo Private Women's School of Fine Arts and became Korea's first female Western-style painter, playing an important role in the art circle of the 1920s.

In the 1920s, the main trend of Western painting was plein-air academism, which showed the mixed influence of classical realism, naturalism and impressionism, movements that formed the base of modern Japanese academism. From the latter half of the decade, the influence of the so-called "new art trends" including late impressionism, fauvism, expressionism, cubism, and futurism began to show.

In the 1930s quantitative growth in Western painting also resulted in its dominance in art theory and philosophy, a trend that continues to this day. Of the works accepted to and winning awards in the Joseon Art Exhibition, Western paintings more than doubled the number of Eastern paintings, including paintings of the four gracious plants (plums, orchids, chrysanthemums, and bamboo) and most artist groups were Western painting groups. The number of Western painting solo exhibitions more than doubled that of Eastern painting as well.

In the early 1930s when this rapid growth took place, art critic Kim Yong-jun (1904–1967) divided Western painting into two schools, the realism school and the subjectivism school. The realism school refers to the academy style painters whose activities revolved around the Joseon Art Exhibition, while the subjectivism school refers to artists of the new movements such as expressionism, which followed late impressionism and reconstructionism. In opposition to these trends were the proletariat artists, who saw these trends as bourgeois art. The proletariat artists aimed to use art as a means of social revolution through posters designed to incite the masses, and reproductive arts such as prints and stage art. This movement continued until the Korean Proletariat Art Federation (KAPF) was disbanded

| Fig. 6.6 Lee Sang-chun, Nitrogenous Fertilizer Factory, 1932, Print, Illustration of "Jilsobiryo gongjang"

in 1935.

The academy school worked around the Joseon Art Exhibition. The academy style, which was introduced in the 1910s, was perceived to be the foundation and tradition of Western painting, and for this reason it spread rapidly through the art scene in general, from art lessons at school to the Joseon Art Exhibition. The academy artists sought to express the aesthetics of ideal sand eternal beauty through the careful observation of the subject, the accurate drawing through study of light and shade and planes, the faithful depiction of texture and character, and the stable composition and harmony of color. Such academic art, featuring the characteristics of the plein-air school and neo-classicism, was led by artists such as To Sang-bong (1902–1977), Lee Ma-dong (1906–1981), Sim Hyeong-gu (1908–1962), and Kim In-seung (1910–2001). After liberation from Japanese rule in 1945, academism continued to dominate the National Art Exhibition (*Gukjeon*).

Proletarian artists sought to become more active through the reorganization of KAFP on April 20, 1930, from a political group seeking to popularize art to a group of Bolshevik artists. Rather than painting pictures for aesthetic appreciation, the activities of KAFP artists generally took the form of more active, direct, and popular forms of art such as prints, illustrations, cartoons, and posters, designed to inform and incite the wider working class. Lee Sang-chun's "Nitrogenous Fertilizer Factory" (*Jilsobiryo gongjang*, <Fig. 6.6>), is an illustration that accompanied the two-part story of the same title by the KAFP writer Lee Bok-man (1908–?), which was published in the *Chosun Ilbo* on May 29 and 31, 1932. The fiery eyes of the protagonist and his expression are filled with his strong resolution, a sign of his labor activism to come.

Modernist art, representing a radical new philosophy opposed to academism, began to appear in Korea in the 1930s. From being a substitute and check on proletarian art, it spread through the adoption of the formal elements of modernism, falling in line with growing moves to separate art from politics and to focus on the autonomy and integrity of aesthetics and subjectivism.

"Moderate modernism," largely inspired by the work of Van Gogh, Gaugin, and Cezanne, which is subjective but at the same time respects the forms of naturalism. Moderate modernism gained popularity through the Joseon Art Exhibition. The major artists of this type of modernism were Lee In-seong (1912–1950), Kim Ju-geyong (1902–1981), Oh Ji-ho (1905–1982), Hwang Sul-jo (1904–1939), and Suh Jin-dal (1908–1947). Kim Ju-gyeong and Oh Ji-ho are associated with the Japanese Western style painting of the Taisho era (1912–1926), which is based on self-awareness of the artist's individuality and other perspectives rising out of late Impressionism. They pursued the visual representation of inner subjectivism. These artists sought to show the strong color of Korean scenery using expressionist brushstrokes, the lines throbbing with spiritual life recalling the stylistic hallmarks of Van Gogh, and reflect discovery of the innate power of colors beyond the visual effect of light, thus revealing the basic laws and principles of nature.

Compared to moderate modernism, which combined subjectivism and objectivity on the basis of individualism, radical modernism flatly rejected the existing naturalist tradition, which was subjective and realistic. Under radical modernism, artists declared a spirit of experimentation, sowing the seeds of semi-abstraction that swept the Korean art scene in the 1950s on the heels of early 20th century Fauvism and Cubism. Radical modernism largely spread through non-government group exhibitions. The pioneer of this movement was Ku Pon-ung (1906–1953).

Ku devoted himself to radical modernism from the early 1930s when he was an art student in Tokyo, presenting his works several times to the art exhibitions of the Independent Art Association, the cradle of Japanese fauvism and epicenter of new Japan-centrism. "Woman" (*Yeoin*, <Fig. 6.7>), presumed to date to the first half of the 1930s, shows the upper body of a naked woman with arms raised over her head and two hands clasped together. The face and body have been deformed and white and yellow paints have been thickly applied over the canvas, with red and green highlights on top. Freed from the laws of color usage ruling the existing naturalism school, Gu explored color for its own sake, and for the effects of pure color contrasts and for the texture of the material.

| Fig. 6.7 Ku Pon-ung, Woman, mid-1930's, Oil on canvas, 47×35cm, National Museum of Contemporary Art, Korea

Kim Whan-ki (1913–1974) also followed avant garde trends such as Cubism and Futurism from his days as a student in Tokyo. "Crockery Terrace" (*Jangdokdae*, <Fig. 6.8>) from around 1936 is an experimental work featuring a native theme that removes all sense of volume in pursuit of a new flatness in art. Rejecting art as the result of visual experience and customs or as expression of the subject, he pursued art as perception of the object, as a process of creation rather than imitation.

Western art in Korea in the 1950s was a continuation of the 1930s. Academy style realism grew even more through the National Art Exhibition while modernism spread rapidly through group ex-

| Fig. 6.8 Kim Whan-ki, Crockery Terrace, 1936, Oil on canvas, 22.2×27.3cm, Private collection, Seoul

hibitions. Native Korean materials and subject matters came to be dominant and a Korean-style Western painting developed. Kim Whan-ki attempted to represent flat, contracted reconstructions of Joseon dynasty white porcelain jars or poetic natural subjects that were favored by the Joseon literati in pursuit of a semi-abstract or folk craft beauty. In his paintings of oxen from the latter half of the 1930s, Lee Jung-sup (1916–1956) forged his own unique style. "White Bull" (*Huinso*, <Fig. 6.9>), a work from 1954, exhibits a strong touch and calligraphic expression. This painting strongly conveys the pain and passion of the artist who suffered in the aftermath of the Korean War. Park Soo-keun (1914–1965) also created a very individual style using a unique surface matiere with the texture of weathered granite or an old earthen wall or straw mat. The figures and the background elements in his work are rendered flat. "Washing Place" (*Bballaeteo*, <Fig. 6.10>) from 1954 features a group of women washing clothes in a stream viewed from the back. On a coarse surface, the subject is

| Fig. 6.9 Lee Jung-sup, White Bull, 1953, Oil on plywood, 30×41.7cm, Hongik University Museum

| Fig. 6.10 Park Soo-keun, Washing Place, 1954, Oil on canvas, 14×29cm, Private collection, Seoul

depicted in straight lines which seemed to be carved rather than painted, compact in form and restrained in technique, portraying so well the lives of the ordinary Koreans who have endured patiently through much hardship. Park Soo-geun's art, unifying subject and technique, shows the model of the ordinary person and is highly regarded as the most unique painter in Korean figurative art.

2) Sculpture

Unlike the Joseon traditions, sculptures in the early modern period comprised mostly of human figures. The influence came from western art. The Joseon Art Exhibition (1925, sculpture was introduced from the 4th exhibition onwards) and the Korean Art exhibition (national exhibition) became the main events for presenting sculpture. Sculpture in Korea at the time broke away from, traditional conceptions on form and received new influences and ideals which coincided and conflicted with Korea's existing ideologies. This collision began with the return of Kim Bok-jin in 1925, after studying sculpture in at the Tokyo School of Fine Art, in Japan. Kim Bok-jin's sculptures were realistic, focusing on form and expression. His beliefs in art theory were orthodox, and he also took on the role of an art critic. The tendency continued on well into the 1930 when realistic sculptures were made by students of Kim Bok-jin such as Lee Gook-jeon, Kim Gyeong-seung, Yoon Hyo-joong, Lee Byeong-sang. These artists did not simply concentrate on making sculptures of the head, but they also produced works expressing the different body parts, the full length sculpture, a group of people and so on. This movement was followed by conceptual artists, often referred to as the first generation sculptors who contributed to educational and social advancements of sculpture in Korea.

Abstract sculpture which began as a purely experimental form by artists such as Kim Jong-young (1915–1982) and Kim Jeong-sook (1917–1991), became more active in the 1950s and 1960s. New materials such as iron were introduced to widen the scope of expression. Soon after, abstract sculpture grew rapidly, and in the 1960s, the National Exhibition competition focused on this style. Thus, abstract sculpture became another major mode of expression in Korean art. The focus was laid on humanism in order to express the innermost spirit of the artists. The trend appears to reflect the effort to seek for the Korean self through abstract expressions.

3) Craft

Modern Korean craft can be understood as a progress in which functional craft transformed into an art form. But it was not an independent transition which occurred within the craft world itself, but rather resulted from the attempt to be westernized. Through this, function and form lost the integrated elements of the past, and lost its balance completely. Consequently, formative expression was preferred over function. Even the skilled craftsmen were in a state of confusion, as they were forced to change their methods. They could no longer rely on the skills of their hands as they were now required to learn how to use machines. The circumstances were such that everything was in a state of change, and this rapid transition in the craft world was not easy for the craftsmen.

The modern period in Korean craft actually when Korea exhibited craft objects at the Chicago World Columbian Exposition in 1893. This was followed by the 1900 Exposition Universelle in Paris, where woodwork, lacquer ware, ceramics, brass wares and instruments from Korea were exhibited. With the participation in these two expositions, the government precipitated the promotion and development of Korean craft. In 1902 the Office of Agriculture and Commerce temporarily changed to operate as the office in charge of passing legislations for expositions. They bought craft objects made by different craftsmen around the country. These were then assessed and awarded to encourage craftsmen. In 1906, the government established an institution for technical skills, and the Hansung Art Production Institute was founded in 1908 by the Joseon Royal court in the Changdeokgung Palace. The Institute continued on in 1920 after the occupation of Japan, for the development of traditional and modern techniques in craft. The name changed to *Yiwangjik* Art Research Institute (李王職美術品研究所) and it reproduced the original forms of Korean traditional craft. There was strong emphasis on the restoration of traditional techniques. However the craftsmen did not have the dedication to pass on their skills to younger generations due to the discrimination for their talents. Thus many discarded their original occupation, and sought after new careers. For this reason, traditional craft was unable to be transmitted to the younger generation. Instead, it continued on as everyday objects for ordinary use. In the 1930s the Korean people who studied at the Tokyo School of Fine Art actively worked centering around the Joseon Art exhibition. Although they were not able to possess a cultural identity, it is possible to understand that they struggled to keep the tradition and ethnicity.

4) Architecture

The majority of architectural constructions built during the modern period consisted of structure for western diplomatic purposes or for commercial developments as Korea at the time was forced to westernize. Westernized buildings such as churches established with the introduction of Christianity, hospitals and educational buildings began to appear. After the Japanese colonization, the government-general established banks, government and public offices, schools and so on. Architectures with Renaissance or eclectic style were increased.

With the opening of Korea from the late 19th century, western civilization including unfamiliar styles in architecture also streamed in, and traditional architecture confronted changes. The new architectural form was introduced heteronomously due to the political situation of the period. The Japanese governmental offices were first established in Wonsan (1880), Incheon (1883), Seoul and Busan (1884). In these cities, diplomatic consulates and offices for government affairs were established consecutively. These were the 2-story wooden constructions, with western style) based on the elementary Japanese technique. Moreover with Christianity, the Baejae school building was established in 1886. Afterwards the Jeong-dong Church (1898), the Myeong-dong Catholic bishopric (1890), Myeong-dong Cathedral (1892–1898), and so on were all built in the Gothic style. Throughout the 1900s, buildings following the development of public transportation facilities such as trams and trains, and western style houses for foreign missionaries, religious and medical institutions related to missionaries were becoming more and more common.

The result of the 1905 Russo-Japanese war, the 1905 Protectorate Treaty, enabled the Japanese to take over Korea. With this they brought specialists from Japan, placing them as managers and operators in government official buildings. The government general building, in particular, was erected from 1916 until 1926 after the period of ten years. This was designed in the Renaissance style in stone. It was the largest construction to have been built during the Japanese occupation period. After the 1930s Korean architects such as Park Dong-jin, Park Gil-yong became prominent. They built university buildings, music halls, school dormitories using stone in the Gothic style. They presented compromised architectural styles between Korean and Western while also including the characteristics of the architect themselves.

2. Dance

1) Re-establishment of Traditional Dance

(1) Re-establishment of Folk Dance and Adaptation for Stage Performance

The first Western-style performance venue, *Wongaksa* opened in Korea in 1908, and it brought about a complete change in court dance and folk dance. The people in charge of dance performances for this newfangled performing theater were *gisaeng* (female entertainers) who belonged either to the court or regional provinces. Performances presented on stage included *seungmu*, *ipchum* (basic dance), *salpurichum* (dance of exorcism), *taepyeongmu* (dance for national prosperity and peace) by the *gisaeng*, and *Nongakmu* (peasants' dance) and masked dances by male performers.

Throughout this time, it was the professional *gisaeng* who developed the traditional *gibangchum* (dance of pleasure house) into a theatrical dance form by presenting them on the Western-style stage, leading to the resurrection of traditional dance. <Fig. 6.11>

After *gwonbeon* (a kind of institution to train and supervise *gisaeng*) was abolished, groups of *gisaeng* established an association and led an active operation, attempting artistic training and working on stage performances. Later, however, such *gisaeng* associations were integrated into *gwonbeon* again and each regional *gwonbeon* invited specialized instructors to teach instruments, dance, calligraphic painting, etiquette. During this period, many dance teachers emerged, one of whom was Han Seong-jun (1874–1942) who earned master

| Fig. 6.11 Images of *Gisaeng* in the Modern Era

| Fig. 6.12 Han Seong-jun

status. <Fig. 6.12>

Han Seong-jun was a person who took the dance of professional entertainers, which was previously performed secretively only in *gisaeng* houses, to the stage, and a pioneer who led in the re-establishment of Korean folk dance. He left a venerable legacy of rebuilding dances preserved until today as Korea's most representative traditional dances, such as the *seungmu*, *salpurichum*, and *taepyeongmu*. He completed dances of a vastly different paradigm from his predecessors by gathering diverse folk elements influenced by *gut* and masked dances, artistic elements from the *gwonbeon*, formal elements from *gungjung jeongjae* (court dance), and stage use elements from the Western theater, and mixing all the elements into the dance. Han's main dance heirs include his granddaughter Han Young-sook and Kang Sun-young, who succeeded *Taepyeongmu* from him.

(2) Succession of *Yiwangjik aakbu* and *Gungjung jeongjae*

The collapse of the Joseon Period triggered the collapse of *gungjung jeongjae*. The early 1900s was a period when court dance was in danger of disappearing due to Japanese colonial rule. With the abolition of *Jangakwon*, the government agency in charge of music, most court musicians and dancers were dispersed and the tradition of court art seemed on the verge of extinction. Fortunately, however, the Japanese government-general kept a minimal amount of staff required for Confucian *jongmyo* and *munmyo* sacrificial rituals; This group became known as the *Yiwangjik aakbu*. Compared to the previous *Jangakwon*, the *Yiwangjikaakbu* was considerably reduced in terms of scale, quantity and quality, but it generated a crucial figure in using this environment to restore *gungjung jeongjae*, namely Kim Cheon-heung. He established the fundamental grounds on which the *jeongjae* tradition could be

| Fig. 6.13 *Chunaengjeon*, Kim Cheon-heung, The Association of Commemorative Services for Simso Kim Cheon-heung

continued through the present day.

Kim Cheon-heung (1909–2007) called the "last *mudong* (boy dancer) of Joseon," held an important position in the history of Korean dance by re-interpreting court music and dance. Among scholars and academics, Kim is thought of as "living dance history" and an "authentic heir of Korean court dance." While Han Seong-jun was responsible for re-interpreting folk dance, Kim Cheon-heung devoted his life to court dance. <Fig. 6.13>

His major achievements are recognized as a holder of Important Intangible Cultural Property No. 1, *jongmyo jeryeak* and No. 39, "Cheoyongmu" and reproducing *gungjung jeongjae* based on ancient written documents. He also presented a new future path for the dance world by introducing several original theatrical dance performances including *Cheoyongrang, and manpasikjeok* on the stage as a live play of original traditional Korean music.

2) Emergence of New Dance

(1) Trends of Korean Dance in the Modern Era

Along with the introduction of new civilization and culture in the time of enlightenment, Western dances like the Russian Copak, began to make their way into the country. With the introduction of diverse foreign dances, Korean traditional dance went through a dramatic change around the 1920s. This change was itself spurred by the shock created by a performance of Japanese modern dancer, Ishii Baku (1886–1926) in Korea in March 1926. The performance set the stage for a new conception and style to emerge in the Korean dance world. The Korean modern dance was designed to fit the Western-style stage; the new styles combined with the Korean aesthetics and themes were referred to as "New dance." In other words, a large number of performers who created new dances by adding elements of traditional Korean dance onto the foundations of foreign dance; performers included Choi Seung-hee, Bae Gu-ja, Park Whae-seon and Jo Taek-won. The representative works of new dance include *chyoribdong* (youngster wearing a straw hat), *buchaechum* (fan dance), *jangguchum* (hourglass-shaped drum dance), *bosalchum* (dance of old female Buddhist) and so on, which were created in the style of a theatrical stage on the background of Korean music and themes.

Dance in 1950s, like other art fields, was in a complete crisis. The dance world was put on hold at that time due to the defection or abduction to North Korea of certain dancers like Choi Seung-hee, and the outbreak of the Korean War. After the war, Korean dance evolved around stage performances based on the work of research organizations. The dancers of this period included Song Beom, Kim Baek-bong, Jin Su-bang, Lim Seong-nam, Kang

Sun-young, Kim Jin-geol, Ju Ri, Jeong In-bang, and Park Whae-seon.

In this period, the differentiation between traditional dance, new dance, modern dance, and ballet were not distinct, and as a result, the world of dance became of hodge-podge of all genres. Most dancers performed traditional and modern dances at the same time or performed ballet, modern dance, and dance from the southern regions, which were popular at that time. This situation persisted until the 1960s when dance was established as an academic subject in academia.

(2) Joseon's Legendary Dancer, Choe Seung-hee

Choe Seung-hee first decided to walk the path of a dancer after seeing the performance of the Japanese modern dancer, Ishii Baku in Korea. Deeply inspired by the performance, she went to study dance in Japan. Upon her return to Korea, she successfully held a returnee performance and soon, at the age of 19, she opened a research institute to pursue her own world of dance.

She established her reputation as a successful dancer through long-run performances not only in Korea but also in Japan, Europe and South America. She promoted Korea through her dances as a world star dancer with the nickname "The Dancer from the Orient."

| Fig. 6.14 *Chyoribdong*, Choe Seung-hee

觸合ふ心の琴線

絢爛 麗人花園に

内台鮮の優しい融和

自分を生かすこと

まづ先決問題

舞踊精進を語る

| Fig. 6.15 Newspaper Article on *Bosalchum*, Choe Seung-hee

Starting out with foreign dances, her work went through evolutions based on a variety of cultural experience. After Korea's independence, she returned to Korea but agonized under accusations that she was pro-Japanese. Then, influenced politically by her husband Ahn Mak, she defected to North Korea. After defection, she created theatrical dance pieces with a strong revolutionary character in North Korea and China. She also put her energy into education and creation, teaching her principles through national dances. However in 1958, her husband was expelled from the Communist Party for political reasons and subsequently Choe Seung-hee was removed from the party as well in 1967. She died in 1969.

Choe Seung-hee's representative dance works include hundreds of works such as *ehheyranohara, chyoribdong, bosalchum.* Her most important achievement was the cultivation of the "New dance," the Korean modern-contemporary dance of the time and also for the international acclaim she garnered as a dancer. Choe Seung-hee, a pioneer of Korean "New dance," was given much attention from all social fields as an icon of the modern woman wearing fashionably bobbed hair and Western outfits, which was an emblem of an elite female at that time. The world of her works was both national and international. Choi Seung-hee gained a great deal of popularity through long performance engagements, which was very rare as a solo dancer, and prolonged foreign tours.

3. Music

The modern period in Korean history is characterized by Korea's opening its diplomatic doors to the world, and the introduction of Western culture and music. Indigenous music of Korea was now termed as *joseonak*, music of Joseon, which included *dangak*, *aak*, *hyangak*, and *minsogak* (folk music), which was set against Western music, called *seoyangak* (Western music) or *eumak* (music). This is similar to the experience when *dangak* was imported during the Unified Silla period, causing the indigenous music being called *hyangak*. After opening the country ports, until as late as the 1930s, *joseonak* was the mainstream music in Korea, while Western music was performed and taught at schools and churches. However, after this point, Western music gradually began to gain more and more popularity in Korea.

1) Rise and Decline of *Joseonak*, the Traditional Music

During this period, the age-old social class system of the Joseon Dynasty was abolished, and music was becoming more and more commercialized. This caused a change in the traditional order of musicians. With the abolishment of the class system, the hierarchical order maintained within Korean music was also undermined. Theaters were being built, with music becoming commercialized, and this caused commoners to enter into the world of traditional music for the ruling class. Court music and other musical genre now came to be performed on modern stages for the general public. As a result, rather than court music or *pungnyu* music, characterized by emotional reserve, folk music, having more liberty in expressiveness and reflecting the state of society, began to be popular. With the fall of court musical institutions, court music became drastically contracted, and *pungnyu* music barely maintained its old form. On the other hand, folk music became more and more appealing to the modern audience and modern folk repertoires were composed for diverse stages and purposes.

(1) Court Music

With the fall of the Joseon Dynasty, court music virtually came to an end. This is because court music was a symbol for the royal court, patronized by the court in order to manifest its grandeur. The numbers of court musicians were drastically reduced and even the few remaining repertoires underwent a remarkable change. The number of musicians affiliated with the court music institute reduced from 1000 to 50, changing its name From *Jangakwon* to *Yiwangjikaakbu* (Music Bureau of Yi Dynasty), which was only a small branch. Among the court music still being played were *munmyo jeryeak*, *jongmyo jeryeak*, "Yeomillakman (slow Yeomillak)," "Boheoja," "Nakyangchun," "Jeongeup" (now it is called "Sujecheon"), "Dongdong" and etc. However, among these, *jongmyo jeryeak*, "Yeomillakman" and "Nakyangchun" came to feature irregularities in rhythm.

| Sound. 10 *Jongmyo jeryeak* in irregular rhythm, "Huimoon," Performed by National Gugak Center

Moreover only parts of "Jeongeup" and "Dongdong" were extracted from their original pieces, and turned into new pieces. These newly changed repertoires are transmitted unto today. Most of the national rituals from the Joseon Dynasty were no longer performed, with only *munmyo jeryeak* and *jongmyo jeryeak* remaining. Therefore most of the *aak* repertoire of the former dynasty has disappeared. The *mumyo jeryeak* that we hear today is the version created during King Sejong's reign.

| Sound. 11 Court Music, "Sujechen (*Jeongeup*)," Performed by National Gugak Center

The role of *Yiwangjikaakbu* was to promote court music to the general public and to educate musicians in traditional music. Performance of court music took place in its contracted form, for occasions such as the *jongmyo* and *munmyo* rituals. Musicians at the *Yiwangjikaakbu* would perform at radio station, in order to introduce court music to the general public, make recordings, and even appear in motion pictures. The center also established a modern music school under its branch called *Yiwangjikaakbuwon Yangseongso* (Educational Institution of the *Yiwangjikaakbu*) for young musicians in court music. In this school, music and theory in court and *pungnyu* music, as well as ordinary subjects for secondary school and western music theory, were taught. With endless effort of *Yiwangjukaakbu* and its musicians, court music tradition has been transmitted until today.

(2) *Pungnyu* Music

Pungnyu music, essentially music for the aristocratic class during Joseon period, suffered even a greater reduction than the court music tradition. In the modern period, it was maintained mostly by male musicians from the former dynasty, students at the *Yiwangjikaakbu* and *gisaeng* (court female entertainers). *Joseon Jeongak Jeonseupso*, a professional school for teaching *pungnyu* music, was founded in 1909 and taught *pungnyu*, *gagok*, *gasa*, *sijo*, and "Yeongsanhoesang," as well as Western music. However, facing financial difficulties, this institute came to focus only on musical performance, with little resources left for education. Afterwards, *pungnyu* repertoires came to be absorbed by the professional musicians at *Yiwangjikaakbu*, and, with *aak*, it came under the category *jeongak* (literally, "proper music").

(3) Folk Music

With the modern performance environment of this period centering on public theatres, the recording industry, and the broadcasting system, traditional folk music of Korea underwent a great change. With commercialization and general distribution of music, professional musicians in the local provinces relocated to Seoul, the capital city, performing in theaters and on professional stages. *Pansori*, which was traditionally performed by one singer and a drummer, came to be performed by many singers, resulting in a new genre called *changgeuk* (theatrical and staged version of *pansori*). As it gained more and more popularity, several *changgeuk* troupes were founded, some of which still continue today, including the National *Changgeuk* Theatre (*Gungnip Changgeukdan*). <Fig. 6.16>

Meanwhile, local folk songs in various provinces were reborn as popular songs by professional singers. New folk songs, *sinminyo*, based on traditional melodies and forms were

| Fig. 6.16 *Changgeuk* Performance

composed. Professional singers created a new song genre *japga*. Unlike folk songs, *japga* were rooted in the professional singer's songs and featured long and elaborate melodies with epic contents.

Meanwhile, *sanjo*, which had been previously performed only on the *gayageum*, spread to other instruments such as the *geomun-go*, *daegeum*, *piri*, and *haegeum*.

2) Influx of Western Music

Western music was imported through Western missionaries and military bands. Western missionaries taught Western hymns and Western music in schools. With the rise of Christianity in 1905, this type of music was spread very quickly in Korean society along with its religion. At the same time, the hymns gave birth to a new type of song called *changga*, the lyrics of which were patriotic and promoted enlightenment through Western civilization. Western music began to be taught in public schools while Korean traditional music was no longer taught. As a result, Western music became prevalent in Korean society. With the establishment of the modern Korean government in 1901, Western style military bands were established, and this also contributed to the spreading of Western-style music. The music performed by military bands became the foundation of Western style instrumental music in Korea. It was during this period that Korean composers with Western musical training made their debut. They composed children's songs, *gagok* (Western style lyric songs), and popular songs as well as music for Western musical instruments in the style of Western music.

(1) Hymnals and *Changga*

American missionaries in Korea first published a hymnal called *chanyangga* (hymns) in 1894, and began to teach hymns to Koreans. The songs included in this book came from the standard hymns of the New Laudes Domini (N.I.D) and the Gospel Hymns Compilation (G.H.C.), in the tradition of American Presbyterian church. These melodies were in the Western major/minor systems, and far from traditional Korean music. In 1909, another hymnal was published, but its contents were similar to *chanyangga* with only one song composed in the traditional Korean style. These hymnals exerted a great influence not only on the religious songs in the Korean Protestant church, but also on the independence songs, anti-Japanese campaign songs, and patriotic songs composed during the Japanese colonial period.

From 1896, *changga* also appeared, which was essentially modern Korea songs composed in a Western style. The melody was similar to that for religious hymns, but the text emphasized patriotism, enlightenment, and secular contents. These songs gained great popularity from 1890s to 1920s, reflecting and influencing the emotions of the ordinary Korean people. Like all popular music, their texts directly expressed the feelings of the people. These songs were later divided into *gagok*, *yuhaengga* (popular tunes), and children songs for targeting respective audiences. During the Japanese colonization, *changga* with patriotic content were banned, replaced by a new style of songs composed in Japan that were officially taught at schools.

(2) Development of *Changga*: Lyric songs, Popular Songs, Children's Songs

Western style modern lyric songs, *gagok*, are the more artistic version of *changga*, especially in terms of lyrics. Early *gagok* were composed by those who received their education from Western missionaries and had musical training through study abroad. Many of these songs were on a highly artistic level and were sung by professionally-trained singers. One of the earliest *gagok* was Hong Nan-pa's "Bongseonhwa." The song is about balsam flower, figuratively standing for the home country under Japanese occupation. After "Bongseonhwa," similar style *gagok* repertoires were composed.

Meanwhile, *changga* changed into a more simplistic and popular style of song. After the failure of the 3.1 Independence Movements, Koreans were experiencing emotional frustration and desperation. Reflecting such feeling were some of the nihilistic songs that became popular among the general public.

One of the offsprings of *changga* was children's songs. The lyrics for these songs were easily spread, contributing to the formation of public opinion and affecting the social atmosphere. Although many such songs were composed, they eventually became banned by the Japanese government, and only Japanese *changga* were allowed to be taught at school.

(3) Military Bands

The first Western style military band in Korea came about when Franz Eckert, a German composer in February of 1901, was invited to Korea. In March of the same year, he established a military band that had their debut in September for the 50th birthday of Korean Emperor Gojong. Although the members only had four months to practice, this performance was a success, after which the band not only performed for military affairs but also for all types of national ceremonies for the royal family and the government. In addition, they performed one or two weekly concerts for the general public. Aside from such concert activities, Eckert composed many pieces for the band, including the national anthem, and taught Western music to many young musicians, which contributed greatly in establishing Western musical tradition in Korea.

The music of the military band helped in emotionally encouraging Koreans under Japanese rule. After the Eulsa Treaty of 1905, the band was dispersed in 1907 when the army was abolished. Yet the royal family kept a small band, under the name *Yiwangjik Yangakdae* (Western music bureau of Yi Dynasty). However, there were financial difficulties in maintaining the band, which eventually was dissolved when Eckert died in 1916. Three years later, in 1919, Baek U-yong, who was a former member of the military band, attempted to reestablish a private band called *Gyeongseong Akdae* (Gyeongseong Band), but this too was soon dispersed due to financial difficulties. After the disbandment, its members entered the *Yiwangjikaakkbu*, working on transcribing traditional Korean music, composing *sinminyo*, commercial music, film music, and popular music. Some of them also taught at schools, establishing their own school bands.

Contemporary Age
(Late 20th Century–Present)

Ⅶ. Contemporary Age (Late 20th Century–Present)

The Republic of Korea was founded in 1948, and democracy was finally achieved, but only after a series of struggles including the April 19 student's revolution of 1960, the May 18 civil uprising in Gwangju in 1980, and the June democracy movement of 1987. To rise up from the ashes of the Korean War, from the 1960s the country focused on rebuilding the national economy and succeeded in achieving miraculously fast economic growth. Such economic and scientific growth continued through the turbulent 1970s and 1980s, which were marked by series of political incidents, namely numerous demonstrations against the military government that had seized power in a coup d'etat by General Park Chung-hee and by General Chun Du-Hwan. In 1992, the military government, which had continued for some 30 years, was replaced with a civilian government, opening an era of advanced democracy. Today, Korea is counted as one of the top ten most powerful economies in the world and has firmly established its place as a leader in the field of information technology. Furthermore, Koreans are now pursuing cultural diversity in a more liberal social atmosphere, and while exercising greater autonomy in acceptance of Western culture are creatively building on and developing traditional Korean culture to ensure its future survival.

1. Art

After the Korean War (1950–1953), formalist modernism, including Art Informel and geometric abstraction, dominated the domestic art scene, a trend that continued through the 1970s. Especially during the 1970s, Korean art became preoccupied with the search for identity, and monochrome painting emerged as the leading trend for artists attempting to find a new "Koreanness" in art that could maintain tradition and at the same time keep pace with international movements. Additionally, a series of young artists had already begun to challenge the modernist aesthetic of "art for art's sake" as early as the late 1960s, and until the end of the 1990s engaged in experimental avant-garde practices, creating diverse works under such headings as "happening," "event," "conceptual art" and "performance art."

Following the military government of the 1970s, when the President was all-powerful, the 1980s were a politically turbulent time when critical outlooks on politics and political organizations led to the rise of critical realism. One of the major trends of the time was *Minjung Misul*, a term that can be translated as "people's art," a movement based on discovering art potential in the self determination and fundamental power of the people. In 1992, the military government, which had lasted for 30 years, was finally replaced with a civilian democratic government. In the art world, the political and ideological issues of the 1980s were replaced by a great diversity of subjects, such as the production of meaning in contemporary consumer society and the identity of contemporary human beings, which were explored through various kinds of art activity using high technology and diverse materials.

1) 1960s-70s: Aesthetics of Modernism and Experimental Avant-Garde

(1) Informel Art

The National Art Exhibition (*Gukjeon*), discontinued during the Korean War, was reopened in 1953 when the war ended, and then became the center of conflict between two groups of artists: the Korean Artist Association (*Hanguk Misulga Hyeophoe*), and the Daehan Art Association (*Daehan Misul Hyeophoe*). The government that came to power after the military coup on May 16, 1961 sought to close this divide in the art scene by fusing the two groups into the Korean Art Association (*Hanguk Misul Hyeophoe*). Around this time, several outsider groups joined together to form an anti-institutional organization named Federation of Modern Artists (*Hyeondae Misulga Yeonhapche*). Stand-

| Fig. 7.1 Chu Kyung, Hardship, 1923, Oil on canvas, 52×44cm, National Museum of Contemporary Art, Korea

| Fig. 7.2 Kim Whan- ki, Rondo, 1938, Oil on canvas, 61×71.5cm, National Museum of Contemporary Art, Korea

ing in opposition to the National Exhibition, they argued that Korean art should be kept in line with the international flow of contemporary art. The 1960s were thus peppered with various movements large and small, more than at any other time in history, bringing about a major turning point in the art scene. At the center of these movements was the pursuit of abstract art by young artists who had received formal art education at university and stood opposed to the conservatism represented by the National Art Exhibition.

While tentative moves toward modernism had been made by Chu Kyeong <Fig. 7.1> and Kim Whan-ki <Fig. 7.2> in the 1920s and 30s, the modernist aesthetic did not truly take root until 1957 when two organizations deliberately seeking modernist aesthetics emerged almost simultaneously: the Modern Artist Association (*Hyeondae Misulga Hyeophoe*), formed by artists such as Kim Tschang-yeul, Park Seo-bo, Jeong Sang-hwa, and

| Fig. 7.3 Nam Kwan, Trace of History, 1963, Oil on canvas, Collage and corrosion, 97.5×130.5cm, National Museum of Contemporary Art, Korea

Chung Chang-sup; and the Modern Art Association, formed by artists such as Kim Gyeong and Lee Gyu-sang. The concept of what came to be known in Korea as "Informel Art" was first put forward in a decisive way at the fourth exhibition of the Modern Artist Association in 1958, where the works showed a search for emotional expression and freedom from illusionistic form, similar to the pursuits of the Art Informel movement in Europe and Abstract Expressionism in the United States. Korean Informel artists used free brushwork, dark hues, and heavy application of paint. Hence, their work was closer to European Informel artists such as Wols and Alberto Burri with their powerful lines and textures, rather than American Abstract Expressionists such as Jackson Pollock and Willem de Kooning, who used bright primary colors and action painting techniques. In contrast to these New York based artists who lived amid a sense of geopolitical security in the aftermath of World War II, the European artists had just survived life at the center of the storm, witnessing the frail barriers between life and death. Likewise, the darkness apparent in the work of Korean artists was rooted in the tragedy of the Korean War and the scars it left behind.

| Fig. 7.4 Kim Whan-ki, Mountain and the Moon, 1960, Oil on canvas, 97×162cm, National Museum of Contemporary Art, Korea

Beginning in the mid–1950s, many Korean artists began studying in France and gained first-hand experience of Art Informel, which dominated the Paris art scene at the time. The works of Nam Kwan <Fig. 7.3> or Kwon Ok-yeon, for example, feature natural drips and blobs of paint, and emphasis on paint texture in the style of Tachist abstract painting. But when compared to the European automatic paintings (where the unconscious mind takes over creative activity) featuring rough powerful lines, splashed and spattered paint, or thick application of paint, the works of Korean artists differ in that simplified forms and symbols seek organic harmony in their composition that is not completely deconstructed. As seen in the works of Kim Whan-ki <Fig. 7.4> and Nam Kwan from the late 1950s and early 1960s, Korean artists of this time, while assimilating the Western Informel aesthetic, were searching for a Korean cultural identity and added traditional motifs such as pottery vessels, the moon, plum blossoms, deer, and gold crowns.

Such efforts to keep pace with international trends by accepting the modernist aesthetic, while also searching for a unique expression suited to Korean sensibilities, were apparent not only in the Western-style oil painting (*Seoyanghwa*) circle, but also in the Korean-style ink painting (*Hangukhwa*) circle. A good example is the group *Mookrimhoe* (Ink Forest Group), which was formed in 1960 as Korea's only avant-garde group using the techniques

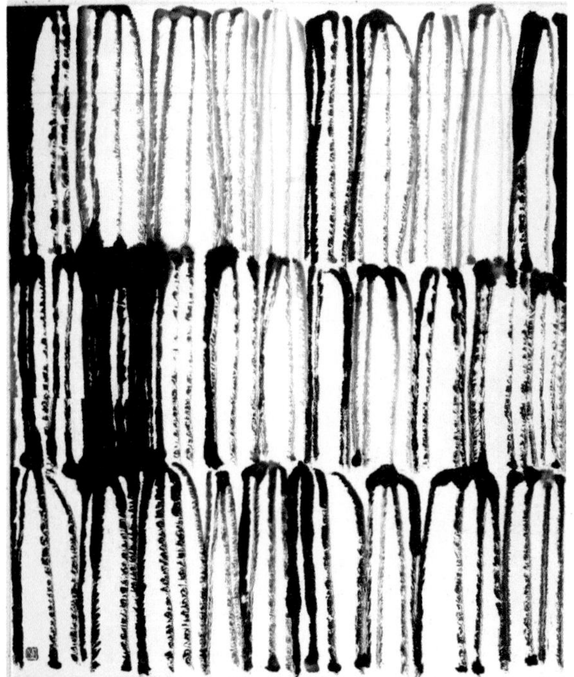

| Fig. 7.5 Suh Se-ok, People, 1983, Ink on hanji, 160×137cm, National Museum of Contemporary Art, Korea

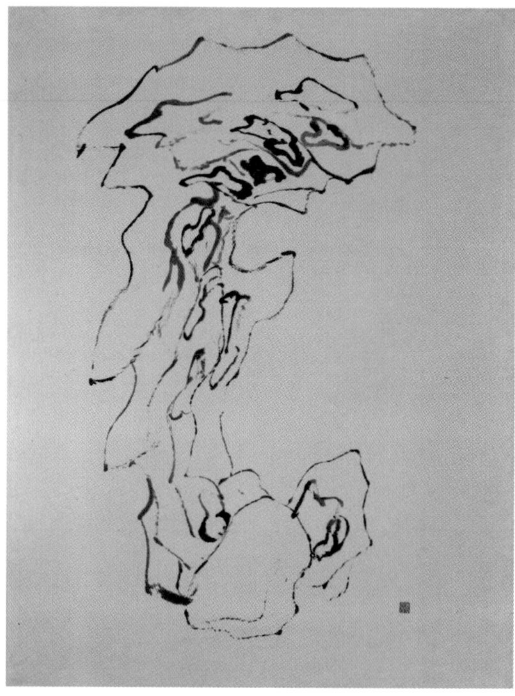

| Fig. 7.6 Song Young-bang, Root of a Cloud, 1969, Ink and light color on hanji, 90×69cm, National Museum of Contemporary Art, Korea

and materials of traditional ink and wash painting, thereby combining tradition with Western art methodologies to express the spirit of Eastern people in abstract language. "People" (*Saramdeul*, <Fig. 7.5>) by Suh Se-ok and "Root of a Cloud" (*Un-geun*, <Fig. 7.6>) by Song Young-bang, who were members of the group, show dots and strokes created with restrained brushwork, and harmony between forms and empty space. The "broken ink" technique (the building up of dense ink washes) and the "spread ink" technique (the natural bleeding of diluted ink washes) are used to create depth and texture. The resulting works have the subtle harmony and high-toned spiritual nature of traditional literati painting and the modern abstract forms of Informel Art. Korean artists continued to seek ways to keep pace with international trends while still maintaining a sense of tradition into the 1970s, a time marked by active debate on the identity of Korean art with the rise of monochrome painting.

(2) Monochrome Painting

After President Park Chung-hee came to power through a military coup, he implemented economic development plans in 1962 to rapidly rebuild the country, which had been reduced to ashes in the Korean War. Park's second term in government, lasting from 1972, when the constitution was revised, to 1979, when Park was assassinated, was a period of turbulence and social confusion arising from the prolonged power of one government. But it also was an era of amazingly rapid economic growth that is sometimes described as "the miracle on the Han River." This was also a time when all sorts of cultural policies were implemented: The Office of Cultural Properties was established in 1961, protection for cultural properties was legislated in 1962, the Ministry of Culture and Information was established in 1968, and a five-year cultural properties development plan was drawn up in 1969 and implemented in 1974. These measures paved the way for more systematic cultural development policies.

Under the Park Chung-hee regime, which strategically used nationalism as a force behind economic and cultural growth, artists had another chance to look back on Korean tradition. Yanagi's theory of distinctive characteristics of Joseon art, which had been applied to the study of traditional Korean art since the Japanese colonial period, was reevaluated and the voice of self-reflection was heard as artists began to question whether they had been critical enough when accepting the aesthetics and methodology of Western art. This mood of self-reflection was extended into the public arena through numerous art magazines, including "Gonggan" (Space), "Hyeondae Misul" (Modern Art), "Gyegan Misul" (Art Quarterly), and "Misul Pyeongnon" (Art Criticism), all of which were rooted in the increased social interest in art and culture that had come with increased economic affluence. In the 1970s, Korean artists began participating more in events such as the Venice Biennale and the Sao Paulo Biennale, and in the process artists naturally began to consider expressing "Koreanness" at the international level.

This was the mood of the 1970s when Park Seo-bo, who had mostly produced works in the Art Informel style, began his "Ecriture" series, covering his canvases in thick white gesso, scratching repeated lines into the surface with a pencil <Fig. 7.7>. During an interview in 1973,

| Fig. 7.7 Park Seo-bo, Ecriture No. 42-78-79-82, 1990, Oil and pencil on cloth, Private collection

| Fig. 7.8 Kwon Young-woo, Untitle, 1980, Cutting on hanji, 163×131cm, National Museum of Contemporary Art, Korea

Park said, "Just as a Joseon Dynasty potter turned the vessel on his wheel with no conscious thought, I endlessly repeat straight lines on the canvas with an empty mind." Through the act of repeated movement, the artist sought the state of "no-idea and no-thought" as if practicing asceticism, suggesting he was trying to succeed the spirit of traditional Korean art through different means such as Western monochrome painting methodology.

Kwon Young-woo, using traditional Korean paper made of mulberry bark, called *hanji*, explored the natural color and texture of the paper as material for his art. Pasting the soft *hanji* in two or three layers, he made use of the bumps and the shadow effect created as the paper was ripped, punctured, and scratched. His works exhibit both the familiarity of Korean sensibilities and the delicate details of abstract form. <Fig. 7.8>

In addition, many other artists such as Chung Chang-sup <Fig. 7.9>, Ha Jong-hyeon, Yun Myeong-no, and Kim Gi-rin produced diverse works during the Monochrome art movement of the 1970s and 1980s. Monochrome painting emphasized the use of white or neutral color, modular units of repeated forms, and "all-over" composition. While the artists were often criticized as imitators of Minimalism, the monochrome painters argued that the flat field in their work was the result of physical action in an attempt to achieve oneness of artistic activity with matter, nature, and the pure energy of nature. They asserted that Monochrome art, therefore, was clearly distinct from Minimalism, which sought to reduce expression to its minimum. However, the whole debate may have been irrelevant. Monochrome art took root as the major trend of Korean art in the 1970s because the artists of the time, like their predecessors, were in tune with the aesthetics and methodologies of international modern art, but at the same time carried out endless experimentation in an attempt to succeed the tradition and emotion of traditional Korean art.

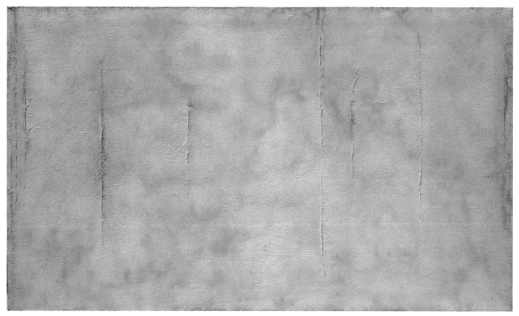

| Fig. 7.9 Chung Chang-sup, Paper Mulberry No.85099, 1985, Dakji on cloth, 140×240cm, National Museum of Contemporary Art, Korea

(3) Experimental Art

In the late 1960s, when Informel Art had become established as the leading trend, some young artists began to challenge this aesthetic with experimental works. Members of the group *Mudongin*, such as Lee Tae-hyun, Kim Young-ja, and Choi Bung-hyun held two exhibitions in 1967: "Exhibition of Experimental Modern Art" in June and "Young Artists' Exhibition" in December, showing on both occasions works that made use of mass-produced objects, discarded items, and popular everyday images. Lee Tae-hyun's "Myeong" series <Fig. 7.10>, consisting of a succession of gas masks or black rubber gloves, or Kim Young-ja's images of a coal briquette and a box of matches blown up to gigantic scale <Fig. 7.11>, presented a head-on challenge to Informel Art, which focused on aesthetic absolutism and internalized subjective vision.

The latter half of the 1960s, when such experimental art activity had emerged in Korea, was a time when Pop Art was the major art trend overseas. Reorganizing values and meaning into a semiotic order to examine consumer society, Pop Art took a cooler and more objective approach than the provocative and expressionist Neo-Dada movement, which had arisen in New York in the mid–1950s in reaction to Abstract Expressionism. On the Paris art scene, by the 1950s Nouveau Réalisme had appeared, a movement that explored the structure and

| Fig. 7.10 Lee Tae-hyun, "Myeong" Breath of Life 1, 1967, Gas mask and knapsack, 140×70×14cm

| Fig. 7.11 Kim Young-ja, Octagonal Box of Matches, 1967, Painted wood, 90×130×130cm

nature of modern industrial society by making use of mass-produced goods, industrial waste, and posters. Comparing the objet installations of Korean avant-garde artists of the 1960s, some critics scorned the Korean experimental movement as an imitation of Neo-Dada and Nouveau Réalisme works from ten years before.

However, the question of who was first to adopt everyday objects and reproduced images in art is not the only standard in evaluating the significance of the art works. What is more important is to evaluate an art work's importance by investigating the historical and cultural context that gave rise to artistic experimentation in each cultural sphere, and how the historical foundations and causes of the times are manifested in the works of art. The emerging Korean experimental art of the late–1960s, a time marked by domestic political turmoil, was an activity that explored artistic issues in terms of form, but more fundamentally was a physical expression of political and social resistance.

The politically-charged use of art in Korea at this time could also be seen in the art form known as the "Happening," which created a stir in the art scene because of its use of provocative imagery and performance. Via the Happening, artists were able to take their work out of the ateliers and galleries and into the cafes, streets, and other places of everyday

| Fig. 7.12 Young Artists Union, Happening with Vinyl Umbrellas and Candles (photograph), 1967. 12

| Fig. 7.13 The 4th Group, The Funeral of the Old Art (photograph), 1970. 8. 15

life. They also broke away from traditional materials such as canvas, paint, and brushes.

The first Happening in Korea took place on Dec. 14, 1967, at the exhibition hall of the Federation of Young Artists when ten young artists performed "Happening with Vinyl Umbrellas and Candles" <Fig. 7.12>. The plastic umbrella, a symbol of the nuclear umbrella, expressed criticism of modern civilization where the fear of nuclear weapons is ever-present, while the candles, symbolic of a pure spirit, expressed the enduring human spirit and will to light the darkness. This happening, which startled conservative elements in the Korean art scene, was followed by others including "Nude and Transparent Balloon" and "Murder by the Han River" in 1968, and "The Funeral of the Old Art" in 1970 <Fig. 7.13>. Happenings became a weapon with which to challenge the rigid aesthetics and arrogance of the art establishment, as well as the tightly controlled social system.

"The Funeral of the Old Art," a happening organized by The 4th Group, a band of artists formed in June 1970, took place on August 15 – Korea's independence day – at Sajik Park in Seoul. Standing before the image of the famous Neo-Confucian scholar Yi I (pen name Yulgok), the artists read a proclamation against the art establishment, and placing the proclamation inside a coffin, they held a street demonstration, holding pickets reading "Death of the Cultured Person." But with the proliferation of student demonstrations, battles with riot police, and other political incidents, the rigid Korean society of the time found it hard to accept such extreme art expression. In the end, all students who took part in the "The Funeral

| Fig. 7.14 Kim Gu-rim, From Phenomenon to Traces, 1970, Ice and plastic bucket, 20×170×120cm

of the Old Art" demonstration were arrested, bringing this particular happening to an end.

If the Happening of the latter half of the 1960s contained some aspects of the Neo-Dada movement, the purpose of which was to create a scandal, then the experimental avant-garde "Event" of the 1970s approached the world with reason rather than emotion, questioning the relationship between nature and human beings, the material and immaterial, and time and place, while showing leanings toward Conceptual Art.

Kim Gu-rim, a member of the AG Group (Korean Avant-Garde Association) that was formed in 1969 and disbanded in 1975, displayed an installation titled "From Phenomenon to Traces" <Fig. 7.14> at the first AG Group exhibition held in May 1970. It consisted of three red plastic tubes, each filled with ice, and a piece of tracing paper placed on top of the ice. The aim was to show a process: Over time the ice melted and the tracing paper floated on the water; then when the water evaporated, the tracing paper sat at the bottom of the tubes. In this work, Kim explored the idea of human reason through analysis; relationships among matter, time, and space; and observation of the process of change over time. Lee Seung-taek, another member of the AG Group, produced a series titled "Wind" <Fig. 7.15> that consisted of pieces of plastic or cloth hung on old trees or ropes in wide open spaces to make them fly in the wind. They prompted the viewer to feel the life and existence of the invisible wind and reflect on the relationship between matter and non-matter, emptiness and fullness, and nature and human beings. These artists who posed aesthetic and philosophical

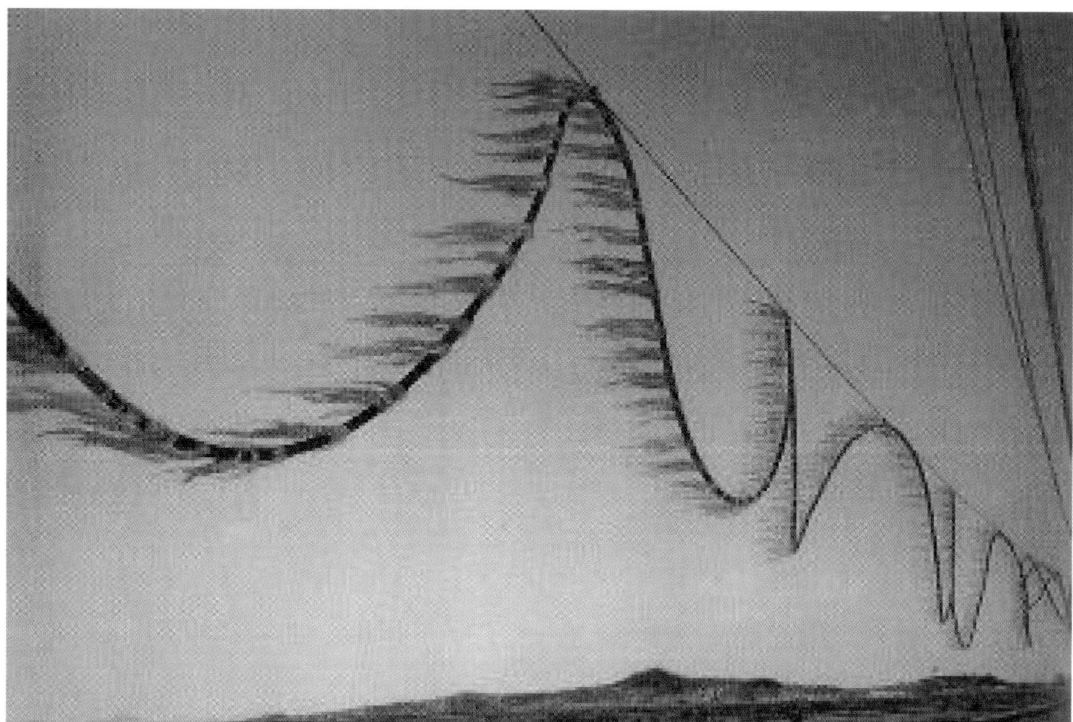

| Fig. 7.15 Lee Seung-taek, Wind, 1971

questions both through the sort of logical thinking associated with the West as well Eastern sensibility can be seen as conceptual artists.

After the Happenings and Events, avant-garde art continued into the 1980s when diverse forms of expression such as art, music, dance, theater, and video were blended together into "Performance." Artists at this time eagerly adopted elements external to the art, such as sound, lighting, and audience participation, as a reaction to the art of the 1970s, which was considered too static and conceptual. An increased number of large events were another reason for this development. The 1986 Asian Olympics and the 1988 Olympics, held in Seoul, created opportunities for artists working alone in different fields to work together on the same project. Such communal art performances, along with people's art, which also had become a significant art trend in the 1980s, reflected the efforts of artists to take art out into the public.

2) 1980s: Critical Realism

(1) People's Art

In the 1960s–70s, Korean art circles focused on experimental art, which was strongly conceptual, along with the formalist aesthetics of modernism. However, by the end of the 1970s, artists had begun to investigate Hyperrealism in their pursuit of a new figurative art <Fig. 7.16>. Kim Tschang-yeul, whose previous works from the 1960s–70s had the characteristics of Informel Art, embarked on works depicting water drops with hyper-realistic techniques in the 1980s <Fig. 7.17>. These works, which show the exquisite harmony be-

| Fig. 7.16 Ji Seok-cheol, Reaction, 1980, Oil on paper, 145.5×97cm, National Museum of Contemporary Art, Korea

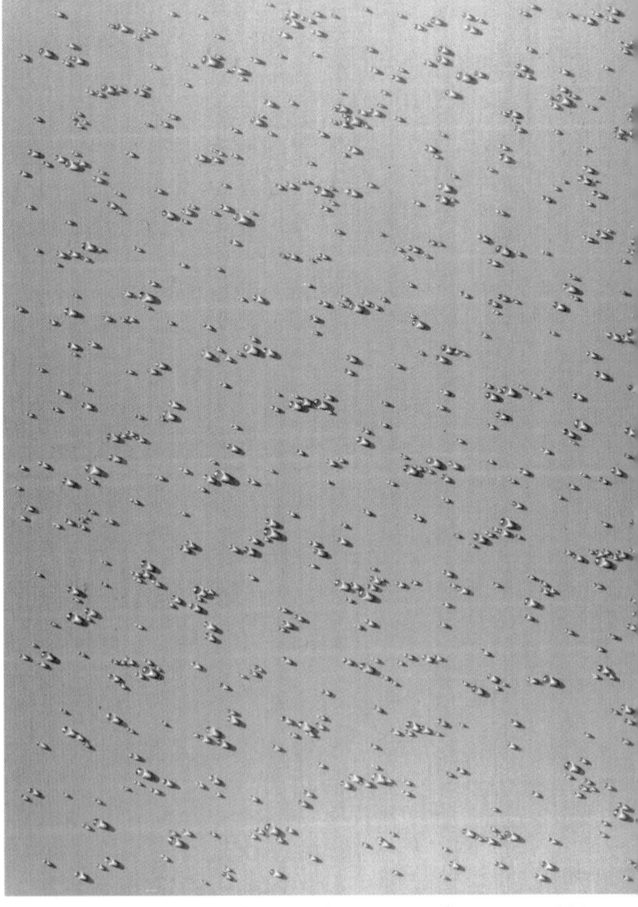

| Fig. 7.17 Kim Tschang-yeul, Water drop, 1978, Oil on canvas, 181×226cm, National Museum of Contemporary Art, Korea

tween water drops that look as if they could roll down at any minute, and the treatment and arrangement of shadows that emphasize the two-dimensionality of the canvas, evoke a delicate sense of life through the elements of water and light. On that point, Kim's works are very original and distinct from other hyperrealist paintings that are generally dry and objective in expression, such as images captured by the camera.

After President Park Chung-hee was assassinated on Oct. 25, 1979, a military coup took place and martial law was imposed in Korea, driving society into great political turmoil. The Korean art scene needed a new style of art that could reflect the spirit of the times and social reality, rather than modernism which pursued art for art's sake. Against this background, an artist group called Reality and Utterance (*Hyeon-silgwa Baleon*) was formed at the end of 1979, aiming to produce works criticizing the reality around them while appealing to realist sensibilities. The artists of this group portrayed the spirit of the people who resisted military dictatorship and the materialism of capitalist society, and the realities and pains of ordinary people's lives <Fig. 7.18>. In "Marketing

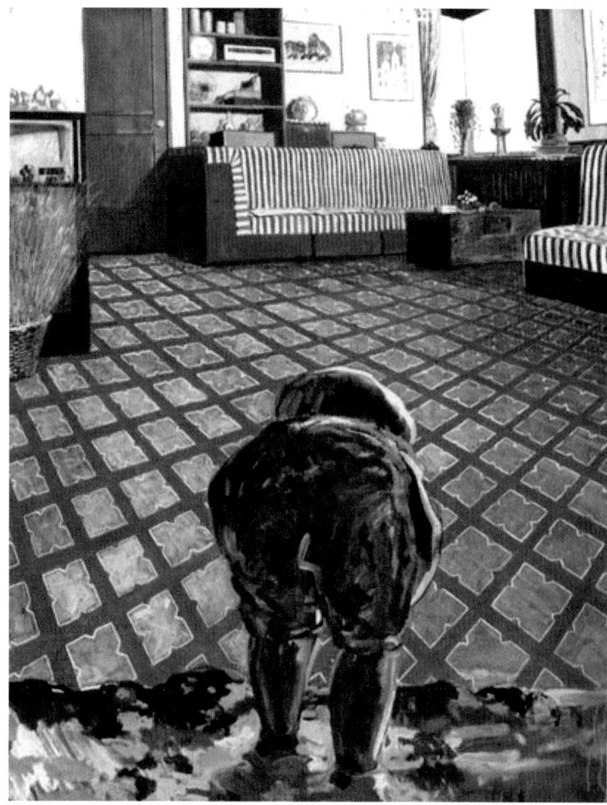

| Fig. 7.18 Kim Jung-heun, Lucky Mono-Lum Creates an Affluent Life, 1981, Oil and acrylic on canvas, 90×65cm

| Fig. 7.19 Oh Yoon, Marketing I - Hell Paintings, 1980, 162×131cm

| Fig. 7.20 Oh Yoon, Windy Place, 1985

| Fig. 7.21 Doo-rung, I go on my land, 1983, Ink and acrylic on cloth

I" <Fig. 7.19> by Oh Yoon, a representative member of Reality and Utterance, one can read a nationalist warning against the indiscreet introduction of foreign culture and criticism of consumer society, where everything is converted into economic value in the form of merchandise. Oh also endeavored to express the images of people who hungered for an ordinary life, simple and wholesome, through crude lines and rough materials on multiple woodprints such as "Windy Place." <Fig. 7.20>

Similarly, the Gwangju Liberal Artists' Association (*Gwangju Jayu Misulin*), established in 1979, organized a theatrical group named Work and Play in the aftermath of the 1980 civilian uprising in Gwangju, presenting themselves as successors to traditional culture. The council also opened a "Civilian Art School" and instituted the idea of public art education, making use of the public-friendly properties of prints. Another people's art group, Doo-rung, worked in conjunction with student activists, laborers, and social activists, and tried to create collective works by opening an art school for the general public in an effort to reject cultural elitists <Fig. 7.21>.

(2) Rise of Feminist Art

Korean feminist art began in the same context as the development of critical realism, which stood against all sorts of power mechanisms suppressing the freedom of human beings in the 1980s, a period marked by countless dark political incidents in Korea. At the time it was difficult for the issue of gender to be included in the concept of community, that is, people or nation, as advocated by groups leading people's art. Feminist artists noticed that point and began to focus on the life and reality of women as social minorities, making an issue of gender inequality in Korean society. Female painters before them such as Ra Hye-seok <Fig. 7.22> and Chun Kyung-ja had been highly acclaimed for their delicate sensibilities and vision of women. That said, the feminist artists appearing in and after the mid–1980s are those considered to have promoted Korean feminist art in the genuine sense with a more aggressive and practical attitude, creating works focused on women's reality, something that had been previously overlooked by people's art.

In 1986, Gallery Min hosted the second exhibition of October gathering (*Shiwol-moim*) under the title "From Half to One." In this title, "Half" represents the incomplete state of woman, who always plays the supporting role of man, and "One" stands for the self that has become complete by at last realizing her identity. "Wise mother-Good Wife" by

| Fig. 7.22 Ra Hye-seok, Cancan, 1940, Oil on canvas, 41×32cm, National Museum of Contemporary Art, Korea

| Fig. 7.23 Kim In-soon, Wise mother-Good Wife, 1986, Acrylic on canvas, 91x110cm, National Museum of Contemporary Art, Korea

| Fig. 7.24 Yun Suk-nam, Mother 3, 1993, Color on wood, 193×119.5×30cm, National Museum of Contemporary Art, Korea

Kim In-soon <Fig. 7.23>, one of the works presented at the exhibition, shows a woman wearing a university graduation cap washing her husband's feet as he haughtily reads the newspaper. This work tells the story of women, who had to obey their husbands to become the good wives and wise mothers demanded by Korean society, no matter how highly educated they were. At the same exhibition, Yun Suk-nam presented a work depicting the exhausting life of an ordinary woman who has to take care of child-rearing and support the family at the same time by peddling things on the street with her young child on her back. Later, Yun portrayed the reality of oppressed Korean women by producing a series of wooden sculptures titled "Mother" <Fig. 7.24>. At *Daedongje*, a public festival held for "democratic citizens of Korea" at Myeongdong Cathedral in June 1987, a number of feminist artists including members of *Shiwolmoim* hosted a collaborative painting activity titled "Creating Daedong Pictures with the Public." Such activities indicated feminist art was headed toward direct interaction with the general public.

The year 1987 saw an array of political incidents. A democratic struggle was waged in June to bring an end to the military dictatorship, followed by labor strife in July and August. The political situation affected the art industry also: As community experience and on-site art were becoming increasingly emphasized, some artists produced hanging pictures used at the scene of demonstrations. It can be assumed that some on-site works were also attempted by feminist artists in the same historical context. In October 1987, the first "Women and Reality: What Do You See?" exhibition took place, but a large-sized hanging picture, jointly

| Fig. 7.25 Doong-ji, Mother as a Laborer, 1989, Acrylic on Cloth, 120×110cm, Ewha Womans University Museum

produced by five feminist artists including Kim In-soon, was confiscated by the Seoul City Police Department. Afterwards, the "Women and Reality" exhibition went on a national tour to be shown at female labor rallies, the sites of labor strikes <Fig. 7.25>, and university student demonstrations. In early 1988, the exhibition led to the organization of an official group named the Feminist Art Society, further solidifying the political position of feminist art. Thanks to the aggressive and practical efforts by its proponents, feminist art had become a major trend in Korean contemporary art, and entering the 1990s, it was further developed by a number of feminist artists who displayed their talents in various ways.

3) 1990s: Era of Diversification

Having witnessed conflict and confrontation between establishment and anti-establishment powers amid the peculiar political circumstances of a divided country, the Korean art community was presented with an opportunity for change in 1993 when the roughly 30-year-long military dictatorship was brought to an end and a democratic government was inaugurated. Diverse discourses and Western art methodologies such as post-modernism,

| Fig. 7.26 Paik Nam-june, Good Morning Mr. Orwell, 1984, Nam June Paik Art Center

| Fig. 7.27 Paik Nam-june, Wrap around the World, 1988, Nam June Paik Art Center

post-structuralism, and feminism were simultaneously introduced in the 1990s, so Korean contemporary art was able to keep pace with the trend of diversification in the international scene, where various modes and expressions co-existed. As the Korean art market grew in the 1980–90s, a large number of art galleries and art publications appeared, which helped Korean artists keep up with various international art trends. In addition, the nation's successful hosting of the 1986 Asian Games and 1988 Olympics provided momentum for the Korean art scene to take more aggressive steps toward globalization.

Paik Nam-June was the artist who established video art as a representative genre of the new era by exploring the artistic potential of television and video, as featured in his first video art exhibition titled "Exposition of Music-Electronic Television," held at Galerie Parnass in Germany in 1963. However, it was not until the New Year of 1984 that Koreans really began to notice Paik's work. To mark the moment when December 31, 1983, became Jan. 1, 1984, Paik set up a gigantic project called "Good Morning, Mr. Orwell" <Fig. 7.26>, based on the idea of turning the world into one global village networked together by satellite and television. In the novel 1984, author George Orwell warned that mankind would face a gloomy future in which technology governs all human thinking as Big Brother controls and dominates the world. However, at the beginning of 1984, Paik tried to show that state-of-the-art technology could instead open up a new era of communication by bringing all people of the world together as one. The work was televised around the world, including in Korea (on KBS). His work achieved acclaim once again through "Wrap around the World" <Fig. 7.27>, which was exhibited during the 1988 Seoul Olympics. Since then Paik's art has exerted great influence on many Korean artists who proceeded to make aggressive use of modern technology such as photographs, video, audio, neon, and computers. <Fig. 7.28>

| Fig. 7.28 Yun Ai-young, Secret Garden, 2001, Video Installation

| Fig. 7.29 Choi Jeong-hwa, Super Flower, 1995, Mixture, 470×420×195cm, National Museum of Contemporary Art, Korea

| Fig. 7.30 Debbie Han, The Battle of Conception, 2004

| Fig. 7.31 Kim Jong-ku, How Can I Measure the Biggest and the Smallest in the World, 2002

In the 1990s, Korea saw the rapid growth of popular culture thanks to the development of high-speed information and communications technology such as the Internet, television, and other mass media. Against this background, artists began to portray a modern society, where barriers between previously distinct abstractions were breaking down, where tradition and modernity, East and West, originality and imitation, concrete reality and virtual reality are jumbled together. They also depict the people of this new society as embodying popular images in line with the code of consumer society. <Fig. 7.29> <Fig. 7.30>

Meanwhile, unlike the feminist artists of the 1980s, who did not hesitate to make direct political comments concerning the social reality of women, those appearing in and after the 1990s talked about women's gender, and cultural and social identity in a more diverse and expanded way. For example, some feminist artists who use the female body as their artistic medium criticized the masculine perspective and expectations of women's bodies that still exist in our society. They raised questions about the dichotomous ways of thinking that divide things between natural/artificial, beautiful/ugly, and showed that the body is not something endowed with an unalterable identity, but a cultural product that constantly changes according to the situation.

Looking at the works of Korean artists, which are now more diverse than ever, it is impossible not to think about the eternal aesthetic question that has been repeatedly asked from the past to the present: What is original art creation? In an era where the creativity and originality of art works is constantly threatened by the ease of mass production, duplication, and borrowing, and in the age of globalization, where all the world's cultures communicate with each other and share information, is it possible to create a unique and original work that can speak for the lives and experiences of Korean artists? Contemporary artists continue their unremitting pursuit of the answer to this question, as evidenced by the works of Kim Jong-ku <Fig. 7.31> and of Moon Kyung-won <Fig. 7.32>, who seek to create new meaning by mixing the traditional and the contemporary. Their delicate screen images re-

| Fig. 7.32 Moon Kyung-won, Passage_Cityscape_Sungnyemun, 2006, Media Installation

semble a traditional landscape painting, but their use of video and computer technology reminds the viewer of the historical significance of the past and present and the meaning of existence in time. The experimental spirit found in such recent works only suggests the endless possibilities of this open-ended journey.

2. Dance

1) The Development of Dramatic Dance and University Education in the Field

(1) The Advancement of the National Dance Company of Korea

After the upheaval of the modern age in Korea, more recent times include the periods when dance was established under the umbrella of fine art. With the establishment of the National Dance Company, theatrical dances with Korean themes and experimental dances created by young choreographers were broadly introduced.

The National Dance Company, Korea's most specialized and representational dance group, was founded in 1962 with the objective of reproducing Korean traditional folk dance and establishing original theatrical dance performances. At the time of its foundation, the company's tendency was to pursue Korean dance together with ballet. This abnormal system continued until 1972, and it was resolved when the system was divided into the National

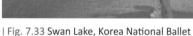

| Fig. 7.33 Swan Lake, Korea National Ballet

| Fig. 7.34 Empty Field, National Dance Company

Dance Company of Korea, focusing on traditional dance, and the Korean National Ballet, centered on ballet. <Fig. 7.33> <Fig. 7.34>

Following the establishment of the National Dance Company of Korea in 1962 many dance companies in Seoul, Busan, and Gwangju began to spring up. At present, more than 20 national and public dance troupes are active around the metropolises of Korea. Since its foundation, the National Dance Company has taken the lead in establishing the form of Korean traditional dance and raising the level of artistic perfection of Korean dance with the participation of renowned Korean dancers, including Song Beom, Kim Baek-bong, Choi Hyun, Kook Soo-ho, Jo Heung-dong, Kim Hyun-ja, and Bae Jung-hae in art directing and choreography. The company continues to work on widening the scope of Korean dance in a serious and innovative manner.

Dramatic dance, which has developed around the National Dance Company, entails original dance with the same dramatic composition and method of direction as in classical ballet while using Korean tales and themes. Since the 1990s, it has sought to produce art-works that can appeal to the public by exchanging with other art fields and incorporating a variety of factors like stage techniques, decoration, visual image, music, and lighting, into the world of dance.

Song Beom (1926–2007), the first director of the company, broke new ground for Korean dance after its postwar stasis during his 20-year tenure at the National Dance Company of Korea, and witnessed for himself the evolution of the medium. During his time at the helm, he put all his efforts into educating his successors and he was able to solidify his own style of dramatic dance. His most representational pieces are "Prince Hondong," "Domi's Wife," "Milky Way" and "Legend of Stars" among others.

| Fig. 7.35 *Buchaechum*, Kim Baek-bong

| Fig. 7.36 Bisang, Choi Hyun

During this period Song Beom worked closely with Kim Baek-bong (1927–) who was Choe Seung-hee's prodigy and was at the forefront of introducing Korean dance internationally. Kim's most renowned works are *hwagwanmu, buchaechum* (fan dance), *jang-guchum* (hourglass-shaped drum dance), *bosalchum* (dance of old female Buddhist). He longed to create splendid works with beautiful lines. <Fig. 7.35>

Choe Hyun (1929–2002) who worked as the most romantic male dancer of his time and served as the director of the National Dance Company is assessed as a multi-talented choreographer working in films and musicals and as an educator. As a choreographer, he pursued diversity by harmonizing the style of male dance and feminine delicacy. His representative works include "Bisang (flight)," "Heohaengch," "Namsaekgwutdong (blue cuffs of a sleeve)," "Gunjamu (dance of a wise man)." <Fig. 7.36>

(2) The Commencement of University Dance as Education

Another event in the modern era deserving of attention is how Ewha Womans University established its department of dance for the first time, opening the door to dance education on a university level in 1963.

In 1953, in the department of physical education, the dance major was for the first time established as part of the educational curriculum and in 1957, dance classes were introduced at the Seoul Arts High School. In 1963, the dance department was officially acknowledged at Ewha Womans University and subsequently, other universities across the country started to set up dance departments at their schools. It can be said that Ewha Womans University paved the way for dance education and established the grounds for the creation of dance. Such education at the university dance departments started to pay off after the 1980s with stage performances by various coterie groups. The most renowned of which include the Changmu Dance Company, Korean Contemporary Dance Group, and groups included in each university.

The first professor at the Ewha Womans University, department of dance was Park Whae-seon who had studied both ballet and modern dance in Japan. The Korean Contemporary Dance Group played a role of locomotive for the modern dance of Korea through active experimental attempts. The Korean creative dance groups of this period in particular, broke away from *hanbok* skirts, tops, and socks and Korean traditional music, and elected to experiment with the innovative nature of Korean dance and its expression. Later, dance departments were also established at Kyunghee University, Hanyang University, Sookmyung Women's University, and Sejong University, among others and are currently leading the dance field of Korea as core of the dance world. Today, these universities act as the heart of the dance world in Korea. There are more than 40 universities with a dance department and 20 art high schools with dance classes. Korea has the largest number of dance departments in universities in the world: a testament to the high level of dance education domestically.

2) Succession of Traditional Dance and the Trends of Korean Creative Dance

(1) Succession of Traditional Dance

Traditional dance in modern times has expanded in terms of quality and quantity. At the state level, the system of preservation of intangible cultural properties was established to protect traditional cultural assets handed down generation after generation in music, dance, crafts and other fields. The most representative works designated as Important Intangible Cultural Properties include the *jongmyo jeryeak* (*ilmu*), *salpurichum*, *seungmu* and *taepyeongmu*. Through the scheme of designating Important Intangible Cultural Properties and acknowledging accomplished artists with superior artistry, many valuable dance forms have been passed down. In the modern era, representative figures who carry the torch of traditional dance include Han Young-sook, Lee Mae-bang and Kang Sun-young. These master dancers are called *myeongmu*.

Han Young-sook (1920–1989) was born in 1920 in Cheonan of southern Chungcheong province. At the age of 13, she entered the path of dance by learning the art systematically from her grandfather, Han Seong-jun. Her *salpurichum* performance at the closing ceremony of the 1988 Seoul Olympics was regarded as the best-ever performance and the occasion introduced the depth and beauty of Korean dance to the world. She led her life devoted to passing down the dances she learned from her father, such as *Salpurichum*, *Seungmu*, crane dance, and other traditional dances. She is known for her Important Intangible Cultural Property No. 27, *seungmu*, No. 40 *hakmu*, *taepyeongmu*, and *salpurichum* that was later designated as No. 97 Cultural Properties, by her disciples.

Lee Mae-bang (1927–) is the living spirit of Korean dance and he is praised for being a true dancer – "a dancer among dancers." Born in 1927 in Mokpo, Lee Mae-bang enjoyed dancing at the early age and started to learn dance in earnest with *seungmu*, *beopgomu* and *geummu* under the guidance of Lee Dae-jo and Lee Chang-jo, who were famous dancers in Jeolla province. Since then, he has devoted his life solely to traditional dance for more than 80 years. He is well known for his performance of Important Intangible Cultural Property No. 27, *seungmu* and No. 97, *salpurichum*. He also excelled in *geummu*, *ipchum*, *janggeummu*, *sapungjeonggam* and *buksori* (drum sound). He is famous not only for his traditional dance with strong artistic traits and techniques based on the dance of the Jeolla region, but for his delicacy as an artist, making all the accouterments necessary for dance a performance on his own including costumes and props. <Fig. 7.37>

| Fig. 7.37 *Salpurichum*, Lee Mae-bang

Kang Sun-young (1925–) is a successor of Han Seong-jun along with Han Young-sook and is an accomplished artist of the *Taepyeongmu*. *Taepyeongmu*, designated as Important Intangible Cultural Property No. 92, is one of the dances that includes the most complicated movements and rhythm among traditional Korean dances. Kang's representative works include "Taepyeongmu," "Chyohon" and "The Compassion of Moran." She also contributed to the development of Korean dance by serving two

| Fig. 7.38 *Taepyeongmu*, Kang Sun-young, National Research Institute of Cultural Heritage

terms as the chairperson for the Arts Association Yaechong. At present, she continues to research *taepyeongmu* and has devoted herself to rising up young talent through education. <Fig. 7.38>

(2) The Trends of Korean Creative Dance

In modern times, traditional Korean dance expanded its boundaries while creative dance advanced in terms of quality. From the late 1970s, the trends in works with dramatical dance styles from the "New Dance" period for large theaters and the trend of Korean traditional dance centered on small-scale works started to change. It is during this period that terminology like "Korean creative dance" emerged and much emphasis was put on developing new dance languages so that the dances could be developed to appeal to broader audiences. Such change and development were accelerated by various coterie group members who majored in Korean dance, including those of the Changmu Dance Company.

In the 1980s, the dance world experienced a quantitative increase. International events, such as the opening and closing ceremonies for the Asian Games and for the 1988 Seoul Olympic Games, became an opportunity to raise the status of Korean dance. In particular, various cultural and artistic events around the Seoul Olympic Games were a good opportunity to introduce the beauty of Korean dance to the world. The choreographers who worked actively between the 1980s and 1990s included Kim Mae-ja, Kim Hyun-ja, Bae Jung-hae, Kook Soo-ho, and Jung Je-man.

In the 1990s and the 2000s, a considerable change took place in the Korean dance world. New dance groups began to appear and attempted to interact with the spectators by developing diverse activities and dance languages. In particular, the Kim Myung-sook Dance Company that focuses on crossover work with other art genres, is said to have broadened the horizons with Korean creative dance by showing the beauty of the lyrical linear curves of Korean dance and attempting the harmonization between diverse art genres and highly developed stage technology. The works of the dance company include "Beyond the Saekdong," "A Moving Mountain," "Love Song of Butterfly," "Sang · Sang," "I Do Not Know." <Fig. 7.39> <Fig. 7.40> <Fig. 7.41>

| Fig. 7.39 Beyond the Saekdong, Kim Myung-sook, Nulhui Dance Company

| Fig. 7.40 A Moving Mountain, Kim Myung-sook, Nulhui Dance Company

Since the year 2000, there have been many different experiments on stage with the growth of the quality in the Korean dance world. In this period, Hong Sung-yup has been recognized for his works "Red Buddha" and "More Shadows than Two," by introducing his own philosophical world onto the stage. Ahn Ae-soon introduced a new style of modern dance by aggressively borrowing Korean themes. James Jeon who leads the Seoul Ballet Theater, has built his reputation by developing fun and more public-orientated versions of ballet.

| Fig. 7.41 I Do Not Know, Kim Myung-sook, Nulhui Dance Company

(3) Internationally Acclaimed Korean Dancers

Since the year 2000, many Korean dancers have extended their stage to the international scene to perform actively and secure their reputations in their own artistic environment. Internationally renowned dancers include Prima Donna Kang Su-jin of the Stuttgart Ballet, Moon Hoon-sook, director of Universal Ballet, Korea and the contemporary dancer Ahn Eun-me, considered to be the Pina Bausch of Korea.

Prima Donna Kang Su-jin of the Stuttgart Ballet (1967–) is one of the most internationally renowned ballerinas that Korea has ever produced. <Fig. 7.42>

In 1987, she was accepted by the Stuttgart Ballet as the youngest and the first Asian Artist. Today she has established herself as the most beloved ballerina at the Stuttgart Bal-

| Fig. 7.42 Kang Su-jin

| Fig. 7.43 Lady of Camllias, Kang Su-jin, Stuttgart Ballet

| Fig. 7.44 Giselle, Moon Hoon-sook

let. The representative works of Kang, who has the nickname "Steel Butterfly," include "Onegin," "Mischievous Daughters" and "Lady of Camellias." Her dancing is said to be beautiful in poise, perfect in technique and accompanied by refined acting. In 1999, Kang Su-jin received the best female dancer prize of Benois de la Danse. She is also a recipient of the John Cranko Prize and the Kammertanzerin Prize. Today she is recognized as one of world's best dancers. <Fig. 7.43>

Moon Hoon-sook (1963–), a Prima Donna ballerina, founded the first private ballet company domestically, the Universal Ballet in 1984. <Fig. 7.44>

In 1992, she was invited as a guest ballerina to the Kirov Ballet to perform the

| Fig. 7.45 Shimchung, Universal Ballet

lead role for Giselle. It was the first time that an Asian ballerina had performed at Russia's Marinsky Theater and with this production she was honored with seven curtain-calls and great international acclaim. She was invited again to perform in "Don Quixote" in 1992, and again in 1995 to perform in "Swan Lake." Through these performances, she helped to elevate the level and capacity of Korean ballet. The Universal Ballet, which has focused on original ballets with Korean themes, has also introduced internationally renowned ballets. <Fig. 7.45>

Contemporary dancer Ahn Eun-me (1963–) known as provocative dancer with a unique and original imagination has been active in creation starting from her first long piece,

| Fig. 7.46 Ahn Eun-me

| Fig. 7.47 Sky Pepper, Ahn Eun-me

"Paper Stairs" in 1988. <Fig. 7.46> Ahn Eun-me most representative creations are "Sky Pepper," "Flower Grave," "Tomato Grave," "Shin-Chunhyang (new Chunhyang)" and "Simpoka Bari." She also served for two terms as the director of Daegu City Dance Company and has been outstanding in her active participation in numerous international festivals, and in an array of spheres such as film, plays and art. Having been appointed as the art director for the Hi-Seoul Festival in 2008–2009, she changed Seoul's City Hall Square into a venue for song and dance in which everybody was invited to participate and enjoy. <Fig. 7.47>

Since 2000, the dance world of Korea has been growing with equal strides in Korean dance, ballet, modern dance, and a host of outstanding creative works. To appeal to a broader public, nationally and publicly organized dance groups joined hands with renowned choreographers. The achievements of ballerinas were, in particular, outstanding. Top honors are being won in international dance competitions by the younger generation in ballet and contemporary dance, generating new stars and also making inroads into the internationally recognized dance groups of Europe and the USA. These shining examples of Korean dance receive international renown and are extending their spheres of influence and activity around the globe. Therefore, it can be said that Korean dance today is cultivating a new form appropriate for the present hour with the active contributions of choreography by middle-aged dancers in their 40s and 50s, combined with the ambitious energy of dancers in their 20s and 30s.

3. Music

During the latter half of the 20th century, Western music and *joseonak* were called *eumak* (music) and *gugak* (national music) respectively. However, the distinction became more and more vague. The Korean government made continuous efforts to promote *gugak*. However, the Koreans who were already accustomed to Western music had difficulties in learning traditional music. With a new generation of *gugak* musicians, who were educated in the modern school system, newly-composed Korean music was introduced and is now moving toward the future. Meanwhile, Western music was officially taught at school, winning the title "music." However, more and more Koreans became critical of Western music's predominance in Korea and new movements to revitalize Korean music were initiated. Now there are efforts to break down the barriers between Western and Korean music, attempting to create a new Korean music.

1) Preservation and Transmission of *Gugak*, the Traditional Music

| Fig. 7.48 National Gugak Center

In order to preserve and protect the disappearing traditional musical traditions, the Korean government founded the National Gugak Center in 1951 and began in the early 1960s to designate several important musicians as "national human properties." Many institutions to teach traditional music were established and many universities opened new departments devoted to *gugak*. Traditional musicians who had such modern training soon tried creating a new type of *gugak*, which was called *changjak gugak* (newly-composed Korean Music), in addition to the traditional repertoires. <Fig. 7.48>

(1) Preservation of Traditional Music

Many traditional genres continue to be transmitted through institutions such as the National Gugak Center, various educational institutions, and the system of important cultural heritage. Some genres tend to be more popular than others. In terms of court music, ritual music such as *jongmyo jeryeak* and *munmyo jeryeak*, banquet music including "Yeomillak," "Boheoja," "Sujecheon" and "Dongdong" and military processional music such as "Chwita" have been transmitted. After the fall of the Joseon Dynasty, *jongmyo jeryeak* was no longer considered a national ceremony, but having been designated as Important Cultural Heritage No. 1, it came to be performed once a year at the *Jongmyo* ancestral shrine along with the religious ritual. *Munmyo jeryeak* is performed at *Seonggyungwan* (Joseon's educational institution, now it is the center for Confucian scholars) each year along with the accompanying ritual. The musicians and dancers of the National Gugak Center perform these rituals and music on stage. "Sujecheon" and "Dongdong" were originally vocal music, but are now performed as instrumental pieces.

Pungnyu music was at first taught at the *Yiwangjikaakbu* and still survives today owing to the important national cultural heritage system. Therefore, those musicians who were designated as human properties for *pungnyu* music were formerly students at *Yiwangjikaakbu*. *Pungnyu* music, presently called *jeongak* can largely be divided into vocal and instrumental music. *Gagok*, *gasa*, and *sijo* are vocal genres, while "Yeongsanhoesang" is the most representative instrumental genre of *pungnyu* music.

Most of folk music genres including *pansori*, *sanjo*, *japga*, *minyo* and *nongak* have been transmitted by the human property system. For *pansori*, both the singer and the drummer can be designated as human properties. *Sanjo* was originally music for the *gayageum*, however it soon spread to other instruments such as *geomun-go*, *daegeum*, *haegeum*, *piri*, and *ajaeng*. Human properties in *sanjo* were labelled for each of these instruments, who in turn created and transmitted his/her own school of *sanjo*. *Japga* was traditionally folk songs sung by professional singers. It is a folk tradition like *pansori* with different singing style. *Japga* from each province had its unique musical features, and therefore human properties in the *japga* category are designated according to region.

(2) Tendencies of Newly Composed *Gugak*

Musicians who received modern musical training composed new Korean music, based on traditional musical features, the first example of which was *sinminyo*. However, this soon spread to all types of vocal and instrumental genres, including solo pieces, concertos, duets, orchestra music, and all types of ensemble forms. Such compositions underwent development according to Korea's social atmosphere.

During the 1940–1970s, Western musical features were strongly recognized along with modernization of the country. Composers attempted to create a new compositional language while actively employing Western musical idioms. The history of newly composed

| Fig. 7.49 Sejong Korean Traditional Music Orchestra

gugak began with Kim Gi-su (1917–1986) in 1941. Since the 1940s, new *gugak* repertoires have been "composed" in Western sense and used Western staff notation. In the 1940s, Kim Gi-su composed "Hwanghwamannyeonjigok" the first piece of its kind written for traditional instruments but arranged in the form of a Western-styled orchestra. The music features Western notation, harmonies, major and minor modal systems and calls for a Western-style conductor. Being a graduate of *Yiwangjikaakbu*, Kim employs diverse Western elements, while basing his music on the court and *pungnyu* music tradition. His compositional style was transmitted to the next generation of composers, making *changjak gugak* sound Westernized. <Fig. 7.49>

Since the 1960s, Hwang Byung-ki composed several new compositions for the *gayageum*, including "Sup (Forest)," "Garado (Gara Island)" and "Chimhyangmu." His music delicately balances traditional elements with the new modern atmosphere and is well-received by modern audiences.

During the 1960s, the first concerto piece for a solo traditional instrument and Western orchestra was introduced and solo recitals and individual composers' concerts soon followed. During the late 1970s, the overall number of composers in Korea greatly increased, making them more and more aware of their former Western-oriented compositional style. This caused many to call for the awareness of a Korean identity in music, which became widely accepted especially during the 1980s.

| Sound. 12 Modern Composition, *Gayageum* Solo, "Chimhyangmu (Dance in the Fragrance of Aloes)," Composed and Performed by Hwang Byung-ki

The 1980s saw the firm establishment of newly composed Korean music. Musical compositions focused on creatively transmitting the spirit of Korean traditional music, aiming to artistically re-construct the traditional genres including "Sujecheon," "Yeomillak" and "Yeongsanhoesang." Composers and musicians strived to reach wider audiences with newly composed Korean music. Popular Korean-styled songs and children's songs for the general public were composed. As the group *Samulnori* became widely popular, folk rhythms of traditional music became emphasized in the new compositions. Meanwhile, Western style compositions have been continuously composed, which includes Western pieces and hymns newly arranged for Korean instruments.

The 1990s saw the rise of ensemble music. Even Western music trained composers wrote for traditional instruments, making the barrier between Western and Korean music more and more vague. The number of small-scale ensemble pieces has increased more extensively than those for orchestras, thereby popularizing Korean music to reach a greater audience. It was during this period that numerous *gugak* chamber ensembles were founded and radio and television programs began more actively broadcasting ensemble music. In the 1990s, music for modified instruments was also composed. Among the traditional instruments, the *gayageum* underwent the most modification, giving birth to a 17- and 25-stringed version. Both were used for pieces that employed Western modal systems. Ensemble groups for same or similar instruments were established, especially among young musicians. Their repertoires, with easy-listening functional harmony, became popular to the modern audience.

| Sound. 13 Modern Composition, *Gayageum* Trio, "Singosan Taryeong," Arranged by Kim Hui-jo, Performed by <Seoul Saeul Gayageum Trio>

| Sound. 14 Modern Composition, *Geomun-go* Ensemble, "Spirit of Goguryeo," Composed by Jeong Dae-seok

The 2000s saw the rise of fusion-style Korea music. Attempts at creating cross-over music with jazz and popular music with traditional instruments were increased. Several attempts at combining Korean music with other Asian music of Vietnam, China, India, and other World music and modern technology-based computer music have also appeared.

Even concerts for traditional musical instruments without other musical elements are getting decreasing. Such newly composed *gugak* is actively performed today. A new generation of composers is creating a variety of musical styles which suit the taste of contemporary audiences. As a result, boundaries for traditional Korean music are becoming more and vaguer, and many feel that Korean music is turning into something totally new.

| Sound. 15 Modern Composition, *Gayageum* Trio, "Pachelbel's Canon for Gayageum Trio," Composed by Pachelbel, Arranged by Baek Dae-ung, Performed by <Seoul Saeul Gayageum Trio>

| Sound. 16 Modern Composition, "*Hakmu* (Cranes Dance) for *Gayageum* and Flute," Composed by Jeong Taebong

2) Western Music in Korea

During the period following soon after the liberation from Japan, numerous liberation celebratory songs (*haebangga*) were composed. They used easy and simple popular song styles to deliver a clear message. However, they gradually turned into songs used by the Communist movement for their demonstrations, and disappeared altogether after the division of North and South Koreas.

Meanwhile, young musicians were returning from their studies abroad composed Western style modern lyric songs (*yesul gagok*), children's songs (*dong-yo*), pieces for orchestras and ensembles, vocal pieces and operas. Modern lyric songs of this period employed traditional poems or traditional folk songs. There were also songs that portrayed social conflicts and the difficulties faced by the oppressed social classes. However, unlike the dark atmosphere featured in music of the Japanese occupation era, more cheerful and futuristic songs were composed for children, which replaced former Japanese style songs and were taught at school.

It was also during this period that many orchestras, ensembles, choirs, and church choirs were founded, for whom many new musical pieces were composed. In January of 1948, "La Traviata" debuted, the first opera to be produced and performed by Korean musicians. It featured most of the top singers in Korea at the time and resulted in great success, calling for an encore performance only three months later. In the 1950s, newly composed operas, such as "Chunhyangjeon (the story of a faithful woman, Chunhyang)" and "Prince Hodong" premiered. During the 1950s, the first musical was performed in Korea.

In the 1960s, a new generation of musicians appeared who gave Korean musicians international acclaimed. They premiered their compositions on international stages and some of the foreign as well as indigenous composers created pieces that combined traditional instruments with Western musical instruments. American modern composers including Alan Hovhaness and Lou Harrison visited Korea and premiered pieces such as "Symphony No.16 for the *gayageum* and String Orchestra" and "New Ode," which used the Korean *piri*. Both compositions exerted great influence on the Korean music scene. In 1962, the first International Music Festival was hosted and in 1965, a concert for modern music was held. In the latter, compositions by Yun Yi-sang and Na Un-yeong were performed. Yun Yi-sang afterwards gained fame in Berlin and continued to compose there. Young musicians such as Han Dong-il, Yi Cheong, Kim Yeong-uk, and Jeong Gyeong-hwa won internationally acclaimed prizes. Meanwhile, popular demands for modern lyric songs increased during this period, thus they became the main repertoire for concerts, media programs and commercial recordings of Western music in Korea. Musical tendencies of modern lyric songs expressed Korean-ness with modern taste. "Geuriun Geumgangsan (*Geumgang* Mountain)" and "Bimok" were the most popular repertoire.

| Sound. 17 Modern Lyric Song, "Geurium Geumgangsan (*Geumgang* Mountain)," Composed by Choe Yeong-seop, Performed by Park Mi-ja

With the number of musicians increasing, their activities spread in all fields of music, both vocal and instrumental. Founding concerts for new ensembles, orchestras, and choirs increased, as well as concerts for solo musicians. Professional singers also increased, which gave rise to opera performances, resulting in the foundation of new opera troupes, including the National Opera Theater in 1967 and the Kim Ja-gyeong Opera Theater in 1968, founded by Professor Kim Ja-gyeong. Sometimes new operas such as "Prince Hodong," composed by Jang Il-nam, were performed, but most operas that were performed in Korea were focused on Western repertoires by Verdi and Puccini. In 1961, the *Yegeurin* Orchestra was founded, causing a new wave in the world of musicals in Korea. *Yegeurin* Orchestra attempted new style musical, such as a trilogy for *gagok*, dance, and popular songs. However, their attempts were not greatly appreciated by the general public. In the 1970s, an independence movement of music, which started as early as 1969, became more active, as more and more Korean musicians performed abroad. In 1969, a Seoul Musical Festival, with the catch phrase 'Make our music with our own hands!' was hosted. This festival featured compositions and performances by domestic composers, premiering 20–30 pieces of new compositions then and in subsequent years. Korean composers during this period also founded the Asian Composers League Korean branch and the *Miraeakhoe* association. Composer Yun I-sang became famous in Berlin, inspiring other Korean composers working abroad. In the field of instrumental music, musicians including Jeong Myeong-hun, Jeong Myeong-hwa, Kang Dong-seok, Seo Hye-gyeong, Baek Geon-wu, and Geum Nan-sae won in international competitions. In vocal music, a new generation of singers such as Kim Yeong-mi received international acclaim.

In the 1970s, compared to the 1960s, an increased number of vocal and instrumental concerts, musicals, operas were composed and performed. With a drastic influx of newly trained musicians returning home from studying abroad, a new vitality in domestic concerts and performances occurred. In 1973, the National Theatre was founded, followed the Seoul Sejong Cultural Center in 1978, opening a new age for domestic art performances. Modern lyric songs, *yesul gagok*, still maintained their style from the 1960s but became more diversified, encorporating several styles of Western, folk, popular, and progressive genres. In the 1970s, thousands of modern lyric songs were composed and performed. In the field of opera, the Seoul Opera Center was founded as a professional troupe, and various opera performances by college students were performed. In terms of musicals, the *Yeguerin* Orchestra was absorbed by the National Gungmingamudan and gained its momentum.

Korea in the 1980s underwent political and social turmoil due to the nationwide pro-democracy movement. However, this had little influence on the field of Western music, which continued to grow in all its fields. However, during this period, some of the Western trained domestic composers started reconsidered musical tendency in Western style. They began searching for music with a clear sense of national identity and a number of scholars, headed by figures such as Yi Kang-suk, began promoting a "discourse on Korean music." Yi criticised the current state of Korean music, which had openly accepted Western modern music without question. He emphasized the need to create music that was "Korean." This was followed by composers such as Kang Seok-hui and Baek Byeong-dong pursuing their own ideas of Korean identity. Such a search for national identity took on diverse directions. There were some who vouched for a totally new type of Korean music by criticizing past importation of Western music, while some thought that 'what Koreans do itself is Korean music already.' On the other hand, some allege that Korean music should be sought out in Korean history and social realities, while some said that the essence of Korean music is in traditional music. Such diverse discourses on Korean music have developed into so-called "*hanguk eumakhak* (Korean musicology)," which is becoming an independent scholarly field.

Since the 1990s, distinction between *gugak* and Western music has begun to dissolve. Instead of thoughtlessly accepting foreign influence or rejecting traditional music, Koreans are beginning to seek for a new creative way. In the period of globalization, Koreans are becoming more and more keenly aware of the need to establish national and ethnic identities. This has caused composers, performers, and scholars to cross over barriers between Western and Korean musical traditions. Since the 6.15 Summit Statement, cultural exchange between South and North Koreas has also increased and given rise to various attempts such as cooperative concerts and co-broadcasting programs. In a word, in present Korea, attempts at dissolving barriers and discovering a national identity are increasing and still in progress.

| Sound. 18 Modern Composition, *Haegeum* Concerto "Dokdo Island," Composed by Jeong Tae-bong

Korean Art History Quick Reference

1. Art

"Dae-Gyeong-Sik" composition (大景式構圖): composition for a large-scale, monumental landscape. A composition where the landscape takes up a large percentage.

"So-Gyeong-Sik" composition (小景式構圖): composition for a small-scale landscape

AG Group (Korean Avant-Garde Association): An art association founded in 1969 and which lasted until 1974. Its founding members included Gwak Hoon, Kim Gu-Rim, Kim Cha-Seob, Park Seok-Won, Park Jong-Bae, and Lee Il. Based on a strong awareness of avant-garde art, the AG Group declared that it would contribute to the development of Korean art and culture by introducing a new plastic order. AG Group published in total four issues of its journal, with Kim In-Hwan, Oh Gwang-Soo, and Lee Il as the main writers. Its opening exhibition was held at the Central Publicity Center (중앙공보관) in May 1970, and also at the National Museum of Contemporary Art in December of the same year. Although there was considerable diversity among the works, they shared strong similarity with the 1960s L'Art Informel movement in Europe, America's Abstract Expressionism, and geometric abstract works.

Amitabul (阿彌陀佛): Amitabha Buddha: Buddha who lives in the Western Paradise, believed to lead sentient beings to paradise after death if he has been called upon during their lifetime.

Amitha-Yeo-Rae-do (阿彌陀如來圖): A painting depicting the Amitabha Buddha granting mercy to mankind while living in the Western Paradise (Buddhist Elysium). Some examples are the Dok-jon-do (獨尊圖, Amitabha), Amitha-sam-jon-do (阿彌陀三尊圖, Amitabha and Two Bodhisattvas), Amitha-gu-jon-do (阿彌陀九尊圖, Amitabha and Eight Bodhisattvas), and Geuk-rak-hoe-sang-do (極樂會上圖, Gathering at the Western Paradise).

Ang-Si (仰視): "Looking-up" perspective. Perspective from under the mountain, looking towards the peak. Belongs to 'go-won' (高遠, high distance) amongst the 'sam-won' (三遠, the three basic compositional methods in Chinese landscape painting), and is used when emphasizing a mountain's height.

Art Informel: The term "informel" originated from the French critic Michel Tapié's description of Wols' work as Art Informel in 1950. He repeated the term in 1951 when referring to works by Fautrier, Dubuffet, Michaux, and Riopelle. The Informel movement, which spread from Europe, can be said to have been the European equivalent to American Abstract Expressionism. Its artists made use of inconsistent and free images, chance brush strokes, and the Mathieu effect to pursue expression and pure aesthetic values within the artist's inner world. In contrast with geometric abstraction, it was also called "lyrical abstraction." In Korea, this term is known to have been first used in 1958 by Bang Geun-Taek in an article published by Yonhap.

Bae-Heu-Lim: Entasis: A method by which a building columns' mid portion is thick and made to thin as it nears the top and bottom. The point after the first 1/3 of the column is made the thickest, and the capital is normally made thinner than the base. This method can be found in ancient Greecestone temples, and was also utilized in Korean architecture over several generations.

Baek-Ho (白毫): The white hair on the sides of both Buddha's eyelashes. They curl to the right. In earlier images of the Buddha, it was either embossed in the form of a small circle, or crystals/jewels were embedded and decorated.

Baek-Ja (白磁): White Porcelain: Ceramic vessels made of a vector with very low iron content. A transparent glaze of the feldspar family is applied and the vessel is fired at a high temperature of more than 1200–1300℃. In Korea, it was produced since the Goryo period together with celadon porcelain, and the stronger white porcelain was produced during the Joseon period.

Bi-Baek-Che (飛白體): Flying white drawing technique. Refers to a brush stroke method by which parts of a thick line being drawn is left unevenly white, depending on the speed of the brushwork and the amount of ink left on the brush. This method can simultaneously express both speed and quality.

Bodhisatva (菩薩): The abbreviated form of 'Borisalta' (菩提薩陀). It refers to a living being who seeks enlightenment from above, and helps the Buddha practice mercy on earth. This being works to be enlightened and eventually enters Nirvana (attains Buddhahood). Initially, it was used solely for the Sakyamuni before enlightenment, but gains the next position after the Buddha as an influence of Mahayana Buddhism. It appears in various forms such as the Mireuk (彌勒, Maitreya), Gwaneum (觀音, Avalokiteśvara), Moonsoo (文殊, the Bodhisattva of wisdom), Bohyun (普賢, Samantabhadra), etc.

Bun-Won (分院): The branch of Sa Ong-Won (司饔院). A tool installed for use in the production of ceramic vessels for the royal court. From during the earlier Joseon period (from the 15th century), the *Bun-Won* was established in the *Gyeonggi*, *Gwangju* province and became the Sa *Ong-Won*'s chinaware production centre. It operated until the latter years of the Joseon period (end of the 19th century).

Bu-Gam-Si (俯瞰視): Bird's eye view. View from mountains in the front or from a mountain peak, of mountains behind. Belongs to 'sim-won' (深遠, deep distance; recession) amongst the 'sam-won' (三遠, the three basic compositional methods in Chinese landscape painting), and is used when emphasizing the depth of mountains, or their overlapping forms.

Bulta (佛陀): Another term for the Buddha, saints and sages who have become enlightened with all truths and who lead and enlighten other living beings. Originally a title for Sakyamuni, but was used for all Buddhas in the heavens and on earth following the development of Mahayana Buddhism. The 'sam-sae-bul' (三世佛) in Buddhism refers to Dipakara, Sakyamuni, and Maitreya.

Byeong-Pung (屏風): Screens or screen paintings. An object spread indoors as a form of windscreen or as decoration. Generally, paper is spread out over rectangular wooden frames. Drawings, embroidery, writings, etc. is glued on to this paper so that the 'byeong-pung' is foldable. There may be between 2 to 12 rectangular pieces in a single 'byeong-pung' and always an even number of such pieces.

Daehan Art Association (大韓美術協會): With the establishment of the Republic of Korea in 1948, the Joseon Fine Arts Association was re-named, expanded, and reformed to become the Daehan Fine Arts Association. Artists Ko Hee-Dong, Do Sang-Bong, Yoon Hyo-Joong, Jang Bal, and others were active members.

Dang-Gan (幢竿): flagpole: A pole where the 'dang' (幢) is hung. The pole's '*gandu*' (the top of a pole) (竿頭) is embellished with a dragon's head. A wooden, stone or metal pole placed in front of a Buddhist temple on which to hang a long and narrow flag.

Dapo (多包): Bracket sets placed on the lintel between pillars as well as on the pillar heads.

Deung-Yo (登窯): A type of rising kiln, made by use of a sloping hill. Fire is made to rise by use of natural wind. Used in places where firewood is used, such as in China, Korea and Japan. Built with heat-insualted bricks of stones or clay.

Do-Hwa-Seo (圖畫署): A government office established during the Joseon period to manage activities to do with paintings. Its tasks were various, as they included being responsible for all paintings demanded by the royal courts. Painting during the Joseon period developed around two main groups: the 'munin-hwa' and the professional artists of the Do-Hwa-Seo. This was because the state continuously trained and developed artists for employment in various national tasks related with the arts.

Do-Hwa-Won (圖畫院): A government institution during the Goryo and early Joseon periods in charge of activities to do with painting. Its Goryo title was used until 1464 (10th year of King Sejo), but the title 'do-hwa-won' is estimated to have disappeared before 1474 when the『Gyeong-Guk-Dae-Jeon (經國大典, Joseon's Code of Laws)』was circulated.

Do-Seok-Hwa (道釋畵): Paintings of Daoist and Buddhist figures. Do-Seok-In-Mul-Hwa (道釋人物畵). Paintings which depict figures such as Taoist 'shin-suns' (hermit with supernatural powers) or Go-Seung (priest of high virtues) and Na-Han (Buddha's disciples) of Buddhism. Classic 'do-seok-hwa' is drawn using the 'baek-myo-hwa-beob' (白描畵法, technique of applying ink-only brushstrokes to the depiction of outlines). Its specialty lies in its spontaneous and simple brush strokes, known as 'gam-pil-che' (減筆體).

Dong-Yang-Hwa (東洋畵, Oriental style paintings or East Asian style paintings): A term used collectively during the Modern Ages for Korean, Chinese and Japanese traditional art.

Doo-reong: An art group formed by Kim Bong-Joon, Jang Jin-Young, Lee Gi-Yeon, and Kim Joon-Ho (real name: Kim Joo-Hyung) in October 1982. Doo-Reong was created by artists who had during their academic years participated in folk culture revival movements such as "talchum" (mask dance), "pungmul" (outdoor performance with music and dance), and theater performances. Popular folk activities such as face painting, wood printing, collaborative mural painting, folk art, graffiti, and mask making were adopted. Such activities allowed artists to downplay their individuality or professionalism while encouraging public participation and the communal experience.

Eo-Jin (御眞): Portraits of kings. This term was established in 1713 (39th year of King Suk-jong) and was not in use in China.

Gab (匣); Gab-Bal (匣鉢); Sagger: When piling plates in the kiln, this was placed on the plates to prevent ash from setting. It comes in various sizes and acts as a form of screen, its fire-resistant clay component preventing fire from directly reaching the plates.

Gak-Bae (角杯): A horn-shaped cup. The cup's saucer was also sometimes made along with the cup. In Gaya, images of animals such as horses were also made and stuck, which enabled the cup to stand.

Gama (窯); Kiln: A heat-treatment facility insulated with refractories to fire ceramics.

Go-Bae (高杯): A cup with a high heel. A formation found in Gaya, Silla and Baekjae ceramics. There are manyexamples of geometric decorations on the heel. After the Unified Silla period, the heel's height becomes gradually lower and eventually disappears.

Go-Sa-in-Mul-Hwa (故事人物畵): Paintings where famous stories of historical figures, or their daily lives are taken up as subject matter. Some examples are 'Haeng-rak-do' (行樂圖, painting of pastime pleasures), 'Tak-jok-do' (濯足圖, Painting of Washing Feet) and 'Gwan-pok-do' (觀瀑圖, Painting of Looking at the Water Fall).

Gol-Ho (骨壺): A Burial Urn for ashes after the cremation of a person. India's cremation practices werepassed on during the transmission of Buddhist traditions, and the 'gol-ho' became established in Baekjae and Silla.

Group Number Four (제4집단): An experimental art association founded in 1970. Its members employed materials which broke free from conventional usage, and incorporated shocking demonstrations as an artistic means to challenge fixed stereotypes, sociopolitical constrictions, and traditional notions of aesthetics. Furthermore, its members emphasized that establishment of genuine Korean culture was the means by which Korean culture could play a leading role globally. Kim Gu-Rim, Jeong Gang-Ja, Kang Guk-Jin, Chwe Bung-Hyun, and Son Il-Gwang were some of its main constituents.

Gu-Reuk-Jeon-Chae (鉤勒塡彩): Technique for outlining and coloring. A method by which the outline is first drawn out, and the insides filled with ink or paint. A style contrasting that of 'mol-gol-chae-saek' (沒骨彩色).

Guaneumbosal (觀音菩薩): Avalokiteśvara Bodhisattva: The Bodhisattva who symbolizes compassion. Avalokiteśvara Bodhisattva is usually placd as an attendant to Amitabha Buddha.

Guk-Jeon (國展, National Art Exhibition): The Republic of Korea Arts Exhibition (大韓民國美術展覽會). Refers to the 30 national art exhibitions in Korea (hosted by the government) from 1949 until 1981. After independence, the 'guk-jeon' produced many promising young artists and enjoyed the greatest authority and honor. However, its tendency to be controlled by conservative academism led to many negative side-effects.

Gwan-Yo (官窯): Royal Kiln; A ceramics factory to make vessels for use in government offices. In Korea's case, appeared in the Joseon records at approximately the 15th century. The state would decide on the form, type and number of ceramic vessels to be made. The material and fuel needed for this was principally to be taken care of by the royal court. The 'gwan-yo' ceramics of the Joseon period was formed under the supervision of Sa Ong-Won (司饔院), which was responsible for all food in the royal courts.

Gwang-Bae (光背): Halo: Materialization of the light radiating from the Buddha and Bodhisattva's head or body. There are several types of 'gwang-bae' – light radiating from the head is known as 'du-gwang' (頭光), and light from the body is 'shin-gwang' (神光) and 'geoshin-gwang' (擧身光). 'Shin-gwang' is expressed together with 'du-gwang' and never alone. 'Geoshin-gwang' is the light emanating from the entire body regardless of whether the Buddha is sitting or standing.

Gwangju Liberal Artists' Association: A gathering started by Hong Seong-Dam in August 1979. This gathering focused on the use of print, which was cheap and easy to reproduce and distribute. The communicative power of print helped the group to expand a folk education movement for the people.

Gye-Hoe-Do (契會圖): Documentary painting of people's social gatherings. A form of 'girokhwa' (記錄畵, documentary painting) pictorially recording the 'gye-hoe' (social gatherings), which were gatherings of elegant enjoyments to strengthen friendship amongst learned officials. Such paintings were produced according to the number of attendants as its purpose was to record and remember scenes from the 'gye-hoe.' Each attendant received a copy to be preserved and passed down the family line.

Hang-Ma-Chok-Ji-In (降魔觸地印): A hand gesture symbolizing the moment when Buddha reaches enlightenment. The left hand is made to face upwards and placed on the leg of the Buddha who is seated cross-legged. The right hand is open and left hanging below the knee. This gesture can only by seen in seated Buddhas and thus, cannot be seen on a standing or leaning Buddha.

Hwa-Bo (畵譜): Painting manuals. A book listing painters (畵家), paintings, and various painting styles. Development of Myung-Cheong-Dae (明淸代)'s printing technology led to the spread of 'hwa-bo' such as the『Gae-Ja-Won-Hwa-Jeon (芥子園畵傳, Mustard Seed Garden Manual) in East Asia, which were used as a common textbook for teaching painting. In Korea's case, such 'hwa-bo' was brought in from about the early 17th century and played a large role in the spread of the 'namjonghwa' method.

Hwa-Cheob (畵帖): Albums. A collection of paintings in the form of a book, where paintings can be viewed by turning over the pages. Generally used for paintings of small size.

Hwa-Guk (畵局): An painting bureau established solely for the arts during the mid-Goryo period.

Hwa-Jo-Hwa (花鳥畵): Bird and flower painting. Paintings which depict a composition of flowers and birds. This includes paintings of flowering grass, grass insects, and 'young-mo-hwa' (翎毛畵), i.e. paintings of birds and animals. It includes various characteristics of Oriental tradition, and its art style can be largely divided into two main styles: 'molgol beob' (沒骨法, boneless manner) and 'gureukjeonchae-beob' (鉤勒塡彩法, the outline was first drawn out and the insides filled with ink and colors).

I-Sang-San-Su-Hwa (理想山水畵): Landscape painting using China's classical 'i-sang-gyeong' (理想景, ideal landscapes) as subject matter. A classic example would be the 'So-sang-pal-gyeong-do' (瀟湘八景圖, landscapes of eight views of the Xiao and Xiang). The 'so-sang-pal-gyung' was much admired by all three countries in East Asia, and gradually lost its 'sil-gyeong' (實景, real landscape) characteristics to become drawn as a symbol for an idealized 'seung-gyeong' (勝景, beautiful scenery).

In-Mul-Hwa (人物畵): Figure painting. Like landscape painting, 'in-mul-hwa' forms an important part of Oriental painting. It progresses from the tradition of Confucian teachings and admonitions (敎化主義) and it can be classified according to its subject character. For example: figures from traditional folklores (故事人物), figures in Daoist and Buddhist religions (道釋人物), portraits (肖像畵), etc.

Ja-Bi-Dae-Ryeong-Hwa-Won (差備待令畵員): Court painters standing by. Amongst the art institutions controlled by the Do-Hwa-Seo, the 'Ja-Bi-Dae-Ryeong hwawon' was temporarily transferred to be in charge of 'eo-jae' (御製, created by the king; writings by the king), 'deung-seo' (謄書, copies) and 'in-chal' (印札, grid lines drawn for book pages). Officially, it was constituted of 10 members who were selected by means of the 'nok-chwee-jae' (祿取才, selection of talented painters for emolument) exams. In 1783 (7th year of King Jeong-Jo's reign), the Gyu-Jang-Gak (奎章閣, Royal Library) was expanded, and the 'Ja-Bi-Dae-Ryeong Hwawon' established within the Gyu-Jang-Gak.

Ja-Yeon-Yu (自然釉); Natural glaze: A type of natural 'hwe-yu' (灰釉, ash glaze). When firing ceramics without applying glaze, ashes from the fuel in the kiln mixes with the clay's constituents and a glass-like substance covers the vessel's surface. Such ceramics with a natural glaze (jayeonyu) can be occassionaly found in hard ceramics from during the end-years of the Silla period.

Jagi (磁器, 瓷器): Term used for high-viscosity ceramics heated at high temperatures between 1,250–1,300℃. Made from clay –more than 50% kaolin, with additions of quartz, potassium and feldspar. Extremely low and strong water vapor permeability as silicates from both clay and glaze completely melt and stick. White porcelain which satisfies all of the above conditions is also designated by this term.

Jeong-Hyeong-San-Su (定型山水): Standardized landscape painting in China. Canonized and recognized as the medieval 'bo-pyeon-gyeong' (普遍景, standard landscape), it pursued nature's fundamental beauty through the classical 'ga-sang-gyeong' (假想景, imagined landscape)'s framework.

Jijangbosal-do (地藏菩薩圖, Ksitigarbha-do): A painting depicting the Ksitigarbha saving mankind from the sufferings of hell. Some examples are the Dok-jon-do (獨尊圖, Ksitigarbha), Jijang-sam-jon-do (地藏三尊圖, Ksitigarbha and Two Bodhisattvas), and the Jijang-siwang-do (地藏十王圖, Ksitigarbha and the Ten Kings of the Hell).

Jin-Gyeong-San-Su (眞景山水): True-view landscapes. Landscape painting during the latter years of the Joseon period which depicted mountains and streams as subject matter. This landscape painting developed from the traditions of the 'sil-gyeong-sansuhwa' and is based in the 'nam-jong-hwabeob.' It also has touches of Jeong-Seon (鄭敾)'s characteristic style. Such a style was widely imitated by artists during the latter Joseon period, and it formed a complementary relationship with the 'jeong-hyeong-sansu.'

Jin-Jeon (眞殿): A hall for portraits of deceased kings and gueens.

Jok-Ja (簇子, a hanging picture or scroll); Chuk (軸): a hanging scroll. Painting hung vertically. It may be hung on columns or on walls, or may be kept rolled.

Joseon Mi-Jeon (朝鮮美展): Joseon Art Exhibition (朝鮮美術展覽會). It refers to the 23 collective art exhibitions from 1922 to 1944, which were hosted by the Joseon Government-General during the Japanese colonial period. They are abbreviated and called 'Seon-Jeon' (鮮展) or 'Jo-Mi-Jeon' (朝美展). They were modeled after Japan's national exhibitions, and played the institutional role of re-establishing Joseon art as colonial art which obeyed colonial rule.

KAPF: Korea Artista Proleta Federation. As socialism spread as a result of the Russian Revolution, this Federation was organized in 1925 as a literary movement organization. It fell apart in 1935.

Korean Art Association (韓國美術協會): After the May 16 coup d'etat in 1961, the fine arts community, which was divided into the Daehan Art Association and the Korean Artists Association, was again united to become the Korean Art Association as a result of government policy to unite art associations. Active members included Park Deuk-Soon, Kim Whanki, Kim Sae-Joong, Lee Bong-Sang, Kim Byung-Gi and Seo Sae-Ok.

Korean Artist Association (韓國美術家協會): An organization established in 1956 by Jang Bal, dean of Seoul National University, who had left the Daehan Art Association after having differences with Ko Hee-Dong, Yoon Hyo-Joong, and other members. Jang brought a significant number of prominent artists with him: Seo Sae-Wook, Lee Sae-Deuk, Park Deuk-Soon, Lee Gyu-Sang, Gwon Ok-Yeon, Kim Hyung-Gu, Gwon Young-Woo, Jang Woo-Seong, and Kim Sae-Joong who were all active members of the association.

Mi-Beob (米法): Painting styles of the Mi family (Mi Fu and Mi Youren). A form of landscape painting established by Mi Fu (米芾) and Mi Youren (米友仁), 'literati' painters of the Northern Song period (北宋代). The 'Mi-jeom-jun (米點皴, Mi-dots, horizontal dots)', where dots are drawn several times over each other to paint cloudy hills and mountains. It is a painting method of conveying the humidness after rain, or the unique characteristics of mist-filled natural landscapes.

Min-Hwa (民畵): Vernacular or popular paintings. 'Sil-yong-hwa' (實用畵, practical paintings for daily life) produced according to ethnic customs during the Joseon period to decorate living spaces and for use in various ceremonies. Its most prominent stylistic characteristic would be its unsophisticated form, its bold and daring structure, strong colors, its formalities and stylistic conservatism.

Minjung Misul (People's Art): Minjung Misul arose in the 1980s with the belief that art can used as a major tool to change the socio-cultural realities arising from Korea's division and subordination to external powers. Reality and Speech, Gwang-ju Liberal Artists' Association, and Doo-Reong were some of the representative Mujung art groups, Artists including Park Bul-Ttong, Shin Hak-Cheol, Oh Yoon, Lim Ok-Sang, and Hong Seong-Dam were active participants.

Modern Art Association: Founded in April 1957 by Korean artists practicing Western-style oil painting, the group resisted established norms of academicism in pursuit of avant-garde art. The group showed a tendency toward combining figurative and abstract language. The group's activity ended in 1961, after its sixth exhibition.

Modern Artist Association (現代美術家協會): An arts association that came into being when the Creative Artists Association and the Modern Art Association revolted against the art establishment during the late 1950s. In 1957, the Modern Artist Association declared its slogan of "anti-Gook Jeon" (Gook Jeon being the National Exhibition competition for promising artists) in opposition towards Gook Jeon's (國展) Academism. Kim Young-Hwan, Kim Jong-Hwee, Kim Chang-Yeol, Moon Woo-Sik, Lee Cheol, Jang Seong-Soon, and Ha In-Du played a central role in the organization.

Mol-Gol-Chae-Saek (沒骨彩色): Boneless manner. A style of painting where ink or paint is applied directly without drawing an outline. A style contrasting that of 'gu-reuk-jeon-chae' (鉤勒塡彩).

Mookrimhwe (墨林會): Mookrimhwe was established in March 1960 as "Korea's only organization seeking avant-garde art in the field of Oriental painting." It had many members, including Park Sae-Won, Seo Sae-Ok, Jang Woon-Sang, Min Gyung-Gab, and Jeon Young-Hwa. The group adopted anti-traditional and anti-representational elements which stood in opposition to conventional art practices. It attempted to break free from conventional material and techniques to achieve works that were not traditionally considered Oriental art.

Mu (無) Dong-In: An avant-garde group established in 1962 by graduates of Hong-Ik University, including Lee Tae-Hyun, Kim Young-Ja, Chwe Bung-Hyun, and Moon Bok-Cheol. During the 1960s, consumption was on the rise due to social policies that made economic development a top priority. There was a growing notion that L'Art Informel, which was rooted in the atypical, was no longer a justifiable form of art of the time. Amid this mood, the Mu Dong-In opened its first exhibition in 1962. Its second exhibition in 1967 received much attention for its use of "daily objets and trash" in art works.

Mun-In-Hwa-Ga (文人畵家): A non-professional artist. This term refers to learned and refined academics or 'sadaebu' (士大夫, literati) artists who drew for a hobby. It is a concept contrasting that of professional artists.

Mun-In-Hwa (文人畵): Literati painting, referring to paintings drawn by academics or by the sadaebu who paint for leisure. 'Munin-hwa' is often referred to in the same terms as 'namjong-hwa' (南宗畵, a Chinese painting of the Southern School). However, there were cases amongst the 'munin' artists (hwa-ga) in Korea who followed the style of professional painters. Thus, it is difficult to simply define 'munin-hwa' as 'namjong-hwa' in Korea's case.

Na-Han (羅漢): The abbreviated form of 'Arhan' (阿羅漢). 'Eung-gong' (應供), 'Eung-jin' (應眞). A title for one who completed the Buddhist practice of austerities, and is worthy of respect. The highest position in Hinayan Buddhism (小乘佛教). It has developed to 16 nahan, 18 nahan and 500 nahan.

Nam-Hwa (南畵): Southern-School style painting. A form of painting much enjoyed by artists in Japan during the 18th and 19th century. It is an abbreviated form of the 'Nam-Jong-Mun-In-Hwa.' Its artistic composition and brushworks exaggerate that of China's 'munin-hwa' and creates a new style of humorous character.

Nam-Jong-Hwa-Beob (南宗畵法): Painting styles of the Southern School. A style contrasting that of 'Buk-Jong-Hwa' (北宗畵, the Northern school painting). It was formed when Dong Qichang (董其昌, 1555–1636) and Mo Shilong (莫是龍, ?–1587) of China classified paintings according to artists' lineages and styles of painting. This was during the end years of the Ming dynasty. Generally, 'nam-jong-hwa (the Southern school painting)' refers to elegant paintings using 'sumuk' (水墨, ink) and 'damchae' (淡彩, pale and light colors) to express inner thoughts. Such paintings were drawn by well-learned and refined academics or 'sadaebu' (literati) during their pastimes.

Nugumsegong (鏤金細工); Filigree: A goldsmith's method of utilizing gold powder or golden threads to create delicate decorations. Patterns are created by sticking small golden seeds on a thin gold plate. This technique was much prevalent in Silla, and was used frequently for various purposes, such as in earrings and bracelets.

Pi-Ma-Jun (披麻皴): Hemp-fiber strokes. A thread-like 'jun-beob' (brushstroke) which appears to be loose hemp-fibers (麻). Generally used when depicting earthy mountains. As one of the most commonly used 'jun' methods, it shares a deep relationship especially with 'nam-jong-hwa.'

Pung-Sok-Hwa (風俗畵, Genre Painting): Paintings of secular subjects (俗畵). Paintings which depict various scenes from common people's daily lives. Such paintings became properly developed during the latter part of the Joseon period, in the 18th century. During this time, the influence of 'silhak' (實學, practical learning) led to high interest in national history, geography, culture, language, and other aspects of actual life, and 'pungsokhwa' together with 'jin-gyeong-sansuhwa' (眞景山水) became new issues of artistic interest.

Sa-Sin-Do (四神圖): A painting which depicts in animal form the gods protecting North, South, East and West. 'Sa-Sin' (4 gods) refer to the Blue Dragon of the East, (青龍), White Tiger of the West (白虎), Red Phoenix of the South (朱雀) and Black Snake-

Turtle of the North (玄武).

Sam-Do (三道): The three wrinkles expressed on the neck of a Buddhist image. Symbolizes the causes and effects in the cycle of life and death ; disbelief, karma, and suffering.

Sang-Nam-Pyum-Buk-Ron (尙南貶北論): Theory of praising the Southern School and deprecating the Northern School. A Chinese theory on painting which highly esteems 'namjonghwa' (南宗畵) and disregards 'bukjonghwa' (北宗畵). It is based in the 'nambukjong-ron' (南北宗論, painting theory of the Southern and Northern schools) of academics such as Dong Qichang (董其昌), and has foundations in the different social positions and painting styles of 'munin' and professional artists.

Sari Jang-Eom-Gu (舍利莊嚴具): Reliquary: A term referring to '*sarigu*' which is a casket used to store the reliced of Buddha or a monk inside a pagoda (塔). It is normally made of an inner and outer chest, with the 'sari-byung' (sari bottle) inside.

Se-Hwa (歲畵): Paintings given to one another as gifts to celebrate the new year. Paintings with functions, such as those attached to doors to chase off demons, and others such as 'gilsang' (吉祥, auspice) and 'gamgye' (鑑戒, moral instructions) form the majority.

Seo-Hwa-Hyeob-Hwe (書畵協會, Association of Painters and Calligraphers): Korea's first association for artists, established in 1918 by 'seo-ye-ga' (calligraphers) and artists in Seoul. There were altogether 15 group exhibitions by the society until its dissolution in 1937 by the Government-General's order.

Seo-Hwa-Mi-Sul-Hoe (書畵美術會, Society of Calligraphers and Painters): An association established as the supporting organization behind the Gyeongseong Seo-Hwa-Mi-Sul-Won (京城書畵美術院, Gyeongseong Calligraphy and Art Academy). The pro-Japanese in Korean society formed its main members, and the Association became known as a gathering for calligraphy lovers. It was within the influence of the Government-General. Its training school was established in 1912, and it hosted exhibitions in 1913 and 1915 before its dissolution in 1919. It formed the foundation for establishing the Seo-Hwa-Hyeob-Hoe (書畵協會).

Seo-Yang-Hwa-Beob (西洋畵法, Western Styles in Art): Western painting techniques. Western painting styles brought in during the latter Joseon period by envoys who traveled to and from Joseon and China. Basic drawing methods to reproduce visual images, such as the shadowing method (陰影法, chiaroscuro) and perspective drawing (遠近法), acted as new factors bringing change to Joseon art styles.

Seo-Yang-Hwa (西洋畵, Western style paintings): A term used collectively during the Modern Ages for European painting which contrasted that of Oriental arts.

Seon-Jong-Hwa (禪宗畵, Painting of Zen Buddhism): Seon-hwa (禪畵). A form of 'do-seok-hwa' (道釋畵) where the ideology and other issues related with Seon-Jong (Zen Buddhism), which is a sect of the Buddhist religion, is used as subject matter. Zen priests (禪僧) drew such paintings as a pastime during their trainings, and it quickly developed to become appreciative art as Zen Buddhism philosophies connected with the sadaebu's mode of thinking. A 'sumuk' (水墨, ink) based 'gampil' (reduced brush strokes) of coarse brushwork is the general.

Shiwol-moim (October Gathering): Credited as the first group to have placed gender issues within a social context, the gathering was first put together in 1985 by Kim In-Soon, Yoon Seok-Nam, and Kim Jin-Sook. Its second exhibition titled "From Half to One," held in October 1986 was one of its major exhibitions.

Sib-Jang-Saeng-Do (十長生圖): A painting widely used in both the royal courts and amongst civilians as a highly decorative piece of work which prays for 'bul-ro-jang-saeng' (不老長生, longevity), meaning 'long life without aging.' It is most common as a folding screen and depicts the sun, clouds, water, rocks, deer, turtles, storks, pine trees, bamboo trees, and the herb of eternal youth. Peaches and the moon are sometimes drawn in together with the above 10.

Sil-Gyeong-San-Su-Hwa (實景山水畫): Topographical Landscape painting depicting actual natural landscapes and celebrated sights as subject matter. Generally refers to the 'sil-gyeong-hwa' (實景畵, real landscape painting) created for practical purposes during the Goryo and early to mid Joseon period. This is in comparison with the 'jin-gyeong-sansuhwa' (眞景山水畵, true-view landscape painting) of the later Joseon period.

So-Sang-Pal-Gyeong-Do (瀟湘八景圖): Landscapes of eight views of the Xiao and Xiang. Landscape painting which expressed the 8 beautiful scenes of China's Dongting Lake (洞庭湖) in Hunan province (湖南省), where the Xiao River (瀟水) and the Xiang River (湘水) meet. It refers to such eight beautiful scenes as the 'San-si-cheong-ram' (山市晴嵐, Mountain Market, clear with rising Mist), 'Yeon-Sa-Mo-Jong' (煙寺暮鐘, Evening Bell from Mist-Shrouded Temple) or 'Won-Sa-Man-Jong' (遠寺晩鐘, Evening Bell from Distant Temple), 'Won-Po-Gwi-Beom' (遠浦歸帆, Returning Sail off Distant Shore), 'Eo-Chon-Seok-Jo' (漁村夕照, Fishing Village in Evening Glow) or 'Eo-Chon-Nak-Jo' (漁村落照, Fishing Village at Sunset), 'So-Sang-Ya-U' (瀟湘夜雨, Night Rain on Xiao and Xiang), 'Dong-Jeong-Chu-Wol' (洞庭秋月, Autumn Moon over Lake Dongting), 'Pyeong-Sa-Nak-An' (平沙落雁, Wild Geese Descending to a Sandbar) and 'Gang-Cheon-Mo-Seol' (江天暮雪, River and Sky in Evening Snow).

Su-Wol-Gwan-Eum-Do (水月觀音圖): A painting of the Gwaneum Buddha, where he is depicted sitting at the riverside and looking at the moon in the water. A painting in the "Chapter on Entrance to the World of Buddhist Law (入法界品)" of the *Avatamska Sutra* (華嚴經) depicting the Sudhana (善財童子) looking dearly at the Gwaneum Buddha living in Mt. Botarakka (補陀洛迦, Potalaka).

Taeng-Hwa (幀畵): A large Buddhist painting on cloth or paper that can be framed or hung as a scroll. Used by Buddhists in various ceremonies and worship.

Theory of Distinctive Characteristics in Joseon Art (조선미술 특질론): Japanese art critic Yanagi Muneyoshi discussed the distinctive characteristics of Joseon art in his 1922 publication *Joseon and its Arts*. This book is made of nine short sections, including "About the Seokguram Sculpture," "Joseon's Art" and "Thinking of the Joseon People," which denounced Japanese oppression. In this book, Yanagi discusses "Ae-Sang-Mi" (sad or heartbreaking beauty), "Bi-Ae-Mi" (sorrowful beauty), "dignified beauty," "beauty of strong will," "the harmony of nature and the man-made," "the combination of virtuous and ugly beauty," "righteous art," "intimate art," "manly beauty" and other Korean artistic elements that can be found not only in architecture, sculpture, and ceramics, but also in Buddhist temple bells and stone pagodas.

Tong-Gyun (通肩): One of the methods by which Buddha's image wears its 'dae-ui' (大衣). Both shoulders are covered.

Video Art: A term widely used for various types of works where visual artists utilize video and television as artistic material. Frank Popper once explained the uses of video art as follows: use of videos to obtain a more permanent record of performance art, use of videos to propagate images and information which could have been easily oppressed by ruling classes, and use of the video camera and monitor in sculptural settings. Although there is evidence that German artist Wolf Vostell created an assemblage in 1959 using television receiver sets, the Korea-born musician and performance artist Nam June Paik is recognized as the pioneer in the establishment of video art as a separate genre in art history. Another representative artist in video art would be American artist Bill Viola.

Women's Art Research Association: Formed in December 1986, the group started as a subdivision of ten female artists from the National Art Association. The group later changed its name to the Women's Art Research Association. Even while standing at the center of Minjung Art, these female artists maintained the autonomy of women's art and carried out a wealth of vibrant activities. Their representative exhibition was "Women and Reality."

Won-Che-Pung (院體風): Painting academy style or style of painting academy painters. Refers to the painting style (brushworks) of professional artists in national art institutions, which had to follow the preferences/tastes of the royal courts. Because court fashion changed every generation, the 'won-che-pung' does not signify a specific style of art, but 'won-che-hwa' (院體畵, Academy Painting) generally refers to the 'nam-song-won-che-hwa' (南宋院體畵, style of the Painting Academy of the Southern Song).

Yeon-Hwa (年畵): Paintings for the New Year. A form of Chinese art. Such paintings were hung on doors and in the interior of common people's homes on the first month of each year. This was in prayer for the year's happiness. It is a 'gil-sang-hwa' (吉祥畵, lucky omen painting) where dwells the people's desires for luck, long life, health, safety, many children and wealth.

Yo-Cheol Beob (凹凸法): Painting technique for rendering the concavity and convexity of an object. A method whereby ink or paint is added such that different stages of brightness and shading occur gradually. This is in order to add a three-dimensional effect to paintings. Originated from Western classic art and reached East Asia as a result of the West's trade with India. Thus, it is also known as 'tae-seo beob' (泰西法, Western painting technique).

Young Artists' Exhibition: An exhibition held at the Central Publicity Center (중앙공보관) in December 1967. The Mu Dong-In group, the "Shin-Jeon-Dong-In" (New Exhibition Group), and the "Origin" group, whose members included Shin Gi-Ok and Kim Soo-Ok, participated together in this exhibition. The exhibition included works which utilized materials reflecting certain aspects of modern consumer society or trends of the time.

Yuyak (釉藥): Ceramic Glaze: Glazing is functionally important for earthenware vessels, which would otherwise be unsuitable for holding liquids due to porosity. Glaze is also used on functional and decorative stoneware and porcelain. In addition to the functional aspect of glazes, aesthetic concerns include a variety of surface finishes, including degrees of gloss and matte, variegation and finished color. A glass-like powder medication used to cover ceramics' surface to add luster and beauty. It is mainly constituted of silicic acid and aluminium oxide, with additions of sodium, potassium and magnesium. Depending on type, lead or zinc may be used as well. Other than decorative effects, it minimizes the clay body's absorbtive capacity, and strengthens the structure.

2. Dance

Akhakgwebeom (樂學軌範): The "*Akjeon*" was the sole standard/guide for music during the Joseon period. This book explained in pictures the various depictions related with the *aak*, *dangak*, and *hyangak* performed during court ritual ceremonies. Other than that, it also lists the order for arranging instruments, costumes and stage mechanisms, dance methodology, and musical theories in detailed form. The "*Akhakgwebeom*" mainly lists theories, systems and rules (法式) related with court music and dance. Thus, it is an important record, especially in this particular field.

Benois de la Danse: A globally acknowledged award, known as "the Oscars of the dance world." In recognition of the great ballet reformer Jean-Georges Noverre (1727–1810), the International Dance Association's Russia headquarters was established in 1991. Kang Su-jin (1999 award winner) and Kim Ju-Won (2006 award winner) are Koreans who were awarded the Benois de la Danse.

Beompae (梵唄): Buddhist ritual music, in other words, the sounds of *beomeum* (梵音), *eosan* (魚山), and *indo* (印度). One of Korea's three main operas, besides *gagok* (歌曲) and *pansori*. It has no steady pulse (rhythm), and is of a mono-tune (單聲旋律). In terms of its existence as a form of religious ritual music, it can be seen as occupying the same vein as the Gregorian chant of the West.

Bupochum: A part of *Nongakmu* (peasants' dance). Generally, a *jing* (gong) is played. The *bupo* dance refers to games played during a dance while a *bupo* made of white fur is attached to the dancer's head.

Chaesun: The name of the boat used as a prop for the royal court dance "Sunyourak," belonging to the *hyangak jeongjae*. This was a large vessel that accommodated some 10 dancers and it was adorned with beautiful pictures and decorations.

Changsa: A song sung in line with dances during court *jeongjae* (a form of court music). It explains the dance's eulogy of the ceremony's significance, and was sung either at the commencement or in the midst of the dance.

Cheoyong: King Heongang of Silla met the son of the Sea God, Cheoyong at Gaewoonpo. Soon Cheoyong was made into the king's subject and he married a beautiful woman as his wife. However a rebellious subject fell in love with Cheoyong's wife and he transformed himself into a human being. The two shared their love secretly but they were discovered by Cheoyong. Cheoyong being wise handled the matter calmly, by singing the *Cheoyongga*: "On my return home, I found four legs. Two, I am certain belong to my wife but the remaining two, who do they belong to?" He leaves his house singing and dancing at ease. On seeing this, the rebellious subject was shocked and immediately he apologized to Cheoyong. He promised he would never step near Cheoyong again, even if he merely confronted an image of him, and he disappeared. After this period, the *Cheoyongmu* was performed based on the tale at the royal court and among ordinary people wearing a Cheoyong mask to shed away evil spirits.

Daebung: A legendary bird of China known to fly 120,000 ri (1 ri is equivalent to 0.393 km) in a single flight. It was believed that the imaginary fish *gon* that lived in the northern seas transformed into this bird.

Daeseong-aak (大晟雅樂): Refers to a new form of *aak* requested by Hweejong (徽宗) of China's Song Dynasty in the year 1105 (Hweejong's 4th year) to the *daeseongbu* (大晟府). *daeseong-aak* entered Korea in 1116 (11th year of King Yejong's reign). Previously,

Hweejong had sent a complete set of instruments, musical scores, dance outfits, and decorations for use in the *Ilmu*.

Dangak jeongjae: This referred to Chinese tunes, musical instruments and dance, and even included the Tang Dynasty's *sokak* and the Song Dynasty's *gyobangak* and *saak* (詞樂). Accordingly, the *dangak jeongjae* referred to a performance, danced along with Chinese music.

Dodanggut music: Gyeonggi Province's shaman music. It has a varied rhythm different from the many shaman musical forms in Korea. It exists in various forms and has a unique instrumental melody. This music carries the Gyeonggi Province's regional characteristics and has an artistic taste unlike the shaman music heard in other regions.

Dongyiin (Dong: East, Yi: Foreigner, In: Person): Name bestowed on the Korean people by the Chinese, which denotes a foreigner from the east with excellent skills in shooting big arrows.

Durae-gut: Instrumental folk music and dance for the commoners. Work and play is combined into one here for people to find pleasure in their labors.

Eumyangohaeng (陰陽五行): Yin, Yang, and the Five Elements. A term explaining the creation and expiration of the universe and all phenomena by means of the Yin-Yang principle (pronounced in Korean: "*eum-yang*") and the transition of the Five Elements.

Gilsamnaegi: A traditional event that takes place around the time of *Chuseok* in Korea. Two teams are established to have fabric weaving competition. The fabric is woven with ramie, silk, cotton, linen and so on.

Gwonbeon: Refers to the *gisaeng* association created during the Japanese colonial period. The *gwonbeon* taught songs and dances to train the *gisaeng*, supervised their activities in the *yojeong* (a Korean saloon/*gisaeng* house), received *hwadae* (charges for *gisaeng* services) and played the role of a mediator for the *gisaeng*.

Gyobang: An institution since the Goryeo period for the education of music and arts. It included a school for *gisaeng* (female entertainers).

Hansam (汗衫): Refers to the extra sleeve added to the end of a woman's *jeogeori* (blouse of the *hanbok*) or *durumagi* (outer coat of the *hanbok*) to enable the lady to cover her hands when wearing formal attire. Originally, the *hansam* was added and used on *wonsam* (圓衫, a form of court attire) worn by the queen and royal concubine. However, it was also used in court dances and masked performances.

Hwoesogok (會蘇曲): A song composed during the reign of King Yourae of Silla and it is known as *Hwoeak*. Although the lyrics for the song were not passed down through the generations, its existence appears in the *Samguksagi*. The king compiled six parts of the song and divided the women into two groups, he then appointed two royal ladies as the leaders of each group. Then the women were made to compete against each other through the *gilsamnaegi*, starting from the full-moon of the seventh month to the 15th day of the 8th month, *Chuseok*. The loosing team was required to prepare a *gamubaekhui* for the winning team. On this occasion, one woman from the loosing team was asked to sing and she expressed her admiration for the winning team with the word "*hwoeso, hwoeso*," from the song. With this she danced and sang. The name, being derived from this, is "*Hwoesogok*."

Hwamunseok: A mat woven with floral patterns that has been produced since the Silla period. During Goryeo times, the *hwamunseok* and ginseng became widely recognized overseas as distinctive products of Korea.

Hyangak jeongjae: A form of traditional court dance, which was created in Korea and passed down for generations. Its name is contrasted to that of the *dangak jeongjae*, passed down from China. The act of bowing at the beginning and end of the dance, and the fact that the *jukganja*, *guho*, and *chieo* are left out are some differences.

Hyangakjapyoungohsu: The renowned writer of the Silla period, Choi Chi-won, composed a poem about the five different entertainments practiced at the time, titled "*Hyangakjapyeongohsu*." The poem comprises five parts, *Geumhwan* (tinkle bells coated in gold used for rolling), *Sanae* (a play wearing a lion's mask), *Woljeon* (a farce with song and dance, similar to the ones performed in China), *Sokdok* (a mask dance influenced by the western provinces of China, where an indigo mask was worn and people in groups were urged to run from one place to another), *Daemyeon* (for this a golden mask was worn and a whip attached with tinkle bell was shaken as a dance act to exorcise evil spirits).

Jakbeop (作法): Buddhist ritual dance. Also called *beommu* (梵舞) as a contrast term to the *beompae*. This form originated from physical expressions of praise for Buddhist morals, with the *Nabichum*, *Barachum* and the *Beopgochum* being some representative examples.

Jangakwon: A government institution during the Joseon period responsible for overseeing music and dance performances in the royal courts. The tradition of such court music continued until the last years of the Joseon period, and was partly maintained when the *Jangakwon* was reformed into the *Yiwangjik aakbu* during the Japanese colonial period. After the August 15 Independence, it was reconstituted as the *Guwanggukaakbu* (舊王宮雅樂部, Old Court Music Institution) and this was later followed with the establishment of the National Gugak Center.

Jangsonggamuak: Song, music and dance for funeral rites. This was usually for ceremonial send-off to the next world.

Japhui: Also referred to as "*Sohakjihee*." It means all manner of crude humor, games and entertainment.

Jimomu: The ancient Chinese called the dance of the Korean people *Jimomu*. Although the precise form of the *Jimomu* cannot be ascertained, it is assumed that the dance involved spears and related to the hunting that preceded the agrarian society.

Jo Chi-hun poem "Seungmu": The light silk, white peaked hat / Gently fold and float Hiding one's blue-tinted shaved head in a peaked hood The light flowing down one's two cheeks / its true fairness makes it sorrowful. In the night, where candles burn silently on the empty stage / the moon shedding on each paulownia leaf, The sky is wide for the sleeves are long, / socks lightly fold up and fly as though turning, Black pupils gently lift / all gather under one starlight in the far skies, Two droplets on peach-blossom fair cheeks / moonlight anguished by worldly affairs. The hand folds, entwines and again folds / like a sacred clasp in the depth of one's heart, Midnight silencing even the night's crickets, / the light silk and white peaked hat gently folds and floats.

Jongmyo Jeryeak: *Jongmyo* refers to a sacred place where the ancestral tablets of successive kings and queens are preserved and where offerings are made. *Sajik* refers to the god of *land* (earth), *Sa* (社), and the god of crops (grain), *Jik* (稷).

Jukganja: One of the *dangak* outfit decorations carried by *muwon* (dance performer) at the start and end of the *jeongjae* (a form of court dance). The person carrying the *jukganja* stood to the front of the last persons on both the left and right, and either entered widely from the first arrangement, or entered separately to stand at the front and maintain distance and position.

Kammertanzerin: A title awarded to those who have accomplished the highest artistic level, similar to England's nobility title awarded to those who accomplish certain heights. The Kammertanzerin is awarded only in Germany and Austria, and is considered a great honor in Europe. In Germany especially, candidates are selected every year in the music and dance sectors. However, the Kammertanzerin is only awarded when there is a candidate worthy of the award, thus adding to its significance.

Kiakmu: A type of mask play based on the contents of Buddhism. It was a silent dramatic mask dance which Mimaji learned from the Wu Dynasty of China and in turn transmitted to Japan.

Moktak: An implement for Buddhist rituals, believed to have been transformed from *moker* (wooden fish). It is used for sutra chanting and Buddhist mass.

Mukhee (黙戱): A play without any talking, similar in concept to a Western mime.

Prince Hyomyeong: Son of King Sunjo (Joseon), who led the golden age of court *jeongjae*. He was later elevated and became King Ikjong.

Samhanak: Music transmitted to Japan from three kingdoms of Korea. The name depicts the music of Baekje, Silla and Goguryeo. Today it is known as *komagaku* in Japanese.

Samul: The word *samul* signifies the four implements used in Buddhist temples for rituals: the *beopgo* (large drum), *woonpan* (cloud-shaped metal plate hit to make different announcements in the temple), *moker* (large wooden fish) and *beomjong* (temple bell). Later these instruments changed to folk percussion instruments such as the drum, hour-glass shaped drum, gong and *kwaenggwari*, a small gong. Hence the name to this particular dance, *samulnori* (Percussion Quartet).

Sandaenori: A mask dance that integrates a combination of dance compositions and transforms any open space, such as a large road or empty grounds, into a stage. It first appeared in the Goryeo period and continued through the Joseon period when it was also performed in the royal court. Later it spread to the ordinary people and developed into a dramatic performance centered around the mask dance enjoyed by the non-ruling masses.

Takmu: According to records on the conventions of Mahan, "seeding was conducted in the fifth month and upon its completion, evil spirits were exorcised. For this, groups sang and danced while drinking. Incessantly throughout the day and night, scores of people danced together. They stood up, followed each other and raised their bodies to the rhythm of the music while coherently synchronizing their hands and feet. They stepped on the land by lowering and elevating their bodies." For the *Takmu*, the dance movement required a person to lower the body while stepping on the ground and also adding in tumbling motions.

The Universal Ballet: A dance company established in Korea in 1984 with the vision of transforming "Korea into the Mecca for world ballet." During the 20 years since its inception, the Universal Ballet has staged more than 1,400 home and overseas performances, a total of 14 complete works and 50 or more single acts, and has progressed to be Korea's representative ballet company.

Theatrical Dance Developed by Song Beom: Story-centered dance which adapt narrative and legendary tales as story-matter formed the mainstream at that time. It is furthermore the National Dance Company's characteristic dynamism, making Korean dance appropriate for large-scale theaters, and it perfected the thick-lined artistic style.

Wongaksa: Korea's first Western-style private theater, established in 1908. It was located at the current Saemunan church site in the Jongro district, Seoul.

Yiwangjik aakbu: A musical institution established to take responsibility for the performance and preservation of traditional music during the Japanese colonial period. This institution was established as the *Jangakwon* (掌樂院), the national music institution since the founding of Joseon, was abolished. It was regularly in charge of music for *jongmyo* and *munmyo* religious ceremonies, and was responsible for the music education of *aak* (classical court music) students. Today, it is known as the National Gugak

Center.

Yunmu: A type of dance conducted in a circle by either standing in form or by moving round in a circular pattern.

3. Music

Aak: Confucian ritual music of Chinese origin.

Ak: An inclusive term to indicate music in Korea including instrumental music, singing and dances.

Akgong, Aksaeng: Male court musicians.

Beompae: Buddhist chant for Buddhist rituals.

Byeongjahoran: The Second Manchurian Invasion of Korea in 1636.

Changgeuk: Revised, theatrical, and staged version of *pansori*, Korean opera.

Chunhyangga: One of the *pansori* repertoires, "The Song of Chunhyang"

Daeakhubo: A music book compilation by Seo Myeong-eung in 1759.

Daehanjaeguk: The Great Korean Empire (1897–1910) in Korea.

Dangak: Music originated from Tang Dynasty, China.

Danojae: A religious rite performed on the 5th of May by the lunar calendar, with offerings made to the gods.

Deungga akdae, Heonga akdae: Two traditional ensembles (terrace and courtyard ensemble) of court rituals. These two ensembles differ in their instrumentation and repertoires.

Euijang: Military armor or objects lined according to social decorum to heighten the dignity of kings or high officials during their travels.

Eulsa Treaty: A Japan-Korea Protectorate Treaty was made between the Empire of Japan and the Korean Empire on 17 November 1905. The treaty in effect made Korea a protectorate of Japan.

Gagok: Long lyric song of Korea.

Gaya: A southern kingdom of Korea during the period 42-562 A.D.

Gochwiak: Court processional music.

Goryeogi: Goguryeo music performed in China's Sui and Tang Dynasties.

Gosu: A drummer.

Haengryeolak: A processional music.

Heungboga: One of the *pansori* repertoires, "The Song of Heungbo."

Hoeryeak: Court ceremonial music for meetings.

Hwacheong, Hoesimgok: Buddhist songs for propagation.

Hyangak: Indigenous Korean court music.
Imjinwoeran: The Japanese Invasion of the Imjin Year (1592–1598).
Jabhui: Acrobatic performances.
Jangakwon: A music institution of the Joseon court.
Jeokbyeokga: One of the *pansori* repertoires, "The Song of Red Cliff"
Jeongak: Literally means "righteousness music," indicate music of court and literati of Joseon.
Jeongwoldaeboreum: National festive day on the 15th of January by the lunar calendar.
Johoeak: Court ceremonial music for morning assembly.
Jongmyo jeryeak: Royal Ancestral Shrine Ritual Music.
Kim Deok-su Noripae: First *Samulnori* group in Korea established during the 1970s with the leader Kim Deok-su.
Minsogak: Folk music of Korea.
Mudeok: Military achievements of former kings.
Mundeok: Civil achievements of former kings.

Munmyo jeryeak: Confucian Shrine Ritual Music.
National Gugak Center: An institute under the ministry of culture, sports and tourism in Korea to preserve and promote Korean traditional music and dance.
Nongak: Farmer's band music, using primarily percussion instruments.
Pansori: Long dramatic narrative song.
Pungnyu Music: Music of scholars and social elite of Korea.
Samulnori: Percussion quartet including *kkwenggari*, *jing*, *janggu*, and *buk*. It is a staged form of *pungmul* or *nongak*, farmers' band music.
Seogyeongbyeolgok: One of the song repertoires in Goryeo *hyangak*.
Sepiri: Slender *piri*, a double-reed oboe.
Simcheongga: One of the *pansori* repertoires, "The Song of Simcheong"
Siyonghyangakbo: A manuscript of indigenous music, written during the period between 1469 and 1544.
Sorikkun: *Pansori* singers.
Sugungga: One of the *pansori* repertoires, "The Song of the Underwater Palace"
Suldae: A thin and short bamboo stick used to perform the *geomun-go*, a six-stringed zither of Korea.
Wonhyo Daesa: A famous Buddhist monk during the Silla period.
Yangban, Yangmin, Cheonmin: Social classes of Joseon Dynasty, ruling and elite class, middle class and low class.
Ye: A person's obligations and courtesy according to Confucian teaching.
Yeogi or Gisaeng: Court female dancers.

Yeongsanhoesang bulbosal: A Buddhist sutra, literally means "Mass to Great Buddha in the Spiritual Mountains."

Yeonhyangak: Court banquet music.

Yesul gagok: Modern lyric songs with European classical style in Korea.

Yin, Yang: The founding principle of Asian philosophy. Represents the dualistic confrontational relationship of the two opposing energies constructing all things in the universe.

Yongbieochenga: A song composed in the 29th year of King Sejong (1447). The song praises the great virtues of the ancestors' achievements in building the Joseon nation.

Image and Sound Source Credits

Art

1. Organization

Korea

Buyeo National Museum (국립부여박물관)
Central Buddhist Museum (불교중앙박물관)
The Central Museum of Kyunghee University (경희대학교 중앙박물관)
Ewha Womans University Museum (이화여자대학교 박물관)
Gyeongju National Museum (경주국립박물관)
The Head House of Yoon in Haenam (해남윤씨 종가)
Hongik University Museum (홍익대학교 박물관)
Horim Museum (호림박물관)
Kansong Art Museum (간송미술관)
Korea University Museum (고려대학교 박물관)
The Korean Christian Museum at Soongsil University (숭실대학교 한국기독교박물관)
Leeum, Samsung Museum of Art (삼성미술관 리움)
Nam June Paik Studios (백남준 스튜디오)
National Museum of Contemporary Art, Korea (국립현대미술관)
National Museum of Korea (국립중앙박물관)
Seoul National University Museum (서울대학교 박물관)
Sosu-Seowon, North Gyeongsang Province (소수서원)

Japan

Daigan-ji Temple (大願寺)
Nezu Museum (根津美術館)
Sen-oku Hakuko Kan (泉屋博古館)
Tenri Central Library (天理大学附属天理図書館)

Tokyo National Museum (東京国立博物館)
The University Art Museum, Tokyo University of the Arts (東京芸術大学大学美術館)

2. Individual

Debbie Han (데비한)
Kim In-Sun (김인순)
Kim Jong-Gu (김종구)
Kim Young-Ja (김영자)
Lee Tae-Hyun (이태현)
Moon Kyung-Won (문경원)
Yun Ai-Young (윤애영)

Music

1. Organization

The National Gugak Center (국립국악원)
Ye Jeon Media (예전미디어)

2. Individual

Im Jae-won (임재원)
Jung Dae-Seok (정대석)
Jung Tae-Bong (정태봉)
Kim Young-Ki (김영기)
Lee Chae-suk (이재숙)
Lee Young (이영)
Park Hyun-Sook (박현숙)
Seo Jeong-Mae (서정매)
Song Bang-Song (송방송)
Yoon Moon-Sook (윤문숙)

Dance

1. Organization

Cultural Heritage Administration of Korea (문화재청)
Kim Myung Sook Nulhui Dance Company (김명숙 늘휘무용단)
The National Dance Company of Korea (국립무용단)
The National Gugak Center (국립국악원)
Research of Jungjai (정재연구회)
Universal Ballet Company (유니버설 발레단)

2. Individual

Ahn Eun-Me (안은미)
Kang Su-Jin (강수진)
Kang Sun-Young (강선영)
Kim Baek-Bong (김백봉)
Lee Mae-Bang (이매방)
Moon Hoon-Sook (문훈숙)

Bibliography

1. Art

Ahn Hwi-joon. *Hanguk hoehwasa*. Seoul: Ilchi-sa, 1980.

Chin Hong-sup. *Hanguk misulsa*. Seoul: Munye chulpan-sa, 2007.

Choi Yeol. *Hanguk kundaimisului yeoksa*. Seoul: Yeolhwadang, 1998.

Chu Nam-chol. *Hangukui mokjogunchuk*. Seoul: Seoul University Press, 1998.

Chung Yang-mo. *Hanguk tojagi*. Seoul: Munye chulpan-sa. 1991.

Hong Sun-pyo. *Joseon sidae hoehwasaron*. Seoul: Munye chulpan-sa, 1999.

Hong Sun-pyo. *Hanguk kundae misulsa*. Seoul: SIGONGART, 2009.

Jane Portal. *Korea: art and archaeology*. New York: Thames & Hudson, 2000.

Jang Nam-won. *Goryo junggi chongja yongu*. Seoul: Heyan, 2006.

Kang Kyong-suk. *Hanguk tojasa*. Seoul: Ilchi-sa, 1989.

Kang Woo-bang. *Wonyungkwa chohwa : Han'guk kodaechogaksaui wolli*. Seoul: Yeolhwadang, 1990.

Kim Hong-nam, ed. *Studies on Korea, A Scholar's Guide*. Honolulu: University Press of Hawaii, 1980.

Kim Kwang-Uen. *Dictionary of Korean Art and Archaeology*. Seoul: Hollym, 2005.

Kim Lena. *Hanguk kodae pulgyo chogaksa yongu*. Seoul: Ilcho-gak, 1989.

Kim Won-yong and Ahn Hwi-joon. *Sinpan Hanguk misulsa*. Seoul: Seoul University Press, 1993.

Kim Young-na. *Modern and Contemporary Art in Korea*: Korean Culture Series 1. Seoul: Hollym, 2005.

Kim Young-na. *20th Century Korean Art*. Seoul: Yekyong, 2005.

Korea Foundation. *Masterpieces of Korean Art*. Seoul: Korea Foundation, 2010.

Lee Kyung-sung. *Hangukui kundaimisul yongu*. Seoul: Donghwa chulpangonhsa, 1974.

Lee Ku-yeol, *Hanguk kundaimisului jeongae*. Seoul: Yeolhwadang, 1977.

Lee Seung-hee, *Yeosunggua jungchiiron*. Seoul: NokDu, 1994.

Mun Myong-dae. *Hanguk chogaksa*. Seoul: Yeolhwadang, 1984.

Oh Kwang-su. *Hanguk Hyundai misulsa*. Seoul: Yeolhwadang, 1979.

Seo Sung-rok. *Hangukui Hyundai misul*. Seoul: Munye chulpan-sa, 1994.

Yun Bum-mo. *Hanguk kundaimisului hyeongsung*. Seoul: Mijinsa, 1988.

Yun yong-i. *Hanguk tojasa yongu*. Seoul: Munye chulpan-sa, 1993.

2. Music

Gwon Do-hui. *Hanguk Geundae Eumak Sahoesa*. Seoul: Minsokwon, 2004.

Jang Sa-hun. *Jeungbo Hanguk Eumaksa*. Seoul: Segwang Eumak Publishing, 1986.

Jeon Ji-yeong. *Geundaeseongui Chimryakgwa 20segi Hangukui Umak*. Seoul: Book Korea, 2005.

Jonathan Condit. "Two Song Dynasty Chinese Tunes Preserved in Korea." *Music and Tradition*. Cambridge University Press, 1981.

Keith Howard. ed. *Korea, People, Country, and Culture*. Hampshire: Ashgate, 2006.

Kim Hae-suk et al. *Jeontong Umak Gaeron*. Seoul: Eoullim, 1999.

Kim Jong-su. *Joseonsidae Gungjung Yeonhyanggwa Yeoakyeongu*. Seoul: Minsokwon, 2001.

Kim Ye-Pung and Jeon Ji-yeong. *Junggukemakui Yeoksa*. Seoul: Minsokwon, 2004.

Korea Foundation. *Korean Cultural Heritage: Performing Art*. Seoul: Korea Foundation, 1997.
Laurence Picken. ed. *Musica Asiatica*. Oxford University Press, 1979.
Lee Byong-won. *Styles and Esthetics in Korean Traditional Music*. Seoul: National Gugak Center, 1997.
Lee Hye-kyu. "Eumak." *Hanguksa*. Seoul: Guksapyeonchanwiwonhoe, 1975.
Lee Hye-kyu. "Ilbone Jeonhaejin Baekjeak." *Hanguk Eumak Nonchong*. Seoul: Sumundang publishing, 1976.
Lee Ji-seon. *Ilboneumakui Yeoksawa Iron*. Seoul: Minsokwon, 2003.
Moon Suk-hie. "A Study on the Interpretation of the Rhythm of *Jeongganbo of* of Old Manuscripts." *Hanguk Eumaksahakbo*, Vol. 45. Seoul: Hanguk Eumaksahakhoe, 2010.
Seo Han-beom. *Hanguk Eumak Tongnon*. Seoul: Taerim Press, 2004.
Song Bang-song. *Korean Music, Historical and other Aspects*. Seoul: Jipmoondang, 2000.
Song Bang-song. *Jeongbo Hangukeumak Tongsa*. Seoul: Minsokwon, 2007.
Song Hye-jin. *Cheongsonyeoneul wihan Hangukumaksa*. Seoul: Duri Media, 2007.
Yun So-hui. *Changjak Gugakui Heureumgwa Bunseok*. Seoul: Gugak Chuncusa, 2001.
Sejong sillok akbo (世宗實錄樂譜: Annals of King Sejong: Scores), around 1450.
Sejo sillok akbo (世祖實錄樂譜: Annals of King Sejo: Scores), around 1468.
Siyong hyang-akbo (時用鄕樂譜: Contemporary Music Scores), around 1500.
Daeak hubo (大樂後譜: Scores of great music-Late Edition), 1759.

3. Dance

Academy of Korean Studies. *Joseon Hugi Gungjungyeonhwangmunhwa*. seoul: Minsokwon, 2003.
Choi Hae-ree. *Changjak Chum; history and nature of a contemporary Korean dance genre*. Honolulu: University of Hawaii, 1995.
Gu Hee-seo. *Hankuk ui Myeongmu*. seoul: Hankukilbosa, 1985.
Jang Sa-hun. *Hankuk Muyong Gaeron*. seoul: Daekwang Munhwasa, 1984.
Jeong Byeong-ho. *Hankuk ui Jeontongchum*. seoul: Jipmundang, 1999.
Kim Cheon-hung. *Wurichum Iyagi*. seoul: Minsokwon, 2005.
Kim Mal-borg. *korean dance*. seoul: Ewha Womans Unoversity Press, 2005.
Kim Myung-sook et al. *Hyomyeongsaeja Yeongu*. seoul: Korean Society for Dance Studies, 2005.
Kim Mae-ja. *Hankuk Muyongsa*. seoul: Samsinkak, 1995.
Kim Myung-sook. "A Study on the Characteristics of Choe hyun's Dance." *The Korean journal of dance studies Vol.10*, 2002.
Kim Myung-sook. "The Artistic World of Lee Mae-bang." *The Korean journal of dance studies Vol. 13*, 2004.
Kim Myung-sook. "The Artistic World of Kim Cheon-hung." *The Korean journal of dance studies Vol. 14*, 2004.
Kim Myung-sook. "The Artistic World of Han Young-Sook." *The Korean journal of dance studies Vol. 22*, 2007.
Kim On-gyung. *Hyangto Muyong Chongron*. seoul: Hanguk Pyeongron, 1991.
Korean National Commission, Unesco. *Traditional performing arts of Korea*. (Seoul) Korea Foundation, 1975.
Korean Society for Dance Studies. *Jungeoneuro dutnun Hankuk Gundae Muyongsa*. Seoul: Dusol, 2007.
Lee Hung-gu et al. *Joseon Gungjung Muyong*. Seoul: Yeolhwadang, 2000.
National Research Institute of Cultural Heritage. *Mubojip-ipchum, Hanryangmu, Geommu*. 1995.
Seong Gyeong-rin. *Hankuk ui Muyong*. Seoul: Sejongdaewang Ginyeom Saeophwae, 1974.
Seong Gyeong-rin. *Hankuk Jeontong Muyong*. Seoul: Iljisa, 1979.
Yi Tu-hyon. *Korean performing arts; drama, dance & music theater*. Seoul: Jipmoondang, 1997.